The Master Thinkers

The Master Thinkers

André Glucksmann

translated from the French by Brian Pearce

HARPER & ROW, PUBLISHERS

NEW YORK

Cambridge
Hagerstown
Philadelphia
San Francisco

1817

London
Mexico City
São Paulo
Sydney

FIRST EDITION

ISBN: 0-06-011639-0

LIBRARY OF CONGRESS CATALOG CARD NUMBER: 78-20164

80 81 82 83 84 10 9 8 7 6 5 4 3 2 1

To the madman who wanted to
swap Brezhnev for Pinochet

Contents

In the Beginning Was
the Interruption

'Science! Everything has been revised. For the body and soul —
as viaticum — there are medicine and philosophy; old wives'
remedies and re-arranged folk-songs. And the pastimes of
princes and the games that they proscribed: geography,
cosmography, mechanics, chemistry...
'Science, the new nobility; and progress. The world is on the
march — why shouldn't it turn?'

RIMBAUD, *A Season In Hell*

1 Panurge Outside the Walls

'Against all other hazards it is possible for us to gain security for ourselves, but so far as death is concerned we inhabit a city without walls.'

EPICURUS

I

Rare, in our times, are rulers who refrain from telling us: 'You are free.' Rare are the subjects who reject the pleasure of feeling free. 'I am free,' says the adolescent of just after the Second World War – only to end up by asking ever more perplexedly: who is this 'I'? To the point of no longer understanding anything about the matter, and least of all whether he is 'free'. Perhaps it would be proper to consider the question of freedom in a different way, not as a question asked of me by me, but as one evoked by a challenge: 'You are free ... ': thus the rulers break in, in a solemn tone.

Is it not yielding too much to their behest to echo it by asking: 'Am I free?' without first of all questioning this voice which at once installs itself in each one of us?

'Do what you will' is the order given by Gargantua, that model leader, to his model subjects, on the threshold of that model of modernity which Rabelais imagined in the Abbey of Thélème. And he stresses that 'in their rule there was only this one clause: Do what you will!'

'Marxism contains a great many principles which amount, in the last analysis, to only one sentence: you are right to revolt,' said Mao Tse-tung, causing himself to be hailed as the Great Helmsman by 800 million model Chinese. The same formula four centuries later.

It shines forth when the modern prince – whether a head of state or the head of a firm – expects to be obeyed in the modern way, addressing his orders to our freedom.

(i) The formula is radical: it refers to the present ('Do') and governs the future ('what you will'). The past is struck off the map, definitively struck off, since repeating the formula means once again starting from scratch. The commentaries illustrate the break thus made – although the rule is reduced, in principle, to the single clause: 'do what you will', the construction and preliminary organization of Thélème installs its inmates in an anti-monastery subject to anti-rules which are no less detailed than those of the traditional type of monastery. Similarly, the Chinese formula is made more explicit as: 'You are right to revolt against reactionaries.' It is a device for making war on the past.

(ii) The formula is revolutionary: it marks that moment when 'everything is possible', as Michelet said of the French Revolution. It defines a group – the inmates of Thélème, the Chinese people – entirely by the one quality that it mentions: the moment when 'everything is possible' is given as his date of birth to each individual belonging to the group. My aim is not 'to plunder men or hold them to ransom, but to enrich them and set them at complete liberty', Rabelais's Kings promised their prisoners. Before the revolution, 'China was a blank sheet of paper' (Mao). Neither priest nor lawyer, neither miser nor syphilitic, the future inhabitant of Thélème must himself likewise be 'blank', unmarked, virgin wax. A new device, an absolute beginning.

(iii) The formula is collectivist: we are free together. Therefore, only the group is free: 'Making use of this liberty, they most laudably rivalled one another in all of them doing what they saw pleased one. If some man or woman said "Let us drink", they all drank; if he or she said "Let us play", they all played; if it was "Let us go and amuse ourselves in the fields", everyone went there.' This society seems doomed to repeat *ad infinitum* its own birth. Communication takes place only in the imperative, as though the original leader was able to yield the initiative only to new, little leaders, found at random, on the spur of the moment, all equally good, and good enough only to be leaders for an instant ('let's drink', 'let's play'). The Thélémites are already Panurge's sheep, before the latter appear in the story. They live in the present: like the past, the future turns out to be abolished, since it contains the threat of unforeseen differentiations. It is the spirit of 'serving the people': a people of 800 million Chinese. It is a device for cutting off differences before they can show themselves.

(iv) The formula is dictatorial. Not only because a leader (Gargantua or Mao) propounds it, with its imperative either explicit ('Do what you will') or implicit ('What all of Marxism amounts to' can be nothing less than the supreme imperative: 'You are right' signifies 'It must happen'). The matter is more serious than that. An insurmountable dissymmetry is established between the one who propounds the formula as a law and the one who accepts it as a rule of life, between the one who orders and the one who obeys. There are no problems for Gargantua or for Marxism: 'You are right to revolt', 'Do what you will' – these things can be said, these orders given, without a forked tongue, without any self-contradiction.

Here we have orders which, when carried out, plunge into the most inescapable confusion all those who submit to them. 'Disobey me,' says the father. If I obey you, I am disobeying you, but if I disobey you, I am obeying you ... Marxism amounts to you-are-right-to-revolt, but are you right if you revolt against Marxism? If so, it's the revolving door again. If not, Marxism does *not* amount to that, and to say so is false. I lie, says the Cretan: if he lies, he is telling the truth, but if he tells the truth, he is lying.

Modern logic has carefully examined paradoxes such as this. All the solutions which have been put forward consist either in ruling out such propositions as nonsenses, absurdities, or in accepting them while making a hierarchical distinction between the proposition and its terms, the whole and its parts, the statement and what is stated. In all cases, an irreversible subordination.

Do what you will, but do not rebel against the one who tells you to, lest you become bogged down in insuperable contradictions. A device that produces only one difference – the hierarchical difference. A device for governing.

(v) The formula is theological. Its origin is religious. Thus spake St Augustine: *Dilige et quod vis fas*, that is: Love (God), serve (God), and do what you will. Removing the connection between the will and God deprives the formula of its religious appearance, but leaves the mark of the cut that has been made: twentieth-century thought remembers that: 'Everything is permitted' means: 'If God is dead, everything is permitted.'

The religious connection vanishes, but not its place in the discourse which claims to decide about 'everything'. We go on talking about God without believing in him with the same authority – that of the rational theology which sought God as the outcome of its logical proofs.

Atheism is theo-logical. Not because it is sometimes caught recalling that 'God is dead', but because it speaks about 'everything', in 'everything is permitted', in the same way in which classical philosophy spoke about God. If our reason can permit itself to declare that God is, its prestige will be the same whether it says God is Perfect, Existent, an Idea, or Dead. If we offer ourselves God by means of a proof, or if we release ourselves from his prohibitions by knowing that he is no more, we can offer ourselves anything, or prohibit anything, that we choose. 'Souls have been abolished', announced zealous activists at work in Russia's provinces in 1924, just as they might have said that bread was being rationed, or sugar subjected to restrictions. Religious and anti-religious policies alike bear the imprint of the strong state.

'Do what you will' expresses the point of view of a God looking at his world, even though the formula excludes God from its explicit considerations. It reinforces the relation of the governor to the governed with that of God to his creatures. If a little boss is a little god, what, great God!, is a big boss?

2

Such is the fable of Thélème. Is it too simple when compared with modern devices for producing authority? It gives the essence of all the political theories that have flourished in our day. We desport ourselves among masters, as tenants of a master who is himself absent. We are fed, clothed and laundered by workers who also are absent. Rabelais is careful to mention that the workers responsible for food and clothing live outside Thélème. Whether one is Ricardian, Keynesian, Marxist,

Weberian, Smithlike, Rabelaisian or even Hitlerite, one is not unaware that present-day societies derive their wealth from the labour they 'organize'. Every political theory contrives, though, to leave aside the problems of domination which are implicit in all organizations of labour: that's a different matter, that's economics. The most revolutionary theories fall down the same hole: Marx speaks sometimes of 'associated producers' taking the place of capital, and more vaguely still of self-management and the gradual elimination of the role played by money. A few, rare reservations: on the pretext of not 'boiling the stewpots of the future' he leaves the future blank, which circumstance has warranted a number of blank cheques endorsed by 'representatives of the future'. His most serious critics in the labour movement, when, for example, they substituted their general strike for the revolution, argued in the same way: everybody stops working, the employers are unable to continue, the control levers pass into the hands of the proletarians and their trade unions, and work starts up again. As before? It would seem so, since nobody thought it necessary to clarify the point – that is, to begin to modify work in the here and now, in order to see what happens. Whether they claim to conserve, to reform or to revolutionize it, the power which all the theories discuss is always situated in Thélème.

Rabelais's fable is lacking, perhaps, in utopian fantasies but certainly not in realism. This place, separated from the production and the producers which sustain it, this place where nevertheless everything is decided, where you 'do what you will', with everything including the lives and the production of those who are not admitted – is it not what is defended, renewed, turned this way and that, by all political theories? There lies their centre of gravity, the fulcrum that will enable them to lift the world, the key, the power that Lenin, Hitler and any and every candidate for the Presidency feels, sees and strives for in the state. When a modern man, possessed of a certain status, talks of conquering the machinery of state (for the good of the greatest number, of the people, of the revolution, or whatever), it is in Thélème that he dreams of establishing himself. In a sense, he is in Thélème already, dreaming, theorizing, terrorizing.

3

The formula applies to every freedom, naming it in a baptism constantly renewed, saying: 'You shall be free.' Free not to listen to it? May one leap out of the circle which it is beginning to close around one and, ignoring it as mere nonsense, get on with one's everyday affairs?

That's difficult. 'Do what you will' is already there in the most everyday affairs: if one did not risk hearing it in unexpected encounters, love would give rise to no romances. Nor would political regimes have any adherents. No one is supposed to be unaware of the modern laws which address themselves only to our freedoms, and speak only of them. The economy itself can get moving only on the assumption that there exists a whole world of 'free workers'. Concentration camps lay down a programme of labour and liberty, 'Do what you will' (*Arbeit macht frei*, 'Work makes you free'): it functions when the dying man self-manages his own death. In China they re-educate people through the self-criticism of mistakes: the more you are re-educated the closer comes the moment of release; if a re-education is nearing its end, that implies your full awareness of the mistakes you have made. When, at last, considering that you have been re-educated, the authorities offer you freedom, can you, being fully conscious of your faults, ask freely for anything but to remain in the camp? That is what you ask for if your education has been successful: and, if it has indeed been successful, the authorities must, showing no less education on their part, agree with you. And so you stay there. But if you do not ask for that, your re-education has failed, and there is no reason why you should be allowed to leave. Do what you will.

One quickly imagines oneself to be cleverer than the booby-trap formula. Forgetting the cloud cast by it, one must go to the things themselves and discover the real relations of force that are concealed in it: have at the bourgeois and the bureaucrat! If their power is not mere paper (even if not constantly at the muzzle of a gun), this is because they make us obey in the name of freedom.

When we go behind words in order to seek the real social

forces, the more we analyse, the more we discover in these forces the words that serve to consolidate them. If it is to rule the world, the bourgeoisie cannot manage without presenting itself in the guise of a universal class that defends the freedom of all. A century later, this observation of Marx's applies even better to the regimes which swear by his name: 'It was all that same invincible theme-song, persisting with only minor variations through so many different trials: "After all, we and you are Communists! How could you have gotten off the track and come out against us? Repent! After all, you and we together – is *us*!"' (Solzhenitsyn, *The Gulag Archipelago*, I). Do what you will: in any case, you will have willed it. Every social force gets its strength from taking over and at the same time threatening the freedom which it 'mobilizes'.

In an outwardly calm society, calm sociologists present the bureaucrat as the employee of a 'disenchanted' rationality. He is not the man who determines ultimate aims, but the man of files competently examined, of objective regulations, of calculated and verifiable deployment of means defined in relation to aims laid down by the legally constituted authorities. And so forth. In the face of the contradictory wishes of the public, he takes up a neutral position. That is even one of the secrets of his pro-liferation: if two administrative bodies get in each other's way, a third is created to administer the conflict between them. Police are needed to police the police-force, there have to be mediators between the public services and the public, and a new service is set up for these mediators. It is useless to call down 'curses on Saint Bureaucratius' (Max Weber): if a bureaucracy is not rational, one rationalizes it by means of bureaucracy, or otherwise one inflicts a 'dilettante' administration on oneself. 'Do what you will with me': that is how bureaucracy gets itself accepted, while letting it be inferred that in order to will, one has to give oneself the means of willing – which signifies willing bureaucracy. The more means, correctly organized, that one possesses, the more one can will. The greater the bureaucracy, the greater the freedom: will whatever you want, but first of all will *me*.

In a society in tumult a 'dangerous social agitator' appears.

The professional revolutionary is no more the man of ultimate aims than the bureaucrat is. Shortly before he took power, Lenin explained that, where ultimate aims were concerned, Marxists and Anarchists agreed – they were all in favour of destroying the state (*The State and Revolution*, 1917). If there was a difference between them, this related exclusively to means: the Marxist accepted these means (the state, dictatorship), whereas the Anarchist seemed to reject them. In short, do what you will, but, first of all, *do*. And the more you submit yourself to the dictatorship of 'doing', the more, later on, will you be free to will.

The bureaucrat and the professional revolutionary are not preachers, they put themselves forward as men of reason: neither of them goes in for prophecy, they claim merely to offer the means of freedom. And if the professional revolutionary is distressed by the possibility of bureaucratizing the future, the bureaucrat constantly takes pride in revolutionizing the present.

The bureaucrat does not proliferate in the bureaucracy only. Before doing that, he proliferates in every individual. Neutral, he neutralizes; he is said to be disenchanted, and he disenchants; modest, he confines himself to means, and makes his own modesty the ultimate aim of everyone. Through him, the formula passes from the imperative into the indicative: what you do, you will wish to do. You will wish it elsewhere, tomorrow, in your private life, in your soul – that is, precisely in what you are making and building here and now. When Gargantua has built Thélème, he can disappear, his rule will stand by itself. Thélème, that means of imposing his rule, reigns over the Thélémites, who are the means of this means.

He who wills the end wills the means, the professional revolutionary hammers out to us. He who wills the means has never finished with them, sighs the bureaucrat. The one is always challenging the other, with both ready to climb into the ring and fight the fight of the century. The dialectic, that of Hegel and Marx, having passed into the public domain, keeps the score. It is the great game of what is 'in itself' and what is 'for itself', of men and things: if they tear each other, it is because they are brothers, but if brothers they are, they must go for each other's guts. Have a care on your left, watch out to your right; the fight is well-balanced provided they avoid deviations. They chase each other, one being the shadow of the other. When they meet they have to be separated, but if they separate it is because they are looking for each other. The professional revolutionary bureaucratizes his game: each adopts the style of the other, right-wing in appearance but leftist in reality, and *vice versa*. After Guildenstern and Rosenkrantz, Bouvard and Pécuchet, Dupont and Pondu, they are the most famous pair in the twentieth-century world of learning.

The title is not what is at stake. The fight exhausts the combatants and the spectators, but not the question. The dialectic thinks it is commenting on a fight to the death in which everything is to be decided: the combatants don't know who arranged the encounter or how it may end, they are wandering about in the space of 'Do what you will'. If each becomes dialectically convinced that the other knows more about it, and that it is necessary to wrest his secret from him, the situation gets tenser for a moment. But let that not prevent them from stepping outside for a breath of air: when they come back, the combatants resume the fight, without knowing why.

They are fighting over a purpose which they do not grasp: the imperative of their conflict hovers high above the fighters. 'Do what you will' was the order . . . Given by whom? Gargantua? The organizer of the show went off, making it known that he was letting things go their own way. He left the scene after arranging matters carefully: Thélème subjects the Thélémites without needing a Prince. There is no lord in Thélème, but this republic does not lack rules, even if they be counter-rules no less finicky, in a symmetrical way, than those which they replace. 'Seeing that in certain monasteries in this world it is the custom that if any woman enters . . . they wash the place where she trod, it was ordained that if any monk or nun happened to enter here, the spot where he or she had stood should be scrupulously washed likewise . . . '

Thélème certainly marked a break. Was this the break between obscurantism and humanism? Between the closed universe of the Middle Ages and the open world of the Renaissance? Historians have greatly modified that contrast, emphasizing the bright side of the Middle Ages and the dark side of the Renaissance; but is not Rabelais even more ironical? His characters pass from the monastery into the anti-monastery; not by leaping from the realm of necessity into the reign of freedom, but more smoothly, by replacing one kind of discipline with another.

4

The walls of the monastery fall, but does this mean freedom? Not without some ambiguity, Friar John observes at once that walls (*murs*) count for something: 'Where there's a *mur* before and a *mur* behind, there are plenty of murmurs, envy and mutual conspiracy.' By knocking down the walls would we not have begun to '"unlock" the disciplines', as the nineteenth century began to do on a grand scale (Foucault, *Discipline and Punish*)?

The Thélémites are free from the traditional hierarchy, but not from *all* constraint: 'If some man or woman said "Let us drink", they all drank ... ' Perhaps they are departing from a space of sovereignty in which the King focuses everyone's gaze upon himself, only to enter that 'space of visibility' in which authority sees without being seen. On condition that his subjects are never caught misbehaving by that invisible eye: a permanent self-discipline, 'a procedure for subordinating bodies and forces which must increase the usefulness of authority while making the Prince redundant'. At the end of the eighteenth century the model prison conceived by Bentham, the Panopticon, introduced a new system of surveillance – the political technology which Michel Foucault, finding it present in the colleges, hospitals, workshops and prisons of last century, has called 'panopticism'.

There is no watch-tower standing in the midst of Thélème, no centre of surveillance. Are the Thélémites isolated from each other so as to be subject only to the gaze of the warder whom they have internalized? Not at all! They 'rivalled one another in all of them doing what they saw pleased one'. Surveillance is mutual; the centre is everywhere and the circumference nowhere. One may leave Thélème whenever one wishes, because no one ever leaves it: 'People who are free, well-born, well-bred, and easy in honest company have a natural spur and instinct which drives them to virtuous deeds and deflects them from vice; and this they called honour.' Thélème is not the Panopticon, nor is it simply a stage leading thereto. It is a universe of display rather than of production, oriented more upon the court of Fontainebleau than upon a factory yard. Altogether, it should be compared to a system of reciprocal control in the Chinese manner rather than to Bentham's isolators.

'There are two images, then, of discipline. At one extreme, the discipline-blockade, the enclosed institution, established on the edges of society, turned inwards towards negative functions: arresting evil, breaking communications, suspending time. At the other extreme, with panopticism, is the discipline-mechanism: a functional mechanism that must improve the exercise of power by making it lighter, more rapid, more effective, a design of subtle coercion for a society to come' (Foucault). Thélème is not *in* history, but it marks a decisive crossroads of history.

The *anti-monastery* is a bunker of the New Age that is to be besieged by the accursed figures from the past: hypocrites, bigots, lawyers, usurers, peevish and jealous old men, mangy creatures, poxed to the eyebrows ... The mechanisms of exclusion operate at the entrance to the abbey, and are reproduced at the doors leading to the ladies' apartments, where perfumers and barbers are always stationed: the men have to pass through their hands before visiting the ladies. Such is the price of liberty.

It is a *training centre* where the question of power is settled, that question which Friar John raised at once, and which dominates the entire project of Thélème: 'How should I be able to govern others when I don't know how to govern myself?' The formula 'Do what you will' introduces secular and obligatory unanimity without there being need for any Prince. Such is the price of equality.

It is an *anonymous construction* in which the master, himself departed, has embodied a law. Already, when the Prince goes away, the stones are called upon to regulate the relations between men. Later, the great rational edifices of prisons and general hospitals will be raised, whereof the 'stones can make people docile and knowable' (Foucault). Thus did Thélème start to speak. Such is the price of fraternity.

A break, a crossroads, a nodal point. All directions are shown, but their grouping forbids us to choose any of them. When freedom is on the horizon, the activity that leads towards it is one of selection and drilling; when it is available on the spot, it is a necessity imposed on all – 'If some man or woman said "Let us drink" ... ' Everyone is equal to everybody else, provided that nobody claims equality with the equalizer. The will of all is the will of each, but the former is named Gargantua whereas the latter is hidden within the indistinguishable Thélémite: the trick is that these two shall never meet.

That which binds them together sets them apart, and therein lies the whole effectiveness of the plan and formula of Thélème. Later on, in this space of paradox, the ruling power will organize itself productively: the antinomy will be put to advantage by being spaced out along the axis of time ('do' today, 'what you will' is for tomorrow) or in the different registers of social life ('Real and corporeal disciplines have constituted the foundation of formal and juridical freedoms'). Later still, the bureaucrat and the professional revolutionary will publish their dialectical duels, each pulling the beam out of his neighbour's eye, both serving as instruments of one and the same disciplinary visibility which watches coldly through their fevered eyes. Thélème already marked that timeless moment when the Prince says: 'You are right to revolt,' while his power, having become modern, puts itself out of reach by means of these words.

5

This construction is not bathed either in the ethereal light of the 'humanist' academies or in the premeditated shadow of the future's concentration camps, Thélème says to itself, with a dreamy laugh.

'I tell the truth.' There is no problem here: if I truly tell the truth, this statement is true; if I don't tell the truth, it is false. The two cases are quite distinct, like Thélémites and 'pious old apes'. Apart from a few details, the abbey becomes the temple of knowledge and of good health: the formula 'Do what you will' does not lend itself to contestation, since those well-born persons who live and talk there could not will anything bad.

If the mere possibility of telling lies or doing ill be allowed in, then everything alters. I say: 'I lie'; that's a paradox. And what if you are already thinking that I may be lying when I say: 'I tell the truth'? 'Do what you will' – but that 'as you like it' introduces not so much the reign of freedom as, sometimes, a shrug: it's all the same because nothing can be put on the same level with anything else.

Inside Thélème everything is good, and outside it everything is false. Depending on whether you hear it from within or from without, the formula will give two versions, one optimistic and the other nihilistic. Except that, if you are outside, you cannot state what is true, and, consequently, to claim that you are inside sounds presumptuous: it's a statement that can't be contradicted and is therefore arbitrary. The paradox leaves us swaying in this intermediate space.

'Get married then; for God's sake!' But: 'Have nothing to do with marrying, then.' Panurge contemplating marriage is perplexed: he faces those risks of being deceived or catching the pox which had been explicitly eliminated by the invisible walls of Thélème. Here conclusions are drawn that have not gained recognition by the Sorbonne for one-thousandth as many as the teachers who have got it on account of the 'therefore I am' of Descartes's *cogito*. Perhaps these conclusions are weightier.

Panurge argues at great length against marriage, answering his own objections: Pantagruel comments each time – 'So, do what you will.' Their dialogue then takes wing: it is as though Bertrand Russell is being predicted here, informing Gottlob Frege (who had just finished his work on *The Basic Laws of Arithmetic*) that one of the fundamental laws which were to provide a basis in truth for all numerical calculation, one of those laws of logic more certain than arithmetic itself, led only to a contradiction. That was a memorable crisis for twentieth-

century mathematicians, the greatest crisis in mathematics, it is said, since the Greeks' discovery of irrational quantities. Apparently driven to distraction by the conclusions of the wise Pantagruel, Panurge, for his part, begins the crisis of 'Do what you will': 'Your advice, if I may be allowed to say so, seems like Ricochet's song to me. It's nothing but taunts and jokes and contradictory repetitions. One of them cancels out the other, and I don't know which to go by.'

Every great paradox alludes to the way in which it is presented, reflects the form in which it is stated. Here Panurge has himself defined the literary devices of Master François Rabelais.

'What ought I to do?' 'Do what you will!' 'But what ought I to will?' is Panurge's rejoinder. Once again Pantagruel brings him back to the formula: 'There are so many ifs and buts about your propositions ... that I can't base anything on them or come to any conclusions. Aren't you certain of your own wishes? That's the principal point ... ' The ball is tossed back again: it's for you to will. Another ricochet?

No, for the question of marriage does not allow free run to the idyll: in it the heaven of Thélème does not entirely conceal the possible hell. Doing 'what you will' presumes that you are certain of your wishes. Where is that the case? At Thélème? Not there! In battles, in great voyages of exploration, in hard problems to be solved. One goes into marriage as one begins a campaign, and not as one enters a monastery. 'The only thing, then, is to put things to the chance, with blindfolded eyes, bowing your head, kissing the earth, and, for the rest, entrusting yourself to God, seeing that you have made up your mind to go in for it. That is the only thing I can tell you for certain,' Pantagruel concludes, before undertaking along with Panurge that great voyage of exploration which was never completed. 'Do what you will' does not mean 'take up residence in Thélème', but 'leave Thélème, for when you are out of it you are already there'.

Thélème accepts you after checking that you are in good health. Outside, you *commit* yourself, nothing is settled in advance, but everything is put at risk, if, as Panurge argues, 'the codpiece is the principal piece of military harness' ... The simplest way to get round a logical paradox is to avoid encountering it, by laying down, for instance (as Russell does), that whatever includes all the elements in a collection must not be itself an element in that collection. Thus, Thélème was not established by a Thélémite but by Gargantua: the element is 'committed' to the collection, but it must not commit the collection of which it is a member. In Panurge's question, on the contrary, both the individual and the race are involved: 'When a man loses his head, only the individual perishes; but if the balls were lost, the whole human race would die out.'

Ever since Plato, the world and human nature have traditionally been divided into three parts: the head, seat of the intelligence, which sees the whole; the lower belly, inhabited by desire which focuses upon the individual and accidental; and, between the two, the heart, which by means of the will subjects the lower to the higher (provided, that is, all is as it should be). Panurge places his dynamite at the centre of this age-old construction. Not in sexual liberation: for him a sex-organ may sin or not sin, but it never preaches. Nor in criticism of the head – our hoary old leader preserves his sovereignty there too easily. More shrewdly, Panurge smashes the bolt, the screen, the buffer-zone called 'the will', and (the height of subtlety), instead of doing away with the will, he lets it appear in its role of intermediary, but stymied in consequence.

'Do you wish to infer . . .,' remarks Friar John when Panurge proposes an interpretation favourable to marriage of the dream he has just had. If there are two contradictory answers to one and the same question, the choice of one or the other of them merely shows the previously existing will of the person who has asked that question. Behind the will to know he reveals the will of the will, and all the more so because one tries to safeguard oneself by knowledge of knowledge. Panurge dreams of a horn: that is the subject of his question. He interprets this horn otherwise than as the cuckold's horn: this is the knowledge of his will. He interprets it as the horn of abundance of knowledge: this is his will to knowledge. 'Do you wish to infer,' says Friar John, 'that the dreams of horned cuckolds, such as Panurge will be, with God's help and his wife's, are always true and infallible?'

What is all this about? Marriage. That is to say, fidelity in love. More generally, fidelity of communication and the communication of fidelity. What can be communicated and what cannot. Ah, if it were only about that! It would then be enough to preach modesty to Panurge: if only he were not to strive after the science of science, he could be told, he might avoid that revolving door. But no, not at all! In the first place, Panurge's problem is not epistemological, it is the problem of how to avoid finding oneself *cuckolded, beaten and robbed*. Moreover, it is through that down-to-earth endeavour that we find ourselves caught in the paradoxes of 'do what you will'.

If he had pursued his explorations further, Panurge would perhaps have discovered, after passing the Kingdom of the Quintessence, offshore from the Isle of the Sandals and of the Order of the Quavering Friars, the archipelago of Marx and Engels. 'Not beaten?' one would have said to him: but this is the question of power – look to France, a political place if ever there was one. 'Not robbed?' That's done in the British manner, by means of the science called political economy. 'Not cuckolded, that is, deceived?' You have to leap in the Hegelian manner which is taught only in Germany. These are, Engels assures us, the three sources of Marxism, and the answer follows therefrom: make the revolution. By doing that, get married, then, by order of Marx!

Upon which certain evil-minded ones would try to explain, quoting examples, that he would none the less, afterward just as before, incur the risk of being beaten, robbed and cuckolded: *don't* get married, then!

'So, of what use to me is all your political science, your economics, and the latest philosophy?' Panurge would exclaim, turning back to get himself determined by the mode of production of his epoch.

Which epoch had, over the present one, the inestimable disadvantage of not knowing the benefits of uniting theory and practice – unless the priestess Bacbuc gave premature birth to the *Theses on Feuerbach*. 'Therefore I do not say to you: Read this chapter, understand this gloss. What I say is, Taste this chapter, swallow this gloss.' And, proffering the little red bottle, she propounded the ultimate version of 'Do what you will':

Trink! She comments in accordance with the best principles of Diamat, as though she had begun her studies at Moscow's Lomonosov University and taken her oral exam at the Humboldt University in East Berlin. Theory is to be drunk (*in vino veritas*), and practice goes on its way theorizing: 'The Holy Bottle directs you to it. *You must be your own interpreters in this matter.*' Adding that by wine one grows divine, and even capable of divination, the drunken priestess did not deceive, especially when she explained that this truth can be translated into all languages – German, included, with the help of Rhine wine: 'The True is thus the Bacchanalian revel, in which no member is not drunk . . . ' (Hegel).

Panurge's version of 'Do what you will' is quite different from that of Thélème. It does not shut one up in an ideal utopia but casts one out upon the road. It gives no guarantee against the risk of being deceived, robbed and beaten – and makes a joke of that. The paradoxes are neither disposed of nor avoided, they go along with the currents, they safeguard one only from the definitive safeguards; and do not constitute a principle of government: of knowledge as of power one can make fun, and one knows how to.

'In the Renaissance, laughter in its most radical, universal, and at the same time gay form emerged from the depths of folk culture: it emerged but once in the course of history, over a period of some fifty or sixty years . . . and entered with its popular (vulgar) language the sphere of great literature and high ideology. It appeared to play an essential role in the creation of such masterpieces of world literature as Boccaccio's *Decameron*, the novels of Rabelais and Cervantes, Shakespeare's dramas and comedies, and others' (M. Bakhtin).

6

Much later, having grown serious again, learned men were to explain laughter. Where did they get the idea that laughter is something that needs explanation? For the thinkers of the nineteenth century, societies become comical only when they are in decline: laughs belong to the end-game. When Aristophanes appeared, the Greek city was sinking, Hegel tells us. He was too serious to suppose that, long before, Socrates was already mocking his absolute knowledge and the Hegelian claims to possess, otherwise than as myth, the discourse that would make itself the creator before undertaking to create. Pupil Marx, always studious, would distinguish between the good people, the tragic ones, those who made the Great Revolution, and the others, the comical epigones, those who produced a (first) Social Republic without making the ultimate Social Revolution. Are those men of 1848 figures of ridicule for a 'consistent' and scientific Marxist a century later? Sartre, after the Second World War, sensed that there was something in common between Fascism and the spirit of seriousness, between the spirit of seriousness and the bourgeois, between the bourgeois and the Marxist.

Laughter moves everything around, crowns fools, de-bags monarchs, sets things topsy-turvy. 'From the wearing of clothes turned inside out and trousers slipped over the head to the election of mock kings and popes, the same topographical logic is put to work: shifting from top to bottom, casting the high and the old, the finished and completed, into the material bodily lower stratum for death and rebirth' (Bakhtin).

The Renaissance a rebirth through laughter? No, not at all, you are confusing matters, insinuates the serious nineteenth century. It's not a question of laughter, but of Science; of Reason, of the spirit-which-reconciles-itself-with-itself; of the Productive Forces; of the Protestant Spirit; of the Great Discoveries; of the New Nations; of Money. Ah, money! Did not Shakespeare himself call it the pandar, the universal whore? Yes, of course, but do not these great things which are held to explain laughter make merry in their turn? At what date did the sciences and the whores set to work without laughing? And the sailors? Seriousness soon descended upon the world after Rabelais, Shakespeare and Cervantes – but *after* them, precisely.

The spirit of seriousness followed that tremendous outburst which cast off all the mooring-ropes, even those of seriousness. Thélème and the universes of erudite and stewed self-sufficiency were laughed at before being suffered in their modern fatuity.

Seriousness cannot explain the laughter that precedes it except as something which it has just shaken off.

Circulation of debts, of blood, of the planets, of witty remarks, voyages, wars, poxes: the whirlwind of 'do what you will', when man becomes the attribute of laughter (and not the other way round). Between the head and the lower belly, the will no longer serves as hierarchical intermediary: the blood is 'the seat of the soul' and, transforming wine into blood, the body proves to be a forge without a master: 'At the forge all the members play their different parts; and their hierarchy is such that one borrows incessantly from another, one lends to another, one is another's debtor.' For the will which questions itself, whether or not to marry is undecidable, but this undecidable is decisive, the will is no longer a buffer, and its slew-round brings all back into the mainstream: 'This is all done by loans and debts one to another; whence it is called the debt of marriage.'

When he comes up against the argument that one cannot live by one's debts, nor indefinitely consume one's green corn, Panurge raises the tone of the debate, and names the adversary: these reproaches come 'from the University and Parlement of Paris, places where you will find the true source and living image of absolute and universal wisdom (*Pantheology*), and of all justice, too. Anyone who doubts this is a heretic ... ' At this point the academics of the twentieth century cannot contain themselves for joy: they have recognized in Panurge's words – true, somewhat incoherent and paradoxical – an outline, which they will not shrink from describing as brilliant (because premature) of the Dialectic, that which 'includes in its positive understanding of what exists a simultaneous recognition of its negation, its inevitable destruction' (Marx).

Does not Panurge himself explain that his circulation of debts transforms the world: he is engaged in 'felling the great trees, like a second Milo, demolishing the dark forests, the haunts of wolves, wild boar and foxes, the dens of brigands and murderers ...; levelling them to make great clearings and pleasant heaths, playing old harry with the timber and preparing the seats for the Eve of Judgement'? Here our rascal is caught in the act, speculating on the ignorance of his contemporaries. He is enriching his discourse with one of the best-known passages in the *Communist Manifesto*, the one wherein Marx begins all his sentences with: 'The bourgeoisie' (or with 'It', meaning the bourgeoisie) and ends them with a list of achievements prodigious enough to make Milo blench: 'has created enormous cities', 'has made barbarian and semi-barbarian countries dependent on the civilized ones', 'has centralized the means of production and concentrated property in a few hands', 'has accomplished wonders far surpassing Egyptian pyramids, Roman aqueducts and Gothic cathedrals'.

Nevertheless, it is to be doubted that Panurge has borrowed from Marx. Not just for the prosaic consideration of their respective dates: any historical and dialectical materialist of our day can cause the bourgeoisie to speak already from behind Panurge – has it not been made to 'accomplish' many another wonder? What matters more, does not Panurge compromise himself by saying that his debt 'prepares the seats for the Eve of Judgement'? This comes in the direct line from Marx: 'Not only has the bourgeoisie forged the weapons that bring death to itself; it has also called into existence the men who are to wield these weapons – the modern workers, the proletarians' (*The Communist Manifesto*).

'"But," asked Pantagruel, "when will you be out of debt?" "At the Greek Kalends," replied Panurge, "when all the world will be content, and you will be your own heir."' Editors put a footnote explaining that these three proverbial expressions all mean 'never'. The way in which this 'never' is signified is important. Goethe commented lengthily upon the second expression, and Freud upon the third. This impossibility does not disappear by virtue of the gesture of a visible king or the decree of a prince who vanishes after assembling the well-born in Thélème and the rest God knows where. Do what you will *and* all the world cannot be content: Thélème is dead, long live the highroad. You will certainly meet a father there, since nobody can be his own heir. May you have a good journey!

7

The Thélémites owed nothing to each other: when one of them said 'Let us drink', they all drank. Consequently, they owed everything, which means too much, to the Father of the Thélémite people. Panurge's economics is not available to worlds that are perfectly complete: debt stands in the way of unbreakable unions, but also of apocalyptic conflicts that are supposed to settle everything: neither the abbey, nor Picrochole's war, nor the eternal haven, nor the War To End War. Consequently, Panurge no longer expects that general crisis of capitalism the imminence of which sometimes delighted Marx and sometimes worried him, for fear that he might not finish his great work, *Capital*, before the bourgeoisie had closed the circle and cleared the paths into the future for the proletariat through a series of crises, collapses and catastrophes: 1853, 1857, 1862, and so on.

Marx studied with a pleasure that is still Panurgical the British system of credit, the most modern of his time, 'where chains of payments and an artificial system for adjusting them have been developed'. But he took care to summon this 'artificial system' before the court of the 'real' crisis, at the moment when the verdict given in the highest court was that there must be payment in cash: 'This sudden transformation of the credit system into a monetary system adds theoretical dismay to the actually existing panic, and the agents of the circulation process are overawed by the impenetrable mystery surrounding their own relations.' This is the great day when all debts will be settled, when the 'theoretical dismay' of the lackeys of capital will be balanced by the theoretical power of Marx and his comrades, just as the 'actually existing panic' will be balanced by the revolutionary dictatorship. A second, and definitive, 'artificial system of adjusting debts'... between powers, this time. It still operates: in 1975 the French Communist Party took care to reissue – on the occasion of *the* crisis – the book that Varga devoted to the general and final crisis of 1930 (which he had the great merit of foreseeing, just as he had predicted a dozen such in the previous decade, and was to predict nearly as many in the following one).

If we substitute for 'payment in cash', 'settlement by force of arms', and 'great battles' for 'crises', we discover what it was that Marx pined for: the sun of Austerlitz and the night of Waterloo. When the time comes, 'where,' asks Lenin, 'can the solution to contradictions lie, under capitalism, otherwise than in force?' Vladimir was to have no difficulty, after the event, in deducing from Marx's construction the necessity of the war of 1914: was this not a particularly bloody 'settlement of accounts'? Marx described, in the manner of Balzac and like Napoleon, the 'contradictions' of capitalism, and he presupposed, looked for and expected the 'final verdict' of the decisive battle.

Recommending that this sort of supreme decision be taken by 'throwing dice', Rabelais breaks with a good century of tradition, both militant and military, and gets himself expelled from many working-class organizations, not the Marxist ones only. In 'the syndicalist "general strike"', counterposed to 'Marx's catastrophic revolution', Georges Sorel saw two 'myths', that is, programmes of action such that 'the new tactics proposed must fit into the drama Napoleon had conceived.' In whatever way it be programmed, a final battle is needed in order to introduce the final solution. One may find Sorel a little bit sectarian in that he forgets the 'reformism' which figures in this same Napoleonic landscape: it is always a question of waging the campaign of campaigns (electoral, insurrectionary or trade-union) in order to get possession of the prize of prizes (the power to decide everything, the state or its substitute).

Here is something to put the wretched Comrade Panurge under the ban of six Internationals: by postponing to the Greek Kalends the final payment of debts, does he not try to hint that the final struggle is never finished? How could it then 'fit into the drama that Napoleon had conceived', and that so many of our revered leaders showed themselves able to put into effect on so many necks that were less venerable (yet had the weakness to be attached to their heads)?

Dubious in respect of his economics which lack an end, Panurge is no less heretical in politics. Has he not taken it upon himself to spread among the working class (naïve and generous of soul, as is proper) that dangerous illusion, denounced with one voice by the élite of reformism, revolution and syndicalism alike: 'eat your corn while it is green', without waiting for the harvest promised by singing tomorrows, or by the unity of national solidarity, or by the requirements of economic determinism? Isn't that egotism, economism, putting oneself first and one's hands in one's pockets, whereas what is needed is to roll up one's sleeves? Accursed working class! It is indeed necessary that the science of socialism be brought to it 'from without' (Lenin), if, 'spontaneously', in its heart of hearts, it tends rather to eat its corn Panurgically. Unless it too, with class-consciousness, dreams of acting the Napoleon.

2 Siegfried Without Knowing It

'Of all civilized peoples, the German submits most readily and permanently to the regime under which he lives and is, for the most part, not at all fond of innovations and opposition to the established order. His character combines understanding with phlegma: he neither indulges in subtilizations about the established order nor devises one himself. This makes him a man of all countries and climes . . .'

KANT, *Anthropology*

'The German working-class movement is the inheritor of German classical philosophy.'
F. ENGELS, *Ludwig Feuerbach and the End of German Classical Philosophy*

As with love and marriage, so with Revolution and the State. Whoever wishes to dodge awkward questions buries his head in the texts. When Panurge is desperate to rescue himself from the 'abysses and dangers' of Uncertainty, he is referred to those who are 'more learned', 'better informed' – to the rule of 'It is written', the refuge of all who are in the grip of hesitancy and scruples.

When Panurge lands on the Isle of Papimania, he is invited to admire, hanging from the roof of the temple, 'a great gilt book, all covered with fine and precious stones'. Opening this book and 'kissing it inside' has to be preceded by a whole ritual. In short, it is expected that one should bow in obedience to the book before reading it, and nobody will be surprised, when he does come to read it, to find that the whole truth, from beginning to end, that the book contains is that he must perform what it commands. Love of texts is what holds up tradition, and not *vice versa*. Explaining Mao by Lenin, Lenin by Marx, Marx by Hegel, Hegel by Moses (why not?) amounts to wanting to believe that the Tables of the Law are reproduced from generation to generation, and that texts, whether degenerated or regenerated, engender new texts by copulation with themselves. This is the usual belief we find embodied in respectable 'histories of ideas', to which those persons resort who prefer to avoid the questions that lurk very Socratically within themselves: don't cudgel your brains, the text provides both questions and answers, commenting on, refuting and transcending itself. Sacred inscriptions are the more sacred in proportion to their indecipherability, observed Hegel (without any commentator taking the opportunity offered to reflect upon the carefully cryptic and allusive style of Hegel himself).

'Obey? Why?' 'In order to be free!' So reply with one voice the Modern Times whose appearance Rabelais hailed joyfully in the guise of the Abbey of Thélème. The experts argue about whether it was industrial, technological, moral, violent or peaceful, gradual or realized at one bound, but none doubts that there is indeed a science of this liberating revolution.

The science of the revolution thus proves to be the subject which is most argued about but least discussed, with several models but only one programme: at the beginning (the 'input') there are your questions, at the end (the 'output') you are free ... to stop asking them. If you don't, you have to start all over again. Are you still wondering? That's a sign that there's something wrong with you, say the experts on politics, the family, sexuality or gardening. The questions you ask are so many symptoms: I question, therefore I lack knowledge, therefore I ask for knowledge. In what does my real freedom consist? A place in a learned text!

It means nothing to say that if the strength of the Prince resides in the weakness of the citizens, then that excuses the Prince. Unless we ask what it is that the citizens give their obedience to. To one person! That's the mange of the personality cult, by which we account for personal power, that mangy thing. Once the dictator has departed, his cult disappears and everything is put to rights. The cause (the cult) vanishes along with its effect (the tyrant). This scenario applies in Russia as in Germany, serving to rub out both Hitler and Stalin. It was all the fault of that big bad man and all those little fools. We won't get caught like that again. But, come now: what was it that those too obedient citizens were obeying? Their own obedience. Their respect, their cult. The Guide is able to guide because the guided let him guide them, damn it! Opium puts you to sleep because it possesses 'dormitive power'. On our way to reaching this point we have been made to forget that Stalin and Hitler secured obedience to themselves *holding a text*. They were accepted as having conquered only when the former succeeded in getting consecrated his one and only History of the Party of the Future and the latter succeeded in the same task with his *Mein Kampf*, as the sole Testament of the Nation of the Third Reich. From then on, until they died, they collected author's royalties from their subjects, paid in human flesh.

Germany we can't shake off: it sticks to our skin, with a mixture of cold sweats. The war in Algeria, the war in Vietnam, the 'socialist' camps: a spectre arises every time to haunt the post-1940 generations, reawakening their anguished contestation, the spectre of a people who went Nazi, after having given its 'beacons of thought' to the worlds of learning, philosophy, music and socialism in the nineteenth century. The most searching, troubling questions take us through that Germany which was for so long 'Europe's battlefield' (Thomas Mann, 1920).

We have been trapped in a text, said Fritz Lang in his *Testament of Dr Mabuse* (1933): a transparent allusion to the rise of Nazism, and at the same time a question about what the real text was that the Germany of that time was engaged in applying literally. Nazism made itself effective through linking what was called *national* with *revolutionary* ideology: but Nazism was not the first attempt to do this, all the German thinkers of the nineteenth century had a go at it – nor is it the last such attempt. In other words, while Hitler's 'personality' finds its place in a text which it thinks it has composed, this text exceeds that personality in all directions. And even if Hitler's reverence for the past entailed little concern for the accuracy of his references – he shamelessly distorted Nietzsche and Wagner – it remains true, nevertheless, that the past, before serving as a pretext, is indeed a pre-text: all through the nineteenth century Germany was premeditating a revolution that should be both national and socialist. Does this mean that we have to denounce an 'original sin' in German thought? Lukács and the Marxists set off along that trail, in search not so much of truth as of a scapegoat. They tied it up with the coarse string of sociology: unlike France, England and, maybe, the United States, Germany did not carry out a people's revolution, and owed its unity to the 'revolution from above' of Bismarck and the Prussian Army. This revolution accomplished in the wrong way was responsible for the irrationalism of Germany's thinkers which eventually burst out into Nazism. Modifying the scenario a little, the liberals have developed the same theme: did not the sociologist Weber say that the Germans' biggest misfortune was that they had not cut off the head of any of their Hohenzollern emperors?

It's only a question of the Germans, of nobody but them! And only in a limited period, not in any other! The Marxists have expounded the same theme, so as to 'localize' Stalin's doings in Stalin himself. But there is, alas, nothing strictly local in the world's succession of genocides, in the colonies and elsewhere, or in the world-wide diffusion of the concentration-camp system. We need to think about these things on a less petty scale.

The cradle of bureaucracy

The 'Germany' where Fascisms are born is not a territory or a population, but a text and an attitude to texts which became established long before Hitler, and spread far beyond the borders of the Holy Roman Empire of the German nation. This 'Germany' is perfectly contemporary, having its seat in the modern heads of the modern world, in the Pentagon in Washington just as in any concentration camp deep in the Cambodian countryside. Perhaps the hypothesis put forward in this blunt way will become plausible in the end, if we re-examine the Germany of last century and its master thinkers, bringing yesterday into relation with today. It ought, though, not to seem totally improbable to start with. Custom requires that text and territory be made to go together: the Rights of Man with France, liberalism with England, the German ideology with Germany. This correspondence runs only one way: from a certain territory a certain text has emerged. Suppose, though, we change the angle of vision: for a Breton, a Corsican, a Basque or (*this* question has now been settled) an Arab, is France really that primary, territorial reality which then, secondarily, expresses itself in texts? Have not these 'natives' experienced in the first place a strategy of the text turned into law and arriving to imprint itself, through *dragonnades* and forced language-teaching, upon a rebellious or alien reality?

The correspondence between text and territory is a matter not of right but of fact, contemporary with the birth of the modern nation-states and the wars of religion, which came to a provisional conclusion (let each region have its own religion: *cujus regio, ejus religio*) that was military rather than metaphysical. Whether royal or revolutionary, the wars which unified the territory – centre against periphery, towns against rural areas, orthodoxy against heresies, language against '*patois*' – forbid us to counterpose a simple 'unification from below' to the unification from above which is supposed to be something peculiar to Germany.

'The Church has no territory' is a maxim of Papal law which has not prevented the oldest bureaucracy in Europe from imposing its texts upon a mass of believers. Quite the contrary – the lack of a territory is taken to be symbolic of the world-wide, extra-territorial power of a Text which is in an absolute sense divine and to which the whole human race is to be subject. Equivalence of a text with a territory – true, for the last five hundred years, and with some exceptions. But it is in the armed institution of the text that we have to see the active side of this equivalence: the text lays down the law for the territory ('territory': 'right to frighten', *jus terrendi*, according to a revealing etymology put about by the Emperor Justinian), and this leads one to think that the peculiarity of the Germany of history and geography has nothing to do with a revolution from above carried out towards the end of the nineteenth century, or with a revolution from below that was lacking at the start of it. It is much more illustrative, over four centuries, of a notable lack of equivalence between text and territory.

To become aware of this it is enough to mention two facts that were decisive for Germany's destiny.

(1) The unity of the Germans existed long before the unity of the German territory. It was affirmed when Luther translated the Bible and addressed his great appeal 'To the German Nation'. He condemned the particularism of the Princes, the ambitions of the Knights, the 'selfishness' of the burghers and the peasants, raising high above them all his 'dear Germany': 'It is for you, dear Germans, that I seek salvation and sanctity' (1531).

(2) The atomization of the territory was contemporary with the process of unification by texts. While the neighbouring states were being formed into nations (England and France), two events transformed the old Germanic Empire for a period of several centuries into a scattering of local absolutisms (the 'regime of little states', *Kleinstatterei*). First came the crushing of the peasants' revolts and the bringing to heel of the mercantile cities which went along with that. Engels, in emphasizing this event, which was indeed highly important, nevertheless gives it undue weight, since in other places repressions that were no less brutal (the war against the Camisards, for instance) did not have the definitive consequences he ascribes to them. It was a second catastrophe that transformed the first one into a destiny: namely, the devastation and massacres which culminated in the Thirty Years' War, a period when the population was not merely decimated but, in all probability, reduced by a third, through the actions of its Princes, aided by all the armies of the young states of Europe. Peace, with the Treaties of Westphalia in 1648, was established over a graveyard: Germany had been the Vietnam of the new powers of Modern Times, a Vietnam which thereafter lay crushed for two centuries.

From this resulted a strange Germany whose text did not correspond to its territory, a Germany that would belong to yesterday and tomorrow but never to today, as Nietzsche said. Measured by the standard of the Europe of national states, it was a special case: 'Instead of forming a national state it is a real dustbowl of territories together with a dream of hegemonic Empire. That is the German paradox *par excellence*.' A German oddity only? No, indeed. While the text 'fits' better in the neighbouring nation-states, they are no less given to dreaming of empires, which in some cases they carve out for themselves as colonies: the dreams of the Foreign Legion do not seem to have been any more tender than those of the Teutonic Knights. The moonbeams of great disasters and the sunbursts of contestations suffice, moreover, for a reappearance of that 'dustbowl' of bureaucratic feudal orders which the great states weld together rather than suppress. Whereas the other states of Europe keep their mouths shut about their methods of domination, the German state goes about with its mouth wide open, since its law cannot manage to devour its territory. This spectacle was for a long time unique, and is even yet revealing in what it tells us about the digestive system of the contemporary powers. Is Germany *monstrous*, perhaps, because it displays in mint condition procedures of government which elsewhere have more of a patina upon them, and so are hidden from our view?

A thing that is presented as being a peculiarly German speciality – the celebrated 'German wretchedness' talked of by Marx and the Young Hegelians – is this capacity for living simultaneously in two separate worlds, the world of ideas and that of facts, of the ideal and of political realism, of mythology and of guns. 'Our German philosophy is merely the French Revolution – but as a dream,' said Heine, ironically: what on one side of the Rhine they do, on the other side they think. Marx faithfully echoed the poet when he spoke of the 'political head' of the French in contrast to the 'philosophical head' of the Germans which led the latter to make up for the 'incomplete works' of their real history by means of criticism, by the 'posthumous works' of their intellectual history. When, later on, German politics became in its turn highly real, but reactionary, Marxists and liberals (before 1940) agreed in simply inverting the duality: Germany was once again to be understood as being cut in two, with politics now becoming its bad side (Prussian, militarist, feudal), while on the other, the good side, lay its humanist, universal, Goethean culture. This time, the philosophical frontier was no longer the Rhine but the Elbe, or the Oder: but the pattern of duality survived.

The German is twofold – cultivated and devilish: Germany is twofold – real and ideal. These are facile explanations, which call for counting on two fingers only. Germany's critics do not hold a monopoly in this procedure: every German head has, at one time or another, been caressed by the idea of discovering a true, sound Germany, completely external, and, as it were, indifferent, to the false 'Germany No. 2' which surrounds it. Still today some small groups faithfully republish the most insignificant of the theories of the pre-war Communist Party, as though it is necessary thereby to join the thread of a totally different, revolutionary history, that of the true Germany. Was the President of the Federal Republic less naïve (in 1976) when he linked the prospects before German democracy with the activity, 'unfortunately not followed up', of 'the shoemaker Ebert'? The socialist founder of the Weimar Republic was at the same time the godfather (this the President forgets) of the repression of the Spartakist revolutionaries by the Imperial Army (1919). The primary and true Germany was pursued by the folk-lore devotees of the nineteenth century even into the forests of the Middle Ages . . .

Explaining Germany by the existence of two Germanies, one good and the other bad, thus proved to reproduce the very myths which needed clarification. Besides, they embraced the wind: the famous German culture was much more subtle, it did not in the least develop in a world external to the barbarism it explored – what was Serenus Zeitblom, the peaceful commentator on Thomas Mann's Doctor Faustus, writing if he was not trying to discern, through his diabolic hero, the integral nature of the German destiny? In the first place, by reference to what unity does one measure the so much criticized duality of the Germans and of Germany?

When Marx speaks of the 'incomplete works' of German history he is comparing them with the 'complete works' of the French Revolution. But hardly has he turned towards *that* than he finds it equally incomplete in relation to the complete works of the proletarian revolution. When he turns back to a Germany which, in 1848, has failed in its imitation of 1789, he explains this circumstance again by a twofold incompleteness: Germany lags behind because there lies ahead of it its future proletarian revolution, which holds it back from accomplishing a revolution that, in a sense, already lies behind it. Does this twofold in-completeness explain the special fate of Germany? Not at all, since Marx at once explains in the same way that the new Em-peror of the French, Napoleon III, is himself also both ahead of and behind an industrial bourgeoisie which has a revolutionary proletariat treading on its heels. And there would be Marxists to speak of the 'Bonapartism' of Bismarck, Hitler and Stalin.

We see that Marx lives in a world in which the history of every country is 'incomplete'. The history of Germany is not at all unusual in possessing this characteristic, since Marx finds the only 'complete works' of history in his own head, and on the shelves of the libraries where they all end up.

An additional proof. The theory of the German ideology was constructed in order to explain the specific situation of the intellectual in a specific history, that of pre-revolutionary Ger-many. Having become the Marxist theory of 'ideology' in general, it has served as an all-purpose explanation – of religion, of madness, of electoralism, of rationalism, of Machism, and so forth. This amounts either to acknowledging that the German situation had nothing specific about it (which runs counter to the initial assumption), or else that, by explaining everything, this theory can explain anything whatsoever (Q.E.D.).

The only gesture that the theory of the 'two' Germanies authorizes is that of closing one's eyes and hiding one's face. The 'good' Germany, virginal and innocent, is always the one where-in the critical commentator takes his stand, which is as much as to admit that his entire theory is aimed only at exorcizing the bad Germany: above all, let her not touch us, or tempt us, or hem us in! After the passage of a few years, the scenery having trembled, the mental trap becomes obvious when a Professor of the Sorbonne is found to have justified in one breath the Tsarist knout and colonialism, in order to attach to these 'complete works' of Western humanism the good Germany, the one which is neither Prussian nor military, but 'cultured': 'This faith in the Enlightenment ... conquered in the eighteenth century not only the most substantial elements in German cul-ture but also the Westernized Russia of Peter the Great. Now, this was the bourgeois idea *par excellence*. When we speak of the Enlightenment we mean also technology and its wondrous achievements ... the great deeds of this Western bourgeoisie, which built vast empires like the British and French empires' (E. Vermeil, *L'Allemagne*, 1945). We measure the price paid for making Germany the special land of duality: elsewhere (in the Western or the revolutionary Thélèmes – which, moreover, are very closely akin) a unity is imagined to exist, the perfection of which draws nourishment from the imperfection of Germany.

The point is to make Germany a sort of foil, an ugly contrast, lest we should recognize in it both the savagery of other powers and the strategies whereby they make their subjects love them. The Europe of states does not dare to look at itself, without make-up, in the German mirror. It does not want to see itself any more in the gaze fixed upon it, upon its rational methods of civilization, government and revolution, by the Algerian or Vietnamese orphan or the fugitive from the Gulag Archipelago. And what if it is the same image? Doesn't it mean going too far in acting the fool today to wish to preserve one half (the good one) of this Germany of fantasy, out of fear lest we may have to decipher therein the old secrets of European power? Is Europe perhaps not, like a heraldic emblem, constructed in the form called 'abyss', with in the midst of it that terrible 'German' face which it has so often shown to the peoples of the other continents?

'There are certain family feelings that are particularly intense, and one of them was the dislike of Germany that prevailed generally in the European family of nations before 1914.' Having noted this, R. Musil, writer in German, found himself fleeing from the Brown Plague into a difficult exile. He goes on, however: 'It [Germany] was, furthermore, aggressive, grasping, boastful and dangerously lacking, like every excited crowd, in responsibility for its actions. But all this was, after all, only European, and it should not have been anything but, at most, a little bit too European for all the other Europeans.' It will perhaps be retorted that Musil died in 1942, the year when the grand manoeuvres of the 'Final Solution' began. Did not the six million Jews who died in the camps signify that Germany's destiny was like no other country's? Could one see in *that* merely something 'a little bit too European'?

Or should one remain firm in Musil's position, being surprised, on the contrary, that the number of victims did not alter by so much as a comma the pre-1914 discourses? (The states which made Germany their scapegoat often collaborated later in the Nazis' crimes.) 'One lets other people exert themselves while one sits there comfortably looking on: that is sport. One lets other people talk the most wildly one-sided extravagances: that is idealism. One shakes off the Evil, and what gets splashed with it is the images of one's displeasure ... But this technique of hagiolatry and fattening up of scapegoats by means of projections into the outer world is not without its dangers, for it fills the world with the tensions of all the inner conflicts that have not been fought out' (Musil, ibid.). Thirty years after the Second World War and the solemn condemnation of the Nazi crimes against humanity, these 'conflicts that have not been fought out' are all around us. The reason is clear: at Buchenwald and Auschwitz the Germans did indeed act *in the European way*, exemplifying a European (even Western, modern, revolutionary) manner of imposing 'final solutions', a manner which was illustrated equally well at Pulo-Condor in Vietnam, under French and then American occupation, and, through half a century, in the Soviet Union's Kolyma.

In two hundred years of colonization and revolution, Europe's ideas and methods have ended by circling the whole world, while, bathing in the blood of its world wars and dreaming of going on with the story by using other continents, the thinking élite of our little headland splits the questions up so as the better to avoid answering them: Germany is Germany, Russia is Russia, South American Fascism is something else again, and so on. It remains true that these strategies of domination which have subjected the peoples to the states and the world to the super-powers are strategies of strictly European origin. There is no point in running off to the antipodes in order to sniff exotic events: nearly fifty years ago the adolescent Nizan discovered that in 'Aden, Arabie' he still found Europe. Since then, the world has been freed from colonialism, by revolution, which means, more often than not, freed from Europe by Europe.

Revolution by means of texts

Imitation of 1789 and 1793 was conscious with Lenin, Trotsky and Mao. In very rare flashes of insight they let their suspicion appear that, far from transcending the 'bourgeois' French Revolution in their 'proletarian' Marxist revolutions, they were only reproducing, at best the experiences of the 'Great' Revolution. When Lenin acknowledges that he has perhaps only painted over the Tsarist bureaucracy a little with some Soviet varnish, or when the aged Mao questions his interlocutors and, very likely, himself as well, about Robespierre, that admission is on the tips of their tongues. But they will not give it voice, out of respect for the 'science of revolution', whose pages are turned when the great moments of history follow one another.

Whatever may be said, revolutions are not contagious. The English, French, Russian, Chinese revolutions all halt, discreetly or not, at the frontiers of other peoples – unless the revolutionary wars become wars of conquest, imperial and imperialist in nature. Taken by itself, each revolution is seen, in its successes even more than in its failures, to be inimitable. Even the revolution of 1789, which offered itself as a universal model, and was greeted as such, found no place where it could reproduce itself. The *apparent* contagion of revolutions is conveyed by the 'science of revolution'. When Lenin in 1917 criticized 'petty-bourgeois compromises' and invented a new form of revolutionary radicalism, he thought simply in terms of applying the 'lessons' drawn by Marx from the defeat of the German revolution of 1848. In the name of those 'scientific' lessons he boldly crammed down the German model over the Russian situation: the Constituent Assembly which he caused to be dispersed was, in his eyes, only a repetition of the garrulous Frankfurt Parliament so despised by the founders of Marxism, who saw in it a 'Constituent Assembly' quite paralysed by the idea of becoming a 'Convention'. The ninety-per-cent peasant Russia of 1917 thus seemed to our materialist thinker to be a second Germany of 1848 (in the image thereof left by Marx, i.e. seen only in the light of a constant comparison with the France of 1789). The 'science of revolution', one and indivisible in the minds of the great thinkers, thus makes it possible to see as the single object of a cerebral passion *the Revolution* which is present in all revolutions and yet resembling none of them.

In 1927 Trotsky, then still the respected leader of the Russian Revolution, appeared for the first time before the Presidium of the Central Control Commission. In the argument that took place they hurled references at one another. Solz, accusing Trotsky, demanded: 'What does this lead to? You know the history of the French Revolution...' Trotsky took the ball at the rebound: he knew all the ins and outs of this scientific dispute.

'During the great French Revolution, many were guillotined. We, too, brought many people before the firing squad. But there were two great chapters in the French Revolution ... In the first chapter, when the Revolution moved upwards, the Jacobins, the Bolsheviks of that time, guillotined the Royalists and Girondists. We, too, have gone through a similar great chapter ... But then another chapter opened in France when ... the Thermidorians and the Bonapartists ... began to exile and shoot the left Jacobins ... Revolution is a serious business. None of us is scared of firing squads ... But we must know who it is that is to be shot and what chapter it is that we are in.'

And there you are! Far away is that Russia in which the first outposts of the Gulag Archipelago were bitterly commemorating their tenth anniversary; windows and doors have long since been shut in the room where these so irreconcilable adversaries agreed 'that they all needed to consult afresh the annals of the French Revolution'. The two colleagues are touching in their realism: not to shrink from firing squads, isn't that the essence of all political realism? The Russian reality of 1927 is thus to be read in the annals of 1793. The question is, on which page is the killing taking place? If it is in the Jacobin chapter, then let the heads roll; but if it is in the Thermidor chapter ... And so history moves forward, turning over the pages of a book.

The game of the law

This passion for texts is not so much a feature of the revolutionary in particular as of the man of power in general. A government maintains itself not by the gun alone but also by the effects produced by a text upon other people. When Stalin asked how many divisions the Pope had, he was pretending to be naïve: he had paid with the blood of others for the privilege of appearing as the unchallenged interpreter of the 'history' of the Communist Party and the sole Vicar of the Spirit of Leninism. A ruling power does not base itself merely upon a certain number of texts added to a certain number of tanks. The history of the Communist Party imposed by Stalin was not just a narrative, whether mendacious or not: it divided up the political world in accordance with guidelines and lines of force, it put forward a methodology for recognizing, classifying and dealing with the enemy, and so on. Texts do not simply serve the exercise of power, they are that very exercise, they subject people. Even more than the chains of slavery, they are part of that slavery. Policemen inside the heads of those who are subjected to them, the great texts of power in Europe are not in the service of strategies of domination, they are these strategies themselves.

The strategy of the text cannot proclaim itself as such. A ruling power does not say that it is a rule *over* before it has claimed to be a rule *of*. The law of France is the will 'of the French people' and the Russian state is a state 'of the whole people' and the dictatorship 'of the proletariat'. In legal terms, the ruling power calls for a game to be played against nature, it summons each and everyone, in the general interest, to 'govern things'. Universal, it is of yesterday or tomorrow but never of today (like Germany according to Nietzsche): it appeals to the tradition 'which has made us what we are', or to the tomorrows which sing and make us all brothers. Since it claims to prescribe the laws by which its subjects are to legalize their conflicts, a ruling power has to be seen to come from somewhere beyond those conflicts: whether its 'truth' is philosophical, historical or racist, it dominates the problems it is supposed to solve, it cannot be governed by the relations between the subjects it governs, and must therefore be governed from elsewhere, like Gargantua instituting the Thélémites before ever they came into existence as such.

At once, the text employed by the ruling power appears not as a 'game against the other one': it recognizes no 'other' apart from the one it excludes ('the barbarians'), in other words, the one it declares it will not play with. However, the strategy of the text cannot be aimed at being a mere 'game against nature': it addresses itself to freedoms which it is claimed are being brought together as such. The ruling power does not rule over men as things, since it needs subjects, but it cannot be reduced to a relation *between* men since it accords itself the privilege of defining the rule of the game, that is, the human status which these men are recognized as possessing. Hence the paradox of the first legislator which every theory of government runs into – facing it or trying to get round it, but never managing to avoid it. 'The people, being subject to the laws, ought to be their author ... The legislator occupies in every respect an extraordinary position in the state ... Thus in the task of legislation we find together two things which appear to be incompatible: an enterprise too difficult for human powers, and, for its execution, an authority that is no authority' (J. J. Rousseau, *The Social Contract*, II, 6, 7).

In face of this paradox, Thélème illustrates the position of the one who dominates: Gargantua provides for the reign of 'Do what you will' and proves his authority by absenting himself: a reign whose author is out of reach appears unchallengeable. The other position, that of Socrates–Panurge, does not aim at providing a foundation for authority but takes it as it is, without foundation, in order to challenge it. Thereby the strategy of the ruling power that wants to lay down the law seems doubly irreducible. There is no 'game against the other one', for he who dictates the law meditates in Gargantua-like solitude. Nor is there a game against impassive nature, for it aims to rule out the possibility of a counter-strategy, that of the challenger whom it names only in order to decree that he cannot exist. Being neither a relation to things nor a relation among men, but regarded as standing logically 'before' the distinction between them, this game of the law wages against phantoms a battle bloody enough for one to be able thenceforth to isolate certain of its character- istic tricks. (More prosaically one recognizes in the game of the law the essential routine of modern bureaucracies, in so far as they make sure of their subjects.)

What are these tricks? What do those men need who rise to power nowadays, apart from a good army, plus brandy and sausages? They need texts.

Being in the good books of the powers that be

A rule is a rule, says the bureaucrat. The sociologist sees in this his 'rationality': the bureaucrat seems merely to be stating that everyone must know what the laws are, and act according to general commandments laid down by an abstract rule. He pro- motes behaviour subject to calculation, combining given means towards a clearly conceived end (what Weber calls action with a rational aim): to add, as Marx does, that more often than not he presents his private interest as the general interest takes away none of the calculating side (whether selfish or not) that we assume him to possess.

Sometimes the bureaucrat seems a man given to calculation beyond the limits of possibility: when he opens his cupboard of rules, we are overwhelmed beneath huge files of official docu- ments, while he whispers in a consoling tone, like a functionary of Kafka's *Castle*: 'That's only a small fraction of it. I've put away the most important pile in the shed, but the great mass of it has simply gone astray.' Hence the suspicion that far from oper- ating in what Weber called a 'disenchanted' world (and Marx a 'sober' one), his 'rationality' introduces us to the modern enchantments: for all that it has been metamorphosed into an undergrowth of procedures, the Forest of Brocéliande has lost nothing of its mystery. It is already ten years since an American minister felt confident that he could rationalize the defence policy of the U.S.A., including the war in Vietnam, by submitting all the budgetary options to 'expert planners who decide rationally on the actions needed in order to attain the objectives chosen'. It is too late now to wax ironical about what was then known as 'the McNamara strategy', except to note that what was important for the minister was not so much to calculate as to convince his public that calculation was feasible. (How could the public, in those days greatly taken with the idea, not entrust to him the arduous task of carrying out these calculations?)

While rational calculation is indeed the ideal that the bureaucrat wants us to share with him, his actual work, which is quite different, consists rather in causing this ideal to be believed in: not so much the man who calculates as the man who guarantees the calculation, he reassures us that the cupboard full of rules will not suddenly burst open to pour forth a Niagara of contradictory regulations – that, on the contrary, everything has been carefully arranged and co-ordinated in there, that his sacred task consists in putting it even more in order than it is, something which is nevertheless still possible. He is the man 'of belief in a single Text' (Legendre, *Jouir du pouvoir*).

Thélème inscribed its rule, in all simplicity, over its entrance. What keeps the bureaucrats busy is deciphering the modern equivalent, quietly acknowledging that this law does actually exist: legislation, regulations, jurisprudence make no sense unless we appreciate that these activities 'keep on producing the same object, always identified as being precisely the same, whether it is styled French law, the bureaucratic system or something else'. The ultimate purpose of bureaucratic systems is to present themselves as *a* system: even more important than application of the rule is the task of getting it accepted that something exists as *the* rule. 'In this way one enters a universe of silence, the universe of the Text, of the Text which knows everything and says everything, asking the questions and also answering them' (ibid.).

Authority does not derive its legitimacy from guns alone. It is not enough for it to make powder speak, it makes the text speak as well: 'One doesn't carry on a dialogue with the law, one makes it speak, using a scholastic method operated by the technicians of this written discourse, just like the old-time glossarists. In our day, though, it is not any longer a matter of the law of the church, of the Empire, of the vassal states, and so on, but of the law of the centralized industrial state.'

The state, bureaucracy, cumulative history, all presuppose in the life of the peoples, observes Lévi-Strauss, that leap forward which was constituted by the invention of writing. The army equipped with guns moves across and mops up, but the army equipped with pens is needed to occupy the ground taken. 'Guns have no minds of their own. If there is a change in the ideology of the men who hold the guns, then the guns will lend themselves to achieving a different purpose for a different master. Whoever forgets this forgets the basic theses of Marxism-Leninism and is foolish' (Mao). In order not to be 'foolish', that is, in order to keep themselves in power, the authorities have not waited for Marxism to codify their wisdom. However, since the guns have been aimed at those capable of causing disorders ('free workers'), Marxism has brought an invaluable contribution to the modern versions of the Text of the rulers.

Twentieth-century scriptures

Marxism? I presume to use the word without any qualifier so as to indicate with unruffled solemnity that intellectual treasure which the bitterest of enemies are supposed all to share – the Russian government, the Chinese government, traitors within, revisionists without. When one-sixth of the globe threatens with thermo-nuclear chastisement one-quarter of the world's population, and it is conceivable that the latter could answer back in kind, what has happened to that 'science of revolution' common to them both? And yet, in all the universities of the West, 'Marxism' is commented on, 'Marxism' is discussed, and sometimes people say they are 'anti-Marxist', with an air of shooting an arrow at some precise target. Where is this target? Is it the red star? The one worn by the Muscovite Marshal who dreams of obliterating Peking, or the same star as worn, more discreetly, by his opposite number in Peking who dreams (also more discreetly) of rendering tit for tat? Is the Marxist the one who will fire second? Or the one who, preventively, will fire first?

Or is it perhaps the third robber? The one who makes a virtue of recording the mistakes of the two others, he who, when the different 'Marxisms' have destroyed each other and a few scattered leaves float above the scene of disaster, will thoughtfully come along and collect them up in order to re-discover 'Marxism'? The worst crimes can be thought of as 'mistakes', not merely by former or future torturers but also by Marxist intellectuals who are some thousands of miles away from the drama itself. Not too ungraciously, they will agree, to close the discussion, that these are indeed crimes, and (coming close to impoliteness to the driving-force of history) even 'horrible crimes' ... But always with a mental reservation: a crime is something more than a mistake, but, all the same, a crime requires an explanation. Behind the crime they postulate the mistake which explains it. As to how this mistake should be described, university teachers and political parties are inexhaustible: economism, voluntarism, dogmatism – the list is infinite, just as the occasions for sin are innumerable: Stalin misread Lenin, or Lenin misread Marx, or Marx read too much Hegel, and so on. Let a hundred schools contend, let a hundred flowers of rhetoric bloom, provided that it be accepted that it is always the same garden that is being cultivated, that of the one-and-only Text, *the* way of using power to which no ruling élite can refrain from referring. All these deviations ending in 'ism', through which tears and blood become matters accounted for and classified, amount to what? To misreadings! Of what? Of the Text!

What have all Marxists in common before they set to massacring each other (and even while they are doing that)? Belief in the one-and-only Text, in 'Marxism'. It is a belief that they share, moreover, with all the bureaucracies of modern states, except that these give different titles to *the* Text. All of them swear by it: 'One does not carry on a dialogue with the law, one makes it speak.'

(In passing, let it be said that the weakness of most so-called critics from the Left of the bureaucracies that proclaim themselves socialist lies in the fact that they, like most sociologists, overlook the point that bureaucracy mobilizes itself around the Text. Since the marrow-bone of these bureaucracies is precisely the Marxist text, in which their critics expect to discover their weapon of criticism, a series of cases of talking at cross-purposes results, with exponential generation of critical criticism. This Marxism, held in common, chimerical but necessary, divided up *ad infinitum* among bureaucrats, critics and critics-of-critics, can itself grow and multiply.)

The game of truth

You either know or you don't know! Hegel (or Plato already before him), addressing Socrates, rules out the third position of *inscientia* (wherein knowing that one does not know can dispense with knowledge). The Athenian court, so far as we can tell, justified similarly its condemnation of Socrates: he does not respect our gods and our authorities, therefore he is conspiring to set up other gods and other authorities, he wants to impose his law in place of ours. Whoever is not with us is against us, Lenin would say, scientifically, as he statistically shovelled masses of 'kulaks, petty-bourgeois, corrupted workers' into the first camps. Why must there be only two parties? Owing to imperfectly suppressed religiosity? An outbreak of moralism? Endemic dogmatism? Behind all that, much closer to common sense, and thereby infinitely more penetrating, lies the postulate of all authority: 'one divides into two' (Mao), and not into three or five, because everything is a matter for decision. There is a right and a wrong, a winner and a loser.

'There may enter in here ... There may not enter in here ... ' So reads the inscription at the entrance to Thélème. Knowledge or ignorance, guilt or innocence, everything is either on the left or on the right. The dichotomies can be complicated and even defy enumeration. 'In every difference there is already a contradiction and ... the difference itself constitutes a contradiction' (Mao). This formula can be understood as one of dangerous radicalism (the schools are different, therefore they contend to the death, and the hundred flowers are blood-red). But this radicalism is a matter of law: the text asks questions and gives replies, and decides everything on the assumption first and foremost, that everything is *capable of decision* by 'yes' or 'no', the third position being excluded and Socrates doomed to disappear.

One of the generally accepted principles of reasoning is the principle of non-contradiction: one cannot assert, at the same time and from the same standpoint, both something and its opposite. Subjecting the behaviour and misbehaviour of its subjects to its non-contradictory judgement, the law annexes them to the domain of cases that can be decided, and proclaims that it acts rationally, is scientific, is indeed the science of decision.

We see why the administration is in such a hurry to postulate a single Text in which all the scattered regulations, decrees and jurisprudence are brought into unity. In the first place, the law must not be contradictory in itself, if it is to decide in a sovereign manner. Secondly, the Text must guarantee to the law that realm of activities upon which it promulgates decisions, and which are therefore matters subject to decision. By applying universally, without question, as though in accordance with simple common sense, the principle of non-contradiction, the law actually endows itself with an extraordinary privilege, namely, that of always disposing of the moment and the standpoint at which it is possible to distinguish between, and to contrast, a thing and its opposite. The problem of the principle of non-contradiction lies there. Not in the subtle definition of the 'opposite' of a thing (as the dialecticians would have us believe, Mao here being Hegel's pupil). Much more important is the 'moment' and the 'standpoint' to which the principle of non-contradiction alludes, indicating that we must take up our position there if we are to employ this principle.

The law sets up its household gods in that place without any apparent difficulty, in the name of common sense, but in fact in an unconscionably privileged situation. Even mathematics (after much labour of formalization and since Gödel) no longer claims to possess that standpoint in relation to itself which would make it possible at a given moment in its development to declare whether it is non-contradictory or not. Mathematics recognizes (in its own way) as capable of expression the 'paradox of the

Cretan' which the Law, in condemning Socrates, definitely does not wish to know. The law's reasoning begins at the point where mathematics concludes its own. '*See, Willem, he admits that he doesn't know the Law, and yet he claims he's innocent*' (KAFKA, *The Trial*).

When we drive the paradox out of the door, it comes back through the window. Claiming that it operates only upon matters that can be decided, the law, when we watch it at work, offers a living proof of the effectiveness of what is undecided and confused – of red tape, in short.

'Administrative inertia, the wall of red-tape-bound formalities, the contradictions engendered by the rivalry between services, camouflaged today by the enigmatic enterprise of co-ordination, all these are not by-products, but realize day by day, in the expanding context of mass-scale management, one of the aims of centralized organization ... In the practice that emerges from this frenzied and sacred doctrine, only the leading figures are able to speak, because they embody the omniscient law ... Everything has to happen in the manner of the colonial set-up in which the ordinary subjects are treated as incapable of speech, being held politically by this wordless condition' (Legendre, *Jouir du pouvoir*).

Here we have to invert the usual way in which things are seen: the blunders made by bureaucratic rationality are more rational and effective than its odes to Supreme Reason. Paper blocks its mouth, the hierarchic lift prevents any physical contact, the uniform, outward and inward, worn by a secretary, together with his 'administrative modesty', prevent one from imagining him naked: 'Here you have your Greek god! Go on, haul him out of bed!' (Kafka, *The Castle*).

K., the indiscreet land-surveyor, asks the village schoolteacher if he knows the owner of the castle. The teacher at once wants to go away; he answers 'Why should I?' Then, pointing to his pupils, he adds, *in French*: 'Please remember there are innocent children present.' Every bureaucracy employs two languages: Latin and the vernacular, the 'distinguished' French and the vulgar Russian of Tsarist Russia, specialized jargon (legal, Marxist, or what not) and everyday conversation. Ordinary language is annulled by a learned language, but this learned language has no secret other than that of annulling ordinary language. Entrenched behind its paper and its formulas, if the law does not speak to the man in the street it is because it has nothing to say to him except that he should hold his tongue. For the accomplishment of this task it is pointless to assume that, behind that stack of files, the law possesses any other knowledge besides that of how to stack files. In view of the number of paper barricades erected over the centuries, a far from negligible degree of practical skill is needed in order to be able to move around among them so as to erect new ones. This science of endless circulation from one office to another constitutes a science of indecision.

The only way of making someone play a game which one is sure of winning is for that someone not to know that this is the situation. The law therefore convinces its subjects of their invincible ignorance because, being totally incomprehensible, it furnishes the living proof of their inferiority: '*The forty volumes of Lenin represent an oppression for the masses*: we can accept that, for the masses have neither the time nor the means today to tackle this type of knowledge, which is an intellectual's knowledge – so what is to be done?' (Sartre, *Situations* VIII). The status of Marxist theory, in which, if we are to believe Lenin–Althusser, every comma matters, is not that of *a* science but rather that of *the* science of decision, the law whose doctors, by misreading or shifting the commas, can determine either Gulag or the unheard-of and never-yet-seen happiness of socialism. A sure sign that these texts are of the kind that authority brandishes.

This strategy functions to the extent that it is not perceived by the subject, who has to believe what the law affirms, that the law knows what it is doing – to believe not that it knows how to make him obey but that it makes him obey because it knows. This end is served, for example, by the artless version of the struggle between master and slave. According to this, in the beginning, the master possesses knowledge, and the slave submits to this by working for him. Through his work the slave changes the world and acquires the knowledge arising from this transformation, whereas his master possesses it without knowing any longer what it is that he possesses. The end follows naturally: the slave who has learnt through his work overthrows, supplants, eliminates (as you like it) the master who has become besotted by his possessions. This version for theoretical infants is remarkable in that it testifies to the mythologies with which the law surrounds itself: I can because I know, I am power because I am knowledge.

Looked at more closely, what happens is exactly the opposite: knowing how to rule means knowing how to render others ignorant and oneself incomprehensible, which presents no problem if one does not understand oneself, seeing that the subjects do not understand that this is the case. The master sustains himself by means of his subjects' ignorance, to be sure: but what sort of ignorance is this? Ignorance of their own ignorance. Stalin did not need to be a genius, but he did need to ensure that his people could not imagine him drunk, and so he censored the film *Ivan the Terrible*, in which a Tsar rolls under the table.

Through assuming that their slavery is justified by the master's knowledge, the slaves grant him what he wants, namely, the justification of slavery by knowledge. By claiming this knowledge for themselves, they thereby claim the justification of slavery: they will fight, of course, but with their chains as weapons. Since knowing how to free oneself and knowing how to work go together, the two will triumph in a slavery organized by an opposite form of knowledge.

Trading in influence

The law is bound to win provided that the subjects play the game. The only strategy needed is thus to oblige them to play. To prepare the subjects to make use of their rights in submission to the law we have the family, the school, the prisons, and all the special branches of knowledge connected with these: pedagogy; moral, religious and civic education; psychiatry; criminology, and so on.

If we watch the law's game as though from outside, from the angle of the way the subject is prepared, we find that the schools, prisons and factories invent a 'soul' for the subject at the very moment when the law (republican and secular) undertakes to judge this. Michel Foucault's *Discipline and Punish* finds in this encounter the birth of the 'disciplinary society'.

And what if we consider the law's game as though from inside? From the theocracy of the Popes to the 'royal divinity' of the Ancien Régime right down to the law of the Republic, secularization of the law has consisted not in doing away with the 'incomprehensible nature of authority' but in censoring any mention of this. When formerly it was divine in origin, authority 'resounded', and its voice was heard like Biblical thunder, unassailable, irrefutable but unintelligible. Today, in its secularized form, authority still derives its effectiveness from being incomprehensible, with the centralized state installed on the Pope's throne. 'The state loves us unfailingly, that is all that it does, loves us ... The public service stipulates this phantasmagoria of the state as a sacrificial offering. On the other side, in the realm of private law, commerce in all its forms prevails' (Legendre).

A third observation: before the law can write upon the presumed *tabula rasa* of revolutions, it needs to have penetrated the brains (presumed to be naïve) of the revolutionary masses. Revolutionary theory comes to the proletarians 'from without', says Lenin: otherwise, the revolutionary class stays sunk in the routine of day-to-day demands and struggles, immediate interests, 'spontaneity' and economism. We ought not to put all the blame for this on Kautsky and Lenin alone, for it is not merely a thesis on the origin of revolutionary ideas which happens to be marked by their particular élitism: it is a commonplace of all modern revolutionary theories to divide the world by contrasting the public (good) with the private (bad). The Chinese masses are called upon to fight 'against selfishness', against individual and material interest and against subjectivism ('petty-bourgeois', of course), in the name of public-spiritedness (preparing themselves to cope with wars and natural catastrophes). Here we come upon the contrast, dear to the bureaucrats of the West, between public law (dealing with matters of state importance, and therefore valuable) and private law (concerned with matters of money and sex, and therefore repugnant) in which Legendre notes 'an interdict laid upon enjoyment'.

The law is external to those who are subject to it, theory is external to the revolutionary class, just as this class is external to the society it revolutionizes. As soon as we postulate that a certain class is the bearer of the law, we conceive it theoretically as being radically alien to those for whom it lays down the law – different in language, race or creed, in whatever ways we care to imagine. Reactionary or progressive thinkers, whether aristocratic, bourgeois or 'proletarian', differ only slightly in the details with which they adorn this essential externality of the bearers of the law. Boulainvilliers defended the privileges of the French nobility, already before 1789, by endowing it with a legal mission, that of preserving the country's fundamental laws from the royal despotism, in the name of a racial legitimacy ('all the Franks were gentlemen and all the Gauls commoners').

The class of the law

This contrast, simply reversed, was to serve to illustrate the pure and firm origin of the Third Estate (Gallo-Roman and urban), as against the Germanic invaders (feudal and rural): 'After the conclusion of the great struggles which took place in the fourth and fifth centuries, ... two races, two populations, which had nothing in common but religion, appear forcibly brought together ... ' says Thierry, following Guizot, the two bourgeois fathers of the Marx-Engels concept of class. It is not so much the 'reactionary' or 'racist' standpoint that should retrospectively be noted in Boulainvilliers as this general approach of setting up one social group as the bearer of the law and thereby removing it from the social whole as though it were 'made of special stuff' (Stalin). The aristocratism of the *grand seigneur* and the dictatorship of the professional revolutionary draw their justification from the same source.

The general rule is that each subject (whether group or individual) *chosen* by the law internalizes the law's externality: that mountain of incomprehensible red tape must become flesh of his flesh, he installs the incomprehensible within himself, and the captive must find himself a 'soul' (Foucault), just as the class finds itself a Central Committee: an observation post watching over the legal frontier between the permitted and the forbidden, or between the public and the private. The subject thus makes himself alien to what surrounds him, as the Third Estate was alien to the disorders of the great invasions, as the conscious and organized working class is alien to capitalist anarchy (and to the petty-bourgeoisie of the feelings), and as the captive is alien to the outside world.

Let not the word 'internalize' give rise to dialectical dreaming: if tribulation there be, it is not that of the mind which becomes painfully reconciled to knowledge of itself, whether this is the individual or the class. Tribulation of the captive, yes, to whom penitentiary changes bring both an 'additional soul' and the renewal of suffering. The law is assumed to be inhabited by an inner knowledge because its outward look is incomprehensible, and ignorance judges thereby of what lies within. It is the same with the subjects of the law. The more they are cut off, the more they are thought to be 'internal': the more the working class is alien to the world it lives in (alien by its hunger, and later by its ideology, its Party, its science, and so on), the more it is internal to the revolution. The heavier his punishment, the more profound is the soul that the prisoner must forge for himself in the depths of his cell: 'a class with radical chains' is needed (Marx). (No, that is not an optimistic commentary by a minister on his umpteenth scheme of prison reform.)

The law compels its future subject to play ... by constructing an interior for him, and making him external to everything else but that.

The operations by which the law mobilizes its subjects are commonplace, everyday proceedings. What matters is to oblige the fellow to play when the organizer is playing so that the latter wins every time. There is 'Operation Struggle-For-Power': play so as to become in your turn the organizer who always wins. There is 'Operation Apocalypse': whatever may happen to you in the game, if you don't play it there will be chaos. There is 'Operation Siegfried': Wagner's Wotan (the law, the state) recruits a hero who is perfectly 'free', that is, who is unaware of the usages, and plays the game without knowing it: the law being incomprehensible by nature, no one will fulfil it better than a fool (in this case made foolish by the law).

Become ambitious, terrify yourself, make yourself childish. In short, stay modern. The three operations for getting the game going are common imperatives in everyday life, and examples are plentiful. The frenzied dread ('Operation Apocalypse') displayed by the French administration whenever the slightest anti-hierarchical contestation occurs is interpreted by Legendre as a repetition of the *castration* of the subjects, who have to stay children ('Operation Siegfried'): touch not the law. The partition of the world between the nuclear super-powers projects a related scenario: one escalates the conflict ('Operation Struggle-For-Power'), brandishing the supreme argument of the end of the world through atomic war ('Operation Apocalypse') until the small countries (Siegfried) accept the order established by the super-powers.

While the strings that control them are similar, the snares of the law do differ in accordance with who is to be ensnared. Even if it carefully brainwashes people so as to reduce them to Siegfried's zero level, the bureaucratic machine always runs the risk of bumping up against irremovable differences: Blacks, Vietnamese, detail workers, Gulag exiles are not at all the same, except in so far as their differences always involve the risk of throwing the law off the rails. One day, the American state discovered that the Vietnamese peasant was not the Prairie Indian of the nineteenth century ... When the law wants to take possession of a particular territory, its game has to be differentiated in accordance with the particular opponent, and becomes specific.

If we want to find out what one or other apparatus of domination expresses, we need to discover *who* it sets out to silence. In itself, the law always ends by saying: 'Shut up!' And the three operations all amount to saying: 'Shut up, Siegfried, or else blood will flow, even unto the Apocalypse!' Apart from these platitudes, the long discourses of the law are induced by those whom it wishes to subject – even though it chooses to be the only one to speak, and sometimes imposes itself in such a way that it has only to say: 'Obey!' And its lengthy monologues are to be deciphered only for what they disregard and what they recognize: who are they getting at, who is the outlaw they seek to bring within the fold by allurements and threats? Law, tell me who you are addressing and I will tell you who you are: the histories of the powerful are all the same, which is why there are only histories of peoples. As for the alleged science of history, whatever its colour, it will always, when seated in the universality of the laws, be taken doubly by surprise. Once, when peoples, by intervening, overturn the pre-established models: the Chinese Revolution did not resemble the days of October 1917. And again, when, in order to stop up the breach opened in this way, the law hits back with the means locally at hand, becoming the Marxism of the heirs of the Tsar, on the one hand, and of the descendants of the Mandarins, on the other.

The Germany within

Once, however, legal fiction and actual history did almost come together, with the law working upon an extensive territory as though upon a blank sheet. Cut up by the fierce birth of capitalism, torn by the wars of religion (thanks to printing and vernacular cultures, these were the first great wars of modern-style fanaticism), wedged between the young nation-states with long teeth and powerful armies, Germany served as the proving-ground of Europe's law.

That 'Operation Apocalypse' was the Thirty Years' War (1618–48): 'No great advanced nation has had to suffer comparable destruction. Germany was thrown back two hundred years in its development. It took two hundred years to regain the economic position it could claim at the beginning of the Thirty Years' War,' wrote the Socialist Franz Mehring, before the war of 1914. But the state of the economy does not give the full measure of a catastrophe in which one German out of every three perished. One might pursue the effects of this terror upon the population in the descriptions given subsequently of the German character. Placid? Serious? Non-political? Musical? Peaceful? Choleric? Metaphysical? Provincial? Barbarous? All these often contradictory characteristics, noted over the centuries as so many 'natural' data – were they not consequences of one and the same terrified shrinking away from authority, the bearer of law and order, the state, and so on? Two psycho-analysts have remarked upon this phenomenon in our own time, using their own special vocabulary: 'One thing alone remained forbidden, and that by virtue of a general consensus, namely, civic courage. The idea of a decision taken in the name of individual conscience, of acceptance of personal responsibility, seemed odious in that it implied lack of respect for the powers ordained by God' (A. and M. Mitscherlich). They record that after Germany's defeat in 1945 the country lived through its mourning as something impossible, as though without thinking about it: ought we not to see, in this a sort of repetition of the first Apocalypse, that which occurred in the seventeenth century? If, after 1945, the German plunged into economic reconstruct-ion, putting everything else out of his mind, was he not finding, in this history starting over again from scratch, the repetition of an eternal German story?

A tradition: that of the 'Operation Apocalypse' which pro-vides the law with a blank sheet. 'Practical activity and its successes would soon hide the open wounds that the past had left. We built anew upon the old foundations, but without consciously linking ourselves with tradition' (ibid.).

With the exception of a few great Romantics, Germany's élite plunged headlong into 'Operation Struggle-For-Power' when the French Revolution broke out. Thinkers, reforming ministers, musicians, enlightened generals, all joined in, and the constituted bodies slowly followed as the nineteenth century advanced. The means advocated were divergent, but the aim was the same: to catch up with and surpass the other nation-states of Europe, to compete with France on the Continent and then with England throughout the world. This aim thus had nothing specifically German about it: Hegel's political model was Richelieu, while Fichte the philosopher and Clausewitz the general began to correspond because they both revered Machia-velli. What, however, *was* distinctively German was that this general European law encountered for the first time a people who had been struck by an Apocalypse – the wound was reopened every time, with Napoleon's *Grande Armée* repeating in Germany the traumatisms of the Thirty Years' War, and giving rise thereby to more terror than resistance, in contrast to what was happening at the same time in Spain and Russia.

A people who had been atomized, and an élite concentrating their efforts upon the state. The fiction of the game of the law became a reality, history a laboratory, and the fitting of the law to a territory seemed likely to be accomplished under conditions of maximum clarity.

Nothing was lacking, not even that subject of the law who, in his free innocence, comes close to submission in its perfect form – Siegfried. The cretinization of a people attained a previously unequalled degree of intensity under Nazism, with everyone participating in accordance with his capacities, right up to the great philosopher and the orchestra-conductor, and including ninety-nine per cent of the administration, the officers, the professions and all the teachers. (Those who resisted or emigrated deserve to be mentioned, but if this is not to serve as a get-out it must be said that they were the exception.)

Never had a people been so completely plunged 'into the imaginary space of the institutions in which the subjects are children' (Legendre): but that space is European. If the German experience is to be instructive, this can only happen if we recognize in it an extreme case of *Europeanism*. A. and M. Mitscherlich note in passing the absence of 'German civic consciousness', understood as meaning readiness to take personal responsibility, individual protest. But when he asks himself about the conditions that made possible the spread of the Gulag Archipelago, Solzhenitsyn also mentions the absence of 'civic consciousness'.

European all through, Nazi Germany does not fail to show what happens when men give unquestioning obedience to the laws. It teaches us by showing what *not* to do. It offers a model which is perhaps unique in its perfection – but *ersatz* versions of which are widespread in the world of today. As a product, it cannot but be of interest, since it illuminates the mode of production of such hells. Cause a people to be placed in an Apocalypse; concentrate the élite upon the sole key to all change, the state, which is to be taken, transformed, revolutionized (the details matter little – it is always the state they begin with); finally, reduce everyone to stupidity, wholesale and retail, mobilizing all forces to this end – through writing, administering, prophesying, haranguing, philosophizing, fighting, serving, working. Who is there who has completely escaped from the German catastrophe?

Nineteenth-century Germany made it a matter of honour to bring European science and culture to their boiling-point. That is good reason for questioning Germany's thinkers. Not so as to 'save' them, as if they saw nothing of what was coming, or as if they had nothing to do with it – that would mean aspiring to do them the melancholy honour of supposing they belonged to another world, or else were blind. Still less to blame them for the scrupulous honesty which caused them to name and describe the mechanisms which they themselves helped to set up: 'The time is coming that will see the battle for world domination. It will be waged in the name of basic philosophical doctrines' (Nietzsche). Let him who knows where he is going presume to reproach them. We need, more simply, to question them, to find out where we have come from, to identify what it is that in each one seeks finally to extinguish contestation, the spark of Socrates and Panurge.

3 The Impossible Mr Socrates

'But now, dear old boy, I'm coming to the most magnificent of my propositions. Imagine *order*. Or, rather, imagine first of all a great idea, and then one still greater, then another still greater than that, and so on, always greater and greater. And then on the same pattern imagine always more and more order in your own head. At first everything's as neat and tidy as an old maid's sitting room and as clean as a Horse-Guards Stable. And after that it's as splendid as a brigade in battle formation. And after that again it's as crazy as when you come out of the mess in the middle of the night and shout orders at the stars: "Cosmos, *shun*! Eyes *right*!" Or let's say, in the beginning order is like when a recruit is still falling over his own feet and you teach him how to pick 'em up. Then it's like when you dream you've suddenly been made War Minister over everyone else's head. But now, just imagine a complete universal order embracing all humanity, in a word, a state of perfect civilian order. Take my word for it, it's sheer entropy, *rigor mortis*, a landscape on the moon, a geometrical plague.'

ROBERT MUSIL, *The Man Without Qualities*, London, Secker and Warburg, 1954, vol. 2, pp. 197-8

Serious thought concerns itself with serious matters: expanding enterprises, growing organizations, states, continents. Apart from those great *ensembles* that occupy the interior of one's thought and cause it to follow the single thread of planning, programming, party lines and reasons of state. An interruption? You've been cut off? You dial the number again.

Most of the gifts which are amusingly described as 'strictly' human have substantial investments devoted to them. Great enterprises neglect neither speech – the secular school, the party school, the trade-union school – nor writing – O offices, O castles! – nor the right sentiments, praise God, nor, God forbid, the wrong ones. Even the imagination, which, ironically, imagined that it was 'in power' in May 1968, concerned itself with changing life: can one imagine a life that doesn't change?

And what's the reason why? There's one reason for the atom bomb, and several for Gulag – no institution among those that are the glory of our century would stop giving reasons for a single moment. Is the reason human? Not unless we muddle too much our feeling of what is inhuman, when the napalm-bombing of the Vietnamese and the dispatch of millions of people to concentration camps are justified by social reasons. We shall have to discover, in the common disregard that the reasoners show for the 'minor' side-aspects of their exercises, the working of one and the same reason – if possible, by losing it. Most certainly, man is a creature fitted to undertake great enterprises.

There remains a little faculty, microscopic, slipshod, disorderly and even tattered, so wretched, apparently, that the experts have not yet found in it any prospect for fruitful investment. Reasonable reasons, constructive imagination, distinguished sentiments, all easily become matters for care and attention on the part of rulers. This faculty was neglected, most probably abandoned because it was useless – this distorted faculty which is still at everyone's disposal and which no one can boast of having sole possession of. To tell the truth, it's hardly a faculty, not even a power: the freedom to interrupt.

'Let's be serious. This is a time for great undertakings. The age of the American challenge. Of the Marxist challenge, which has set 250 million Russians and 800 million Chinese on the march – perhaps against each other. Civilization today is a mass affair, with mass-production, consumption in tonnes: we expect our wars to be world-wide, our civilization to embrace the whole planet. A world like this calls for thinking on the millionaire's scale: speak as a technician, and all the plans and programmes will give forth their drum-rolls: speak as a Marxist, and continents tremble already in the calculated tremolos of your voice. But don't interrupt any of us with your interruption.'

'And yet, when a student interrupts a minister, talking to him about sex, and when the minister, in the course of his speech, advises the student to jump into the swimming-pool, and then when, soon afterwards, students interrupt the traffic, followed by workers who interrupt their work – you have the biggest strike in world history, ten million interrupters!'

'You're on about May 68 again! Whether your thinking tends to the left or the right, you will of course agree, that that was the "nonesuch" revolution. And, consequently, it was nothing at all. A psycho-drama, say the right-wing thinkers. Folklore, say the heroes of the left. The "events" is how the entire press refers to what happened.'

'That's just it! Interruption produces an event. An event described as such, apparently, for want of any better way to describe it, in desperation, out of failure to know what to say about it. Interruption upsets concepts. Who knows where it's going or whence it comes? The event has not ceased to be an event because you can't categorize it. There are other events in the same style which we can compare with May, so as to get a better notion of it. There was one unnoticed in France, so far away it was in terms of kilometres, and intellectually in terms of light-years, a matter that was undoubtedly of world importance and yet at the same time pure folklore, and a gigantic psychodrama for the thinking of serious persons: the war in Vietnam was stopped. By the Vietnamese, of course. There was nothing new in that, save for the Pentagon strategists: Napoleon was halted by the guerrillas of Spain and Russia, wars of national liberation have been with us a long time.'

But what was not foreseen, what was without precedent, was that America's war was stopped by the youth of America itself. An army which was the leading army in the world, the most powerful in history, was smashed from within, by means of songs and drugs, by clergymen, rabbis and priests who argued, by poems and by hand-grenades chucked into officers' messes. There was an interruption in the official speechmaking and reviewing of troops, in the highly strategical calculations of the prevailing wisdom. The napalm-bombing of Vietnam was cut short by ten years. The effectiveness was demonstrated of a spiritual atomic bomb: the most up-to-date war machine proved unable to resist this concentration of critical masses.

This combined force of contestation, the effect of which was on the scale of the nuclear weapons it proved able to halt, is too difficult for us to grasp. What is there in common between the junky, drugged to the eyebrows, and the Catholic, Roman to the depths of his soul? What they were opposing in their contestation, and would describe in very varying ways, was the Devil, one of them would say, perhaps, but what was it for the other? Vileness? Paregoric kids of all lands, unite! (W. Burroughs).

Let everyone use his own words to designate that which, here and there, was interrupted. Provided that no one forgets to interrupt. The Soviet dissidents are showing, at the cost of their sanity and their torn bodies, that resistance can put a spoke in the wheel of the biggest police machine. When he studied the origin of the concentration camp system in Russia, Solzhenitsyn put forward the counter-proof: the absence, at the outset, of individual protests, what he calls the failure of civic spirit, permitted the cancer of police measures to proliferate. The roots of this lack of concern have nothing specifically Russian about them: all the élites of Europe rushed headlong into the military slaughter of 1914.

Serious thought is free to suppose that the Russian resistance, the break-up of the American Army, the contestations in the West, are all so many disconnected events, each of them merely local and ephemeral. Yet it is not impossible to see them as scattered efforts which, though unaware of each other, are nevertheless convergent, in that they all aim to put a stop to the fatal course being followed by our century, and, in it, by a mankind which is less eternal than ever before: two world wars, many sorts of fascism, colonial massacres, variants of concentration-camp socialism imposed on a milliard human beings, and games with thermo-nuclear power when the promoters of this history want to take a rest in the seventh decade.

Embracing all that in one glance, considering it as a whole, is not yet within our capacity. We prefer to discuss these evils one after the other, talking of the errors of socialism, on the one hand, and the failures of liberalism, on the other. These subtle distinctions don't stand up: nothing resembles one charnel-house better than another charnel-house, and one can't tell from a smashed-up body whether the torture to which it was subjected was 'socialist' or 'capitalist'. This is why the élites of our century now nearing its end have been seized by a belated sense of decency, and scenes of violence are being censored on television.

Interruption, history's secret, the mainspring of civilization, the locomotive of expansion!

This shocking remark is likely to seem too way-out to delicate academic ears. Two learned authorities may be quoted in support of it: the most classical of bourgeois economists, Ricardo, and his pupil, the most Marxist of Marxists, Marx himself. In the middle of the nineteenth century the British workers, after a decade of very hard struggle, won a reduction in the working day, together with increased wages. The employers reacted by modernizing their equipment, so as to reduce the amount spent on wages. Marx pointed to this as being 'capital's general method': 'Ricardo correctly observed that machines are in perpetual competition with labour, and very often their introduction has to wait until the price of labour has risen to the proper level...'

O development, sacrosanct in both Russia and America, of the productive forces and technology! The introduction of these new machines that are so fascinating has to 'wait'. What about invention, then, what about research and development? Well, they too may have to wait ... until the price of labour has risen to the proper level. To the proper level, that is to say, thanks to the not-at-all-proper methods used by the British workers of that time, discovering a thousand and one ways of interrupting work. Interruption, the stimulus to industry and commerce, that's the universal driving-force patented by the firm of Ricardo and Marx, whose reputation is already established.

Recent examples could be adduced to extend further the field of application of this 'general method'. After the tremendous social upheavals that accompanied the great crisis of 1930 and the two world wars, the property-owners were obliged to reduce the cyclical magnitude of unemployment and the gravity of its consequences, just as they had had in the previous century to shorten the working day. Hence new 'methods' in the orientation of investment, intensification of factory work and consumption on a mass scale. Note this, the real driving-force of expansion is to be found in strikes and demonstrations, in street politics. History furnishes the counter-proof: those economies which are not shaken up by this massive contestation become stagnant – look at the socialist countries, whose only advancing technologies are those of armament and repression.

The economy itself, that which our experts watch like an oracle, which our rulers worship as Destiny, and which the rest of us are adjured to submit to as to a fatality, thus functions only if its 'laws' can be interrupted. The market, which continually upsets the living conditions of the masses, has itself to be upset by the masses if it is to continue to expand. If they are left to themselves and sheltered from all dangers, whether internal (social) or external (foreign), the so-called mechanisms of the market go slack. Whenever a bourgeoisie reigns unchallenged over the world market and over its own people, it rots on its feet: becoming triumphant, it declines. 'The bourgeois waxes fat as his riches increase and as he accustoms himself to live on the interest of his capital, to be held in the vice of luxury, and to lead the life of a country gentleman,' observes the historian Sombart, recalling the twilights of Italian (sixteenth-century), Dutch (seventeenth-century) and British (eighteenth-century) capitalism. The bourgeois does not automatically raise up his challenger, but he has need of a challenger if he is to restore his strength. Which shows that bourgeois seriousness is not so important as contestation.

This is only a half-proof, for the trap is about to close: doesn't contestation have the effect of strengthening what is contested? If interruption breaks up a discourse, doesn't it do this only to inaugurate a new chain of reasoning? 'The spirit that always denies', Mephistopheles presents himself as 'a part of that power which always wills evil and always procures good' (Goethe). Hardly has one discovered that contradiction lies at the foundation of those very persons who loathe it (the serious persons of sociology, politics and economics) than one is held captive by this realization: one's denial has served only to provide a better foundation for them! Seen in this way, history is presented by Hegel as a gigantic trick played by Reason: taking short cuts through the 'bad sides' and given to evil company, it nevertheless goes forward, 'from setback to setback, until ultimate victory', echoes Mao Tse-tung. Mephistopheles the challenger must draw in his claws: if he is right to revolt, then it's because his revolt serves Reason in the end. He's a good little devil. Is there no irony in this?

What is involved here is important, and calls for close critical examination. In reply to workers' resistance in the first years of this century, the engineer Taylor invented the 'scientific' organization of work. Are we to conclude that the outcome of anarcho-syndicalism was mass-production methods? The violent struggles of the unemployed of the 1930s led, in a roundabout way, to the organization of the 'consumer society'. Is the latter to be seen as the true significance of the former? The anti-war struggle of America's youth upset the careers of a few Presidents: was that all it meant? Is every contestation eventually buried by what it challenges and what it has transformed through its struggle? Or is there a kinship between those who engage in contestation, a kinship running right across the board? Each one of them is the child of his time and bears its mark, even if they all perceive in each other a vague family resemblance. As the faces sink back into the past the photos fade and comparisons become less certain.

It is in vain that we try to decipher a single face in these yellowing snapshots. Contestations recur without needing to resemble each other. The Indians whom Pierre Clastres (*La Société contre l'état*) found in the heart of the Amazonian forests were 'right to revolt' even before Western Reason approached their neighbourhood. They rose up against the shadow cast ahead by the State Power which they discerned in the ambitions of their chiefs, whom they therefore curbed: this can be understood, given the conceptual resources they possessed, which, though different, were neither better nor worse than ours. It is pointless to line up the Guayaki Indians with Spartacus, Gavroche, the Kronstadt sailors, and so on, in a single line, in the vain attempt to discover a single head, 'human nature'. Since contestation always means preserving differences, those who engage in it cannot but differentiate themselves from each other. What they have in common is what confronts them.

What, then, is similar in the attempts made during the last
two centuries to cut down contestations? All of these attempts
appeal to a Reason which can be called bourgeois only if one
applies the same description to the 'socialist' regimes. The
feeblest of racialist governments need a so-called racialist knowledge, just as the anti-popular dictatorships need a science that
can be called proletarian. This Reason argues against, refutes
and silences contestation. This it always does by involving the
given contestation in an order. It may be a future order: the
child and the proletarian must stop playing, must learn to
become leaders. Or it may be a counter-order: for the antisemite
the Jewish vagabond was the agent of an invisible state just as,
for the rulers, all internal opposition was exposed as being the
instrument of external forces. Or else, in between the two, a
confused order: the person who challenges the established state
of things needs to be educated and re-educated, perhaps in a
psychiatric hospital. Or, at the extreme limit of what is think-
able, an absent order: the challenger is then nothing at all, and
will be treated as such, as an animal.

The argument always follows the same line: he who challenges
has an idea at the back of his mind, he is insinuating a certain
Order. He is a double agent, he destroys in order to replace, he is
a plotter, an agent of the future or of a foreign power – if not of
the one, then of the other. The line followed is that of the Great
Trials: the challenging of an order can be conceived only as
being carried out on behalf of another order. For the Government of Reason there can be no simple-minded challenger. And
if he is too simple-minded, he will be given treatment.

The argument of the argument is given by Hegel. Not in his
capacity as a 'great philosopher', for there is no standard in this
matter. Perhaps because he was an intellectual, much affected
by a revolution coming from without, asking himself how, after
the events of 1789, the world, his country, Germany, or he himself could go on governing themselves, or in what new way they
must do this. People argue about whether Hegel was a reactionary or a secret progressive, but he certainly claimed the status of
a functionary. He was the first philosopher to function as a
functionary conscious of himself: 'Philosophy with us is not, as

it was with the Greeks, for instance, pursued in private like an art, but has an existence in the open, in contact with the public and especially, or even only, in the service of the state'. This does not put Hegel on the right rather than on the left, nor does it bury him as the philosopher of the Prussian state, or even the 'last of the philosophers' (Marx). When a master-thinker calls himself 'realistic', he stresses that this reality to which he wants to adapt us is contrasted with 'Greece' – thus, he is thinking on the scale of several centuries. Hegel seems rather to have thought of himself as the first modern philosopher: the state that he serves is often as yet only a state that exists in his mind. He would have been satisfied to hear the most famous of 'professional' revolutionaries declare that one cannot make the revolution without the science of revolution, and that one cannot possess that science without the key thereto, Marx's *Capital*, and that one cannot understand those stout volumes unless one has assimilated the whole of Hegel's *Great Logic*. He would not have been greatly surprised, given the changing times, to find France's strongest concentration of professional Marxists and Leninists in the National Union of Teachers in Higher Education, even if this very Hegelian community sometimes takes liberties with its founding father. Hegel would know how to recognize his own: the only way to deal with a challenger is to Hegelianize him, even unknowingly.

The argument of arguments comes forward arrayed in white linen: Socrates is impossible. The mission assigned to him by the oracle of Delphi was simply contradictory: to establish that, knowing nothing, but knowing that he knows this, Socrates is the wisest of men. Socrates was the first to point out that this formulation was an embarrassing one – he who constantly bogged down his partners in discussion in this difficulty which became impossible to get out of (*aporia*): 'My hearers always imagine that I myself possess the wisdom which I find wanting in others.' Socrates went ahead, talking about knowledge as Panurge talked about marriage: you know that you know nothing, so marry knowledge, but ... So don't marry, his 'Daimon' intervened. Hegel didn't want to let himself be caught so easily: *he* was not practising philosophy as a 'private' matter. It is a matter of state, which is settled like this: Socrates has had contact with a foreign power without realizing it: if he asks questions, it's because he knows the answers; if he criticizes the competent authorities, it's because he thinks he must be more competent than they are: if he seems to be unaware of the goodness of his leaders, does this not mean that he considers that he has something better to propose? If he raises the question of power, he must want power! Not for himself? Then for some other! Tell me to whom these disorders are advantageous, for whom the chestnuts are being pulled out of the fire: Hegel follows the trail without difficulty – Socrates is merely Plato's understudy.

Plato is not lacking in theories about how a state should be ruled. This is solid stuff, one can discuss it, go into it, it's not neither fish nor flesh nor good red herring, like Socrates' 'I know nothing'. Hegel's *Principles of the Philosophy of Right* thus corresponds to Plato's *Republic*. It is between men of learning that problems are clarified, especially if it is a matter of the question of questions, the one that is never called in question: launching a periodical, founding a theoretical review, making friends with a tyrant, recasting the whole of philosophy – *Why?* In order to educate better the future leaders and to guide the men of power: Plato and Dionysius, Aristotle and Alexander, Hegel and Napoleon, Lenin and Lenin ... Faced with the most civilized of the Greek states of his time, Socrates behaved, according to Hegel, in a revolutionary way (*'als Revolutionär'*). Was he not accused of atheism as well as of worshipping new gods, and, even worse, of corrupting the youth and bringing disobedience into families and between generations? And was he not quite legally condemned in accordance with the most democratic constitution in the world of those days, that of Athens? Moreover, he confirmed his own condemnation, by declining to ask for pardon. Did not this mean that he admitted his guilt? Of course, says Hegel, but why not? 'This silence may indeed be considered as moral greatness, but, on the other hand ... ' More Hegelian than Socrates, Bukharin was less 'one-sided': after drafting the Constitution of the U.S.S.R. he 'confessed' to his acts of high treason...

'A most important figure in the history of philosophy', 'a world-famed personage', 'a mental turning-point' – what tributes laid at the feet of the man 'in whom the subjectivity of thought was brought to consciousness'. In asking a general to define courage, a politician to define virtue, a poet to define beauty, and a priest to define faith, Socrates paid poisoned homage to the competent authorities: 'His attitude of pretended ignorance encouraged the others to speak.' Accepting all their answers in order to lead them, still by way of questions, to refute themselves, 'letting the destruction from within develop of itself', Socrates destroyed the authority of tradition. With, as Hegel puts it, 'a seeming ingenuousness', he questions respectfully, listens attentively, then interprets the answers he has been given and shows their contradictoriness: 'He brought the individual under the force of his dialectical vacuum-pump, deprived him of the atmospheric air in which he was accustomed to breathe, and abandoned him. For such individuals everything was now lost, except in so far as they were able to breathe an ether. Yet Socrates no longer concerned himself with them, but hastened on to new experiments' (Kierkegaard). This little game was only half pleasing to Hegel: the 'negative side' ought to have been accompanied by an 'affirmative side' which would have revealed that the former was only 'a seeming ingenuousness'.

Such were the flowers that Hegel laid upon the tomb of Socrates. The philosopher who embarrassed his city embodied the future, since his city did indeed fall into fatal difficulties. But the state embodies the existent eternity of the spirit. A tragic duel, ending in the death of both the combatants. Though Socrates' obstinacy may testify to his genius, it remains 'one-sided', in Mao's word, and therefore blameworthy. Hegel tells us this with all the flatfootedness needed in order that a twentieth-century ear may recognize here some well-known voices: 'But no people, and least of all a free people like the Athenians, has by this freedom to recognize a tribunal of conscience which knows no consciousness of having fulfilled its duty excepting its own consciousness ... For the first principle of a state is that there is no reason or conscience or righteousness or anything else, higher than what the state recognizes as such. Quakers, Anabaptists, etc., who resist any demands made on them by the state, such as to defend the fatherland, cannot be tolerated in a true state. This miserable freedom of thinking and believing what men will is not permitted . . . ' (Hegel).

Behind the Socrates whom he honours we divine that Hegel imagines another one – a Quaker, an Anabaptist, a romantic, an ironist: in short, a challenger. The two figures have only a distant relationship to the historical personage whom Hegel re-draws in his own way in accordance with much more up-to-date preoccupations. It is not, strictly speaking, the revolutionary Socrates that worries the master-thinker: he perceived, through the pattern of 1789–93, that revolutions were 'self-destructive' outbreaks of liberty which transform the earth all the better in so far as they remove themselves from its surface. The Socrates he honours therefore marches towards his own death: like any other good revolutionary, he has built a bridge between two orders – in his case Greece and Christianity. In the meantime he has had his period of stabilization, his N.E.P. The positive truth of Socrates, for Hegel, is Plato, who knows that he knows. There remains in the background that other one, that shade of contestation who lives in the margins of history as this is related by Hegel, the evil spirit whose elasticity 'projected one individual after another outside of the substantial reality of the state', himself along with the rest. In his basket floating between heaven and earth, as Aristophanes depicts him, he still flouts, with his 'I know that I know nothing', Master Hegel, who is all puffed up with knowledge conscious of itself. Kierkegaard, stifling in Hegelianism, evokes this shade: mankind has need 'of a light diet of Socratism'. Hegel exorcizes this shade with his logical guillotine.

If he disturbed the markets so much, was it not so as to put an end to disturbance there? If he reduced the whole world to silence, was it perhaps so that in this even silence one might at last be able to hear the dialogue between those who know and who do not go to the markets? Socrates, outwardly the ironist of 'I know nothing', concealed his real skill: his 'maieutic' method was that of the midwife. Did he not bring to birth

Plato's 'I know'? His irony, Hegel argues, was merely a rocket bearing knowledge: this 'numb-fish' attacked common sense in order the more securely to establish Platonic science. If he had been in a position to show his gratitude, Socrates would probably have bequeathed his body to such an advocate as this: one who is so well able to treat the living as the dead ought to be capable of passing off the dead as the living. This would be pointless, though, if Socrates disappears into Plato, and Plato, in turn, into Hegel and the irony which is obvious in the first two, but involuntary in the third, vanishes in the ultimate picture

We have no right, says Hegel, to be sceptical regarding philosophical science. Scepticism should be directed against common sense, in the service of true knowledge. If it undertakes to attack science, it finds itself in a vicious circle. 'Some of the ancients said that all is vanity and that this proposition includes itself' – but that, Hegel says, was only so as to mock vulgar notions and introduce philosophical self-knowledge: otherwise it would have been merely 'inconsequential', 'a flashy assertion', 'a conceit', 'a joke (*Witz*)', and that sort of incongruity is reserved for the moderns, when they are not Hegelians. Historians can show up the falsification; the Greek sceptics did indeed attack, if not philosophy 'itself', which they perhaps did not know existed, then at least philosophical knowledge which they considered to be dogmatic. Never mind, what matters is to demonstrate that the challenger who asserts his ignorance is *logically* impossible.

The logical impossibility of Socrates – 'I know only one thing, namely, that I know nothing' – is well-known, since it does not differ from that of the liar who says 'I am lying'. Hegel solves the difficulty in a banal way by splitting Socrates into two. On the one hand, Socrates No. 1 who 'knows nothing', on the other, Socrates No. 2 who knows. Number 2 (Socrates-Plato) possesses knowledge that Number 1 (Socrates–Socrates) lacks, the knowledge of Number 2 being hierarchically superior to that of Number 1, whom he controls: 'I know that I know nothing', means that 'I, Number 2, know that I, Number 1, know nothing.' In ordinary Marxism this is formulated as: Number 1 has become conscious in Number 2. In Marxism *à la*

Althusser it would be: Number 2 has created the scientific theory of Number 1. In modern logic we distinguish between the different hierarchical levels of language (Russell's types and orders, the metalanguage and language-object of Carnap, Tarski, etc.). The meta-I knows that the I-object knows nothing. In the everyday world we say: there is the expert and that on which he exercises his expertise, there is the doctor and the patient, there is the officer and the troop.

Unlike Hegelian Marxism and good society, modern logicians have had the honesty to recognize that such an admirable solution through division is, to say the least, lacking in elegance: it solves the problem only by forbidding it to exist. If language is cut up into strata completely separated from each other, so that in each case the higher level reveals the truth of the lower (which is incapable of expressing it), the paradox does indeed disappear, in the sense that it can neither be uttered nor heard: 'I say' (at the higher level), 'I lie' (at the lower level). Your ear cannot be focused in two directions at once, and therefore that will never sound paradoxical to you. Since the entire interest of these theories lies in their claim to deal with a paradox (which one has first had to hear and understand), modern logic has somewhat turned away from this chopping activity and, with increased subtlety, has not failed to attain some interesting results concerning the *limits* within which a language can be logically verified and checked. These are limits which Hegel did not venture to encounter.

For him, Socrates No. 1 (who doesn't know) can never challenge Socrates No. 2 (who knows): *I know* is 'stronger' than *I know nothing*. When Socrates seems to be challenging, it is really Plato who is speaking. This proof of the non-existence of Socrates is the first and last word of Hegelian wisdom, its alpha and omega. It is impossible to ask oneself, as though from outside, whether or not one knows: thinking and being are all one, and have nothing outside them: here, opposing the too 'external' sceptics, Hegel appeals, in his arbitrary way, to Parmenides, to the beginnings of Greek philosophy. Hegel's target, behind the sceptics, is Kant. Had not the latter, a half-century earlier, declared that one could not, on the basis of the Idea of God, prove that God exists ('ontological' proof), any more than he regarded it as permissible to proceed from the idea of one hundred thalers to one hundred real thalers, in actual cash? Today, any and every speculator rejects *that* distinction, just as Hegel gets rid of the previous one by letting it peremptorily be known that the highest wisdom no longer accepts 'the contrast of a thinking subject with an existing object'. Thereby we have at once the proof that Socrates does not exist and that God exists. The person who thinks cannot put himself 'outside' of what he thinks about, except by wiser and truer thought: one can deny wisdom only in the name of higher wisdom, and God only in God's name. Let it be noted for the benefit of sensitive souls: Hegel in this way introduces not belief in God but belief in proof, which has much more devastating consequences nowadays.

The logical murder of Socrates is of ritual significance for Hegel, since he tells us what the ultimate wisdom is to which, he claims, he is going to introduce us. Because Socrates is, for him, only a mask for Plato, it is his *irony* that is to be criticized, that irony which claims to say, without knowledge though not without a smile, that it does not know. Irony of ironies, it is from this strategic location that all Hegel's critics set out, whether they realize it or not – the existentialists, the Marxists, the aesthetics and the poetics, the couldn't-care-less fraternity and the all-that's-gone-with-the-wind school. In each case, the starting-point is something – existence, social life, a man, a woman – that is placed outside the realm of Hegelian knowledge, the observation being made (with smiling pen) that knowledge must, on the other hand, be already in it if it is to possess even a shadow of existence. The Hegelian sage replies, also smiling, that the person who waxes ironical about knowledge presupposes its presence. Refutations and rejoinders increase and multiply, so all that is left is a cloud of Socrateses, unfortunately each more serious than the next.

Socrates is impossible if the paradox is impossible, if limiting (saying: 'I lie') means already going beyond the limit (having a true point of view on this lie). Existentialist criticism, since Kierkegaard, has started this hare, but only in order to weep over man's misery in the paradoxical situation. Its tears are still Hegelian. Subjectivity lies in sin, in withdrawal, in failure in face of a true discourse. I am a traitor in a true story, faced with a discourse that is less treacherous, even if dirtier, than I am. I am impossible, but I am. The 'petty-bourgeoi's, the unhappy consciousness, would go on repeating with Éluard: 'all that matters is to say everything, and I haven't the words'... Where do we get this idea that saying everything is all that matters, if not from this desire for absolute knowledge which all the worthies of the twentieth century cultivate in the poppy-fields of the *Great Logic*? In order to rid oneself thoroughly of absolute knowledge it was thought necessary to take seriously something else, namely, religion (Kierkegaard), politics, history or society. But taking seriously religion or anything else means taking it Hegelianly – and getting back, full in the face, the paradoxes that one had eliminated from one's wise thought.

Thus Kierkegaard: 'Hegel has sought in vain, so it seems to me, to vindicate a positive content for Socrates ... Had his knowledge been a knowledge of something, his ignorance would merely have been a form of conversation. Thus his irony is now complete in itself. To this extent his ignorance is both to be taken seriously and not to be taken seriously, and upon this point Socrates is to be maintained.' In simpler terms, Socrates' irony, his 'art of questioning', consists in trapping someone's knowledge in its own claims, allowing it confidently to spread out its net and then to point to the meshes which are missing, to reveal it as being moth-eaten by prejudice, undermined by contradictions. Socrates has no need of any 'higher', 'positive' science in order to see, test, note and challenge this science which is no science. But the pupil remains enclosed within the master's categories. Kierkegaard adds: 'To know that one is ignorant is the beginning of wisdom, but if one knows no more than this is it is only a beginning ... ' Here the century starts to turn back on itself – that is, into the Hegelian knowledge which it claims to have rejected or surpassed. 'The beginning of wisdom, but only the beginning!' Hegel said no more than that, and even said it word for word: the dialogues of Socrates leave us unsatisfied, without solutions or conclusions, in perplexity. 'This perplexity thus has the effect of leading us to reflect: this is Socrates' purpose. This purely negative side is what is essential. It is with perplexity that philosophy must necessarily begin ... '

The thinkers of the last two centuries often claim to start from a doubt which each one wants to present as more 'radical' than that of the others. They ascribe the origin of doubt either to Descartes (Fichte), to Socrates (Hegel and Kierkegaard), or to the bourgeoisie which has 'opened their eyes' (Marx, in the *Manifesto*). It is of little importance on what screen the origin of doubt is projected, all that matters is to get to the roots of things – the more radical it is, the more serious will be the knowledge that it introduces. Doubt stands at the beginning, at that starting point which, precisely, one *leaves*. Forward, towards *serious* religion, *serious* politics, implacable self-criticism? Hegel has been transcended because he has conquered the world: what remains is to know *what* it is that he has equipped with such effective armour. Dear dialecticians: what if it was the ideas of the heads, the rulers, the masters of these last two centuries that Hegel gathered together and systematized, in order to hand them down to you (the most subtle of methods) as your revolutionary dialectic?

Through Socrates the undesirable we make out the target aimed at by the Hegelian war-machine. The master sketches the glorious portrait of this hero of self-knowledge: incised in the background we see outlined the shadow of the challenger who is to be exorcized. In order to realize the objective of the century – order, the better future, the best of worlds – the intellectual machine-guns are massed, and when they rake the ground, legions of shades start up which know that, if they know nothing, nobody around them is any wiser than they are.

Should we admire the courage of the 340,000 Germans and the 360,000 Frenchmen who were massacred at Verdun without flinching too much? Or that of the official authorities who find, over half a century later, something still to celebrate in that killing-ground? We know now that Verdun was a trap laid by the German General Staff, who speculated on the symbolic value possessed by the place in the eyes of France's rulers. Through their sense of prestige the latter did not fail to let their army be reduced to mincemeat there. We know that the opposing armies both thrust themselves into this trap – the generals with their heads, the soldiers with their bodies. From this gigantic charnel-house, harbinger of others to come, arose the smell of many sciences, those of the generals, the Presidents and the Emperors, those consecrated by public education (compulsory, like military service). Are we going to outdo that, to improve on it: will a stronger science take account of the knowledge buried there under its own devastation? Or ought we to begin to admit that we don't understand, and to be astonished? 'The natives, after all, have to be bludgeoned into doing their job – they've still got that much self-respect. Whereas the whites carry on on their own, they've been well schooled by the state.' When he drew up his balance sheet, *Journey to the End of the Night*, Céline was a magnificent case of *inscientia* ('The war, in fact, was everything that one didn't understand'). Later he was to get 'educated' and to *march* forward, believing that he knew, guided by an unwelcome, racist science.

For all that, 'Ferdinand Bardamu', placed there all alone on his battlefield, seeing that he can see nothing, introduces us to the realities of our century: how many G.I.s were to say, like him, that 'in this sort of business, there's nothing for it, the only thing to do is to shove out of it.' How many soldiers in colonial armies, in the S.S. and among the Gulag guards, did *not* tell themselves that, being unable to hear a voice capable of whispering it to them – in particular, their own voice?

The troops that fought in the war of 1914 had lined up behind them a cordon of gendarmes whose task it was to shoot down any deserters. The same standard method was used when the Red Army crossed the ice to punish the mutinous sailors of the Kronstadt Commune (1921). Power is at the end of *two* guns, the second being aimed at the man who is aiming the first one. There would never be enough weapons or soldiers unless there was a gun in the brain of the last man in the series. Alongside the smart Socrates, the hero of knowledge *à la* Hegel, we see a shadow, the shadow of the deserter. The telescopic gunsight of the century is fixed upon him: when all knowledge is mobilized, to say 'I know that I know nothing' means to desert. Do we need a supreme science of science in order to perceive the failures of the other branches of knowledge? In what are called the exact sciences, the hypothesis is not needed. Where human affairs are concerned, it becomes comical, but is generally accepted. If we take various events of our century – world wars, colonial wars, fascisms – and check to see what the scientific augurs had to say about them, pity or fatigue soon makes us give up the examination.

Is a higher knowledge, capable of judging both itself and other branches, the privilege of a small number of élites? Is there not, rather, in the sciences, above them and outside of them, a knowledge of ignorance that is shared much more democratically? Is it not this that causes Socrates, 'Ferdinand Bardamu' and the G.I. deserter to say 'I know nothing, but *that* I do know'? A rare disease, but fortunately a contagious one.

One can't say 'I lie' unless one knows what is true, or say 'I don't know' without being a well of science, or find that something 'is bad' or 'is false' without having an idea of the Supreme Good, or look at a heap of ruins otherwise than with the architect's vision . . . Really? Ruins give way beneath our feet, rubble collapses on our heads, torture makes us shiver, without any commentary being needed, and blood speaks for itself: the wars of Picrochole seem wrong before any allusion is made to the idylls of Thélème: the practical truth of calamities is appreciated without reference to the ideal truths of theoretical paradises – and we are better agreed on the former than on the latter.

To be able to say 'I lie', feeling or knowing what one is doing, but without having to proclaim oneself possessed of a higher knowledge: to be able to share this *inscientia* and declare it to be just as common among ordinary people as language is, this is what is ruled out not only by Hegel, and along with him all the German and world-scale speculation of the twentieth century, but also, along with them, by the suns of reality: the sun of the Lie which rises in the East and that of the Lie-to-oneself that sinks in the West.

It is up to anyone not to conceive that a socialism that hatches

out concentration camps is a lie; it is up to anyone to consider
that he has nothing to learn from a resistance which, faced with
this monstrosity, applies an all-round strategy of 'rejecting the
lie'; it is up to anyone not to listen to this: 'What cynic would
venture to object aloud to such a policy as *non-participation in
the lie?*

'Oh, people will object at once and with ingenuity: what *is* a
lie? Who can determine precisely where the lie ends and truth
begins? In every historically concrete dialectical situation, and
so on – all the invasions that liars have been using for the past
half-century.

'But the answer could not be simpler: decide *yourself*, as *your*
conscience dictates. And for a long time this will suffice. Depending upon his horizons, his life experience and his education, each
person will have his own perception of the line where the public
and state lie begins: one will see it as being altogether remote
from him, while another will experience it as a rope already cutting into his neck.' Look for yourself . . . The civilizations of the
Lie, whatever the crudeness of the falsehood and the savageries
they impose, have need that their subjects should lie to themselves, or, more precisely, should not let themselves think
'nothing could be simpler' – 'I am lying'. To that end they cultivate also in every individual the dialectical and scientific way of
getting out of it. More subtly pluridisciplinary, having swapped
the monotony of monolithism for the paint-pots of the experts in
social science, this same culture makes it possible, in a different
climate, to effect a saving: the authorities are spared the need for
certain crude forms of lying in proportion to the surplus-value
they collect from the lying-to-themselves which is practised by
their subjects. The axiom of modern authority is, at bottom, as
easy as pie: you can't get yourself off the hook by any 'I know
that I know nothing' – just be good and keep quiet. Any confession of ignorance has to be a confession of obedience: only
authority, inside each individual, says 'I know'.

'Voices from under the rubble': under this title some Russian
dissidents begin their reflections upon a historical experience
that was long left uncommented on. 'Voices', and not science, or
prolegomena to a theory of theory. 'Rubble', and not mistakes

in calculation recorded by a more up-to-date method, not a laboratory experiment in which the dilapidated state of the material used, together with some clumsiness on the part of the lab-boy, resulted in unfortunate incidents that can henceforth be avoided if only one modernizes the apparatus. The art of not seeing the rubble forms part of the rubble, just as the theory which does not allow one to see it accumulating forms part of that process: in this case, not only the different varieties of Marxism but every device for 'rationally' forbidding us to admit our own ignorance.

'I am not unaware that I am unaware,' we are told by Socrates, prophesying; by Panurge, hesitating whether he should marry; and by Bardamu, the insubordinate. Their 'hail and farewell' would cause us to share in their *inscientia*, but for the ban imposed by those who are unaware that they are unaware. Who are they? To identify them it is enough to read the obituaries of famous men, or to meet some leader: any and every man of power *believes himself*. From Socrates to the G.I. deserter, the sharing of *inscientia* and the deliberate fraternization of ignorances constitutes an experiment in democracy, the only one known.

The last two centuries have done their best to silence those voices which accompany knowledge even into its rubble. The theoreticians meanwhile proved that such voices were impossible because contradictory. Knowing one's own lack of knowledge is a paradox, but this spark becomes a self-refuting contradiction only in a world that has previously been asepticized, the world of the Great Wisdom. An old dream of domination, in which all the sciences, scattered, imperfect, non-speculative, would come to have their value recognized and their efficacity blessed before the supreme tribunal of Science, judge of itself, and self-knowledge. An old desire, from Leibniz to Husserl, for a '*mathesis universalis*', never met with except in the form of the depression it inflicts on the other branches of knowledge. The latter retain, however, the not inconsiderable advantage of *not* guaranteeing themselves against the questions posed by conscious ignorance. It is therefore not these that directly suppress the voices and conceal the rubble: for *that* purpose a science was needed that was sufficiently sure of itself to proceed to carry out the theoretical assassination of Socrates the challenger, and to declare that it alone is competent to know who is ignorant of what.

The Four Aces

'It is also true that you hardly ever really gave me a whipping. But the shouting, the way your face got red, the hasty undoing of the braces and the laying of them ready over the back of the chair, all that was almost worse for me.'

KAFKA, *Letter to his father*

1 The New Greece and Its Jew

'We both know, after all, enough typical examples of Western Jews, I am as far as I know the most typical Western Jew among them. This means, expressed with exaggeration, that not one calm second is granted me, nothing is granted me, everything has to be earned, not only the present and the future, but the past too – something after all which perhaps every human being has inherited, this too must be earned, it is perhaps the hardest work. When the Earth turns to the right – I'm not sure that it does – I would have to turn to the left, to make up for the past...

'It's more or less as though someone, each time before taking a walk, had not only to wash and comb himself and so on – this alone is indeed tiresome enough – but he also (since, each time, he lacks the necessary for the walk) has to sew his clothes as well, make his shoes, manufacture his hat, whittle his walking stick, and so on. Of course, he's not able to do this very well, perhaps they hold together for the length of a few streets ... And in the end he probably runs into a mob engaged in Jew-baiting in the Eisengasse.'

KAFKA, *to Milena*

The eternal youth of thinkers

Young Professor Fichte, in the days before he was accused of atheism and dismissed for being a Jacobin, reconciled the students' secret societies of Jena. He drew their attention to Paris, where terrors were being experimented with that were more interesting than those they were directing against each other. Immediately after 1789, the poet, the philosopher and the other, more mystical philosopher were simply Hölderlin, Hegel and Schelling: students, but, above all, future orators of the future German revolution, for which, we are told, they had planted a Tree of Liberty. Thirty-five years later, 'Young Germany', Heine and the left-wing intellectuals (they were called the Left 'Hegelians') were all proclaiming: beware of our philosophers! 'These doctrines served to develop revolutionary

forces that only await their time to break forth and to fill the
world with terror and with admiration ... Ye have more to fear
from a free Germany than from the entire Holy Alliance with
all its Croats and Cossacks.' Thus spake Heine to his French
friends.

Later, Nietzsche was to inaugurate the last third of the century: 'The Germanic spirit is returning to itself ... The weight-
iest of philosophies: Kant and the German Army.' When the
same man, fifteen years later, blamed himself for having 'fabled
about the "spirit of Teutonism",' it was in despair of Germany,
in the name of 'the German spirit which not so long before had
the will to the lordship over Europe, the strength to lead and
govern Europe', and which, now that Bismarck and Wagner
were growing old, had just 'resigned, and, under the pompous
pretence of empire-founding, effected its transition to medio-
critization, democracy and "modern ideas"'. From one end of
the century to the other the amazing freshness of German
thought reminds us of that of young leaders looking for troops
to command. 'We have commotions of every kind going on
within us and around us, but through them all the German head
quietly keeps its nightcap on and silently carries on its operations
beneath it' (Hegel).

Why Germany?

There were other young leaders without troops, wandering
across two centuries, and across Europe and the world, who
identified themselves with Napoleon, and then with Lenin.
Sometimes they met up with organizations, revolutions and wars,
but, unless proof to the contrary can be provided, these cohabi-
tations ended in misunderstandings, without anyone really
knowing who betrayed whom – did the Revolution betray one of
its leaders, or did its leaders betray a (not 'the') revolution? The
German master thinkers did not go to the antipodes to find their
truth, calling on other centuries or other continents to bear
witness for them, they did not explore the modern 'beyond' of
revolutionary exoticism, or unconditional loyalty to a distant
country, so as to come back as heroes and prophesy for the other

side of the earth. They stayed put on their own little plot of reality, Germany and Europe. 'Here is the rose, dance here!' (Hegel). They cultivated it so thoroughly that their hundred flowers have gone all round the world, carried by heroes and prophets who have only ever been *their* representatives. To the point when history and the world, having become German, leave us only one thing to learn from the master thinkers, and for the rest to refer to our usual newspaper – the only thing that they teach us without wanting to: to unlearn the role of leadership.

At the corner

It was Germany's misfortune, surrounded as she was by youthful and warlike modern states, that for centuries she had no state of her own. That happiness was to be found in giving oneself a state became a fancy cherished by all the national and revolutionary élites of countries engaged in freeing themselves – 'in process of development' or 'fighting for national liberation'. The 'German spirit' means the idea that, in order to build a state, it is necessary to bring into play all the forces of history and culture.

This is why Germany is waiting at the corner for every freedom-struggle: there is no fatality as to what the result of this encounter will be, the only fatality, whether conscious or not, lies in the encounter itself. It depends on those who are fighting whether they will be armed *by* it or *against* it. In any case, it is not without some benefit to know the enemy, who is one of the most intelligent in the world, since among his thinkers are Fichte, Hegel, Marx and Nietzsche.

Who asks the questions?

In order to be able to question an intelligent person it is not necessary to be stupider than he is – or to be more intelligent. All that is needed is to find a different way of being informed. Socrates' Daimon made him no promises, but only held him back from giving spontaneous approval to the competent authorities in Athens. There was nothing terribly original in that, and nothing brilliant, either, as Plato would have liked to suppose, in order to present it as something peculiar to Socrates: the scum of the city shared those insolent attitudes of his. Hence a problem for which the experts have never given up trying to find final solutions. May the smoke rising from the most recent of these solutions serve us as Daimon.

Don't confuse !

The master thinkers were not Nazis. Fichte remained a revolutionary in the French style: against Imperial France as occupying power it was the people that this weaver's son called to arms, while disapproving of the xenophobic and reactionary Pan-Germanism of the students. Hegel became a liberal official, in the service first of Napoleon, then of a Prussia that was reformed and, by the standards of the time, enlightened: perhaps he also remained a secret revolutionary, as Heine thought, a notion that has engendered many a university thesis right down to our own day. Marx and Nietzsche were capable of insulting the Germans with a verve that only a few other Germans have equalled.

With Nazism these men have only one direct and obvious link, namely, *antisemitism* – in their case not in a vulgar but in a refined form. All the thinking heads of nineteenth-century Germany were born with that caul on.

To begin with Hegel. He began the century, and his career, by contrasting the beautiful unity of Greece, wherein all were brothers, with the ignominious alienation of the Jews, who know only the relationship of master and slave, a vengeful God and submissive Man. Then Marx: no academic perfume can blow away the furiously antisemitic stench of his *On the Jewish Question*. Finally, Nietzsche brings up the rear, lifting higher than ever his tragic Hellas, above the bog of the Judeo-Christian bad consciousness. The question is not confined to Germany, for these ideas have gone all round the world. (Paradoxically, it was not until Heidegger that a German philosophy appeared that was not antisemitic: on the road to Greece it is Rome, not

Judaea, that blocks our way – the Imperium Romanum, with its translations no less destructive than its proclamations of peace...)

The height of perversity

Antisemitism is no speciality of the Germans, either in this age or before or after. But what is distinctive is that the master thinkers declare that they are what they are – 'Germans' or 'revolutionaries', depending on which aspect they take more seriously – only in inverse proportion to what they are not, namely, Jews. Hegel concludes his first (unpublished) political manifesto with these words: 'Once man's social instincts are distorted and he is compelled to throw himself into interests peculiarly his own, his nature becomes so deeply perverted that it now spends its strength on variance from others, and in the course of maintaining its separation it sinks into madness, for madness is simply the complete separation of the individual from his kind. The German people may be incapable of intensifying its obstinate adherence to particularism to that point of madness reached by the Jewish people – a people incapable of uniting in a common social life with any other. The German people may not be able to carry separation to such a pitch of frenzy as to murder and be murdered until the state is wiped out. Nevertheless ...' (*The German Constitution*). It's all there: the madman, the pervert, the egoist, the stubborn individualist, murder and suicide, privilege and stupidity, war and dispersion – the Jew. Let not the smoke from the crematoria tickle our nostrils unduly at this point: Hegel is not an antisemite of *that* sort. He wants a modern law that will take cognizance only of 'a universal person', and courts before which 'a man counts as a man in virtue of his manhood alone, not because he is a Jew, Catholic, Protestant, German, Italian, etc.'. There is no contradiction here with his opinion previously expressed. In order to establish a modern law and state, the German has to kill the Jew within himself. Hegel does not rule out the possibility that the Jew too can become modern, that is, can kill the Jew within *himself*.

With the master thinkers it is as with the majority of the Germans. Every inhabitant comes to see us with his Good Jew: all right, so far as the others are concerned, but not that one – which would mean, given sixty million Germans, that millions of Jews would go scot-free, said Himmler to his S.S. It is not fair to accuse the master thinkers of having organized the concentration camps: rather, of not having *dis*organized them in advance. Their antisemitism prepared the way not for Nazism but for non-resistance to Nazism.

I think, therefore the madman doesn't think

Descartes says that he doubts everything, he imagines that his senses may be deceiving him, that the world does not exist, that he is dreaming – but all the same, he is not one of those who think their bodies are made of glass, for 'they are mad, of course, and I should be mad in the eyes of men if I were thought to be following their example'. On that point he has no doubt. The subject who thinks cannot be mad because 'madness is precisely the condition in which thought is impossible', observes Foucault. This reciprocal exclusion (which was quite a new idea) of reason and madness went along with the idea (also new) of imprisonment on the grand scale for all deviants (unemployed, freethinkers, lepers, syphilitics, madmen ...). In the classical period this was done in the name of Western Reason: 'While *man* can always go mad, *thought*, being the exercise of the sovereignty of a subject who sets himself the task of perceiving the truth, cannot be mad. A line of demarcation was drawn which was soon to make impossible that experience, so familiar to the Renaissance, of an unreasonable reason, a reasonable lack of reason' (Foucault).

By what obscure process did the Jew come to place himself alongside the madman in the exclusion-area of Hegelian reason? In order to become 'lord and possessor of nature', rational Cartesian man shuts away the madman: in order to become lord and possessor of a rational society, why does he have to drive out the Jew? I am, therefore the Jew is not. The Reason of the classical age never locked up the 'madman' only. Is the politics of Reason which has become 'consciousness of self' aimed at the Jew alone?

What does a Jew lack ?

The Jewish Jew lives, according to Hegel, in 'a state of total passivity, of total ugliness'. This definition is neither racial nor aesthetic, but political. In contrast to the beautiful independence of the Greeks, free citizens in the free cities of Antiquity, the Jew is, from the start, an animal without a fatherland. 'The state is an institution not consonant with the Judaistic principle, and it is alien to the legislation of Moses.' While the German has, in order to unify his fatherland, to build his state, the Jew has no fatherland, for he has never, since Abraham, wanted to have a state.

Here a difficulty arises for one who, like a master thinker, identifies people with nation and nation with state. The Jews furnish a living proof of the falsity of such an identification, for they have been a people for two thousand years without any state to show for it. To formulate the problem is to answer it: the Jews find their unity in denying that of the other nations, 'the soul of Jewish nationality' is hatred, '*odium generis humani*'. The whole story of Abraham, who 'wanted *not* to love', is that of an endlessly repeated separation: his family leaves its homeland, and he leaves his family in order to be 'a wholly self-subsistent, independent man, to be an overlord himself', through becoming 'free from all relationships': which presupposes that any relationship with nature, oneself or other peoples is one of pure hostility – like his God, seen by Hegel as all-powerful, unique and vengeful, 'the product of his thought raised to be the unity dominant over the nature which he regarded as infinite and hostile (for the only relationship possible between hostile entities is mastery of one by the other)'. The entire history of the Jews is a repetition of Abraham's exodus.

Self-assured and arrogant, and therefore anarchistic, the Jewish people wants everything and is satisfied with nothing: 'Instead of a people which was dominant in idea, it became one dominated in reality'. Never mind what history shows – the

ruination of the Jewish states proves that the Jews bring their
own state to ruin, and two thousand years are short-circuited in
this *will to dispersion* that Hegel calls mad and Jewish, in comparison with Reason and its State.

No life outside the state

The Jews are anti-state, says Hegel. Or, more simply, they are a
state within the state, suggests Fichte, among others. He began
to write after the outbreak of the Revolution of 1789, and so was
the first after that event: 'In the midst of all the countries of
Europe there is situated a powerful state, animated by hostile
feelings, which is constantly at war with the others, and which,
in some of them, subjects the citizens to frightful oppression: I
refer to the Jews. I believe, and hope to show, that if this state is
so redoubtable, that is not because it forms a separate and
strongly united state, but because it is based upon hatred of the
whole human race.'

This observation is made by Fichte at a definite stage in his
argument concerning the revolution, when, to justify the latter,
he undertakes to define 'the people'. His reference to the Jews
introduces a list of exclusions, in which the people assume
sovereignty over against the privileged orders and estates (the
Church, the nobility, the petty princely courts of Germany).
Apparently, the mention of the alien Jew is brought in by means
of a play on words: the Jacobin philosopher passes unnotice-
ably from the concept of an order or 'estate' (for example, the
nobility, or the Third Estate: in German, *Stand*) to the concept
of a 'state' (in German, *Staat*). The figure of the Jew, against a
background of ancestral horror, is fixed in the new guise of *the
enemy within*. A state within the state, filled with enmity towards
those around him, the Jew must emigrate ... thereby legitimiz-
ing the expulsion of the clergy and the nobility, if they should
show themselves hostile to the revolutionary states.

By means of these *Reflections on the French Revolution*, published anonymously, Fichte meant to arouse his people, who
were oblivious of their own misfortunes and touched by those of
Marie-Antoinette and other crowned heads. One needs to learn

to give proper direction to one's pity: 'If you ate yesterday and, being hungry now, you have bread only for the day, then give some of it to the Jew who is hungry along with you, if he did not eat yesterday. In doing that, you will perform a very good action: but, as for granting those people rights of citizenship, I cannot, for my part, see any other means to it than cutting off all their heads one fine night and replacing them with other heads in which no Jewish idea is to be found. Otherwise, I know of no way to defend ourselves against them, except by conquering their Promised Land for them and sending them all off thither.' The project of exporting all the Jews of Europe to Madagascar was considered by the Nazi leaders, with all their characteristic seriousness: but they found it more diplomatic, simpler and more economical to use the crematoria of Auschwitz.

The German sickness

As the nineteenth-century doctors follow one another at her bedside, the diagnosis does not alter: Germany's trouble is that she is without a state, and this sickness is deep-rooted. Its root lies in 'what has been the chief fame of the Germans, namely, their drive for freedom. This drive it is which has never allowed the Germans to become a people subjecting itself to a common public authority, even after every other European people had become subject to the domination of a state of its own making.' Hegel, at once proud and horror-stricken, sets his people at the crossroads. Either 'the stubbornness of the German character' will harden the opposition between freedom and the state, following the example of the eternal Jew, that wretched wanderer over the face of the earth, or else this stubbornness will be overcome, the individual Germans will 'sacrifice their particularisms to society', and they will find 'freedom in a common, free subjection to a supreme public authority'. After killing the Jew within him, the German is to become, so far as modern life permits . . . a Greek.

The chronology of the German sickness is always, at bottom, the same – for the young Hegel (*The Spirit of Christianity and its Fate*), for the old Hegel (*The Philosophy of History*), or for

Nietzsche (*The Birth of Tragedy*). The new Germany must grasp the torch from a Greece swept aside by the 'victory of the Jewish world over the weakened will of Greek civilization'.

In these great Hollywood sets, world history puts on disguises: 'the Jew' serves to exorcise the question of the 'drive for freedom', and behind an imagined Greece we see outlined the modern state. As for the plot, this is freely inspired by some events in Paris which were much in the news: one, two, three revolutions.

The Revolution and the State

It matters little how the history of the world is written, if one does not discover on what blank sheet it is proposed to inscribe this history with variants which, though numerous, are all *on the world scale*. The super-productions begin and end with a proposition that never changes its form: *all history boils down to . . .*, or *history is merely the history of . . .* The writers vary as they choose the principal hero of this one-and-only play: it is the history of . . . self-consciousness, of the class struggle, of the Blond Beast. For such projections it was necessary to have a blank screen.

A Germany burdened with states within the state (orders, principalities) was not 'a blank sheet', Hegel lamented, thinking his thoughts, all his life long, in the light of a revolutionary radicalism. He conceived the events in France as the moment when it was 'perceived that man's existence centres in his head, that is, in thought, inspired by which he builds up the world of reality'. Whether loved or loathed, or treated with indifference, the Revolution was the starting point, not the finishing point: thought proceeded amid the heat of its fires, and the rational state was to be erected on the ground cleared by its Terror. The young Hegel found justification for the tyranny of Robespierre, which he carefully distinguished from the 'despotism' of the Ancien Régime. Later on, he was to share with Goethe, Marx and Nietzsche a fierce admiration for Napoleon. What the Revolution of 1789 taught all of them was that nothing must resist the modern state, which, if necessary, will reconstruct everything from scratch.

Given the traditional pedantry of a public that had not been revolutionized, the lesson was to be translated into Greek before being applied in German: '... only the iron fist of the state can force the largest masses to dissolve, so that there may then necessarily take place that chemical separation of society which accompanies its new pyramidal structure. But whence arises this new power of the state, whose aim far surpasses the understanding and the egoism of each individual? How was the slave, that blind mole of civilization, *born*? The Greeks have revealed this to us, through the instinct they had for the law of nations, which, even at the highest point of their morality and humanity, did not cease to proclaim in brazen voice such maxims as: to the victor belongs the vanquished, with his wife and children, bodies and goods alike ...' (Nietzsche).

The State and the Revolution

A Marxist was to celebrate with more discretion the 'iron hand of the state', even if his fist was no less heavy: 'Marxists will never, under any circumstances, advocate either the federal principle or decentralization. The great centralized state is a tremendous historical step forward from medieval disunity to the future socialist unity of the whole world ...' (Lenin). This passage is indeed remarkably innocent, with the centralized state seen as merely the stage between the Middle Ages and the radiant future.

The need to pass through such a stage was for Marx and Engels a matter beyond dispute, and from it they deduced an exhaustive categorization of the world's nations and peoples, arranged hierarchically according to whether they were 'historical' or not. Those peoples ('nations') were historical which were capable of providing themselves with a modern, rational state. Unhistorical were the others ('nationalities') who, in order to survive, had to become assimilated to the first-mentioned; such were the swarm of Czechs, Serbs, Gaels,

Bretons, Basques ... 'relics of nations mercilessly trampled underfoot in the course of history'. Not to mention what Engels calls 'this meanest of all races', the Jews of Poland. As for the remaining continents, apart from the United States, Persia and Afghanistan, they seem doomed to the darkness of barbarism.

Marx, in London, was not ignorant of the fact that the state unites its territory and colonizes the world with the bloody savagery of primitive accumulation. Ireland – half-assimilated, half-colonized – showed that the method did not vary. That observer knew the mechanisms of domination were horrible, but his horror did not cause him to flinch from them: 'However much the English may have Hibernicized the country, the breaking-up of those stereotyped primitive forms was the *sine qua non* for Europeanization. The destruction of their archaic industry was necessary to deprive the villages of their self-supporting character' (Marx on the colonization of India).

The only nations, the only civilized communities, the only bearers of the future are those peoples who can build and defend a state under the conditions of the modern world, that is, in Western Europe. Marx and Engels showed some leanings towards a statist and dictatorial strategy for the proletarian revolution, leanings that were modified by their compromises with the facts or with other revolutionaries. Did they, in their minds, see the state as a mere stage, 'from the standpoint of socialism', or did they, rather, see socialism through the spectacles of the state?

The philosophical baptism of Karl Marx

Accused by the German thinkers of incarnating perversion of the social instinct, the Jew was at the same time emancipated, and while his religion was condemned, it was no longer *that* which made him condemnable: though the Anti-State he was no longer the Anti-Christ. More than ever he haunts modern society, but this haunting is no longer religious in character, and is sustained by explanations that are more realistic, in the sense that reading the newspaper every day (what Hegel called 'that morning prayer of modern man') is realistic.

Marx's materialism did not improve upon the realism of Hegel. The latter described as 'the bourgeois spirit' the Jewish temptation experienced by the German who isolates himself, cultivates his particularisms, and, in general, conceives reason of state within the categories of private property. Each of the German states, and each inhabitant, maintains with the whole a relation which 'is something particular, in the nature of property' that is, which is optional, depending on the will of a 'small property-owner'. Consequently, the whole ceases to exist: 'Associations of this sort are like a heap of round stones which are piled together to form a pyramid. But they are perfectly round and have to remain so without any dovetailing, and so, as soon as the pyramid begins to move towards the end for which it has been built, it rolls apart . . .' (Hegel).

Identifying, like Hegel, the *Jewish question* with the question of private property, the young Marx remains logical in turning private property into a new Jewish question: the property-owner will be expropriated so that society may recover its coherence, whatever is private will be driven out so that the world may again be common, communist – a world of 'associated producers', as he was later to put it. By denouncing 'the *chimerical* nationality of the Jew' as 'the nationality of the merchant, of the man of money in general', the young Jew Marx Hegelianized, and simply passed his entrance examination for what he later spoke of as the cafés of Berlin.

Perhaps he bought this right of entry extremely dear, since he never ceased to pay instalments on it. 'The Jew has emancipated himself in a Jewish manner, not only because he has acquired financial power, but also because, through him and also apart from him, *money* has become a world power and the practical Jewish spirit has become the practical spirit of the Christian nations' (*On the Jewish Question*). Marx, on the contrary, emancipated himself in the German manner, that is, he never stopped emancipating himself from the allegedly Jewish manner of emancipation. His critique of that Jewish manner became a critique of political economy, and money, as the 'world power', was to be denounced as *Capital,* giving its name to his major work.

It was not the cafés of Berlin that he entered, but, through them, the closed world of the master thinkers, which he never left. We sense here the origin of the modern condemnation of the Jews. Is it from this beginning that we get the identification of the march of the wanderers around the world and the world market of capital? Who begins to confuse the Jew with money if it is not the state, enlightened in the Hegelian manner, which sees in these frontier-crossers one and the same danger, that of its own decomposition? If the Jewish question and the question of Capital fit together so precisely, is this not because they conceal one and the same unspoken question, that of the state?

Is it really *communism* that Marx counterposes to the power of private property? Or is it merely the *public* domain – nationalization, the power of the state? The chapter on the state which Marx planned to write is missing, as though by chance, from *Capital*. Is it a matter of chance if, focusing all hatreds upon individuals, from the Jew to the property-owner, the state gets itself forgotten and escapes any challenge?

Why do the Western élites take two centuries to see the state as the biggest property-owner? Because all condemnations of *private* property were levelled in the name of the *public* spirit, in the name of that same state! Marx shifted hatred of the Jew on to hatred of money. The Nazis shifted it back. Whether the movement be forward or backward along the rails of hatred, it is the modern state that provides the steam.

The new order

When they were talking about it, the German state did not exist. After it had come into being, the master thinkers had only bad things to say about it. The state thus remained a concept but not an ideal: what was conceived in it was the reality attributed to the neighbouring real states. The state was a machine. If commentators were amazed, a century later, to discover a young Fichte who was ultra-liberal, almost libertarian, this was because they had not read him properly. The relentless critic of the Ancien Régime was in step with the new order of the legal machine. ' It is the law that must rule through the Prince, and he must be subject to it ... As Prince, the Prince is a machine animated by the law, and is lifeless without it.'

The phrase has polemical force: the Prince bows to the law, the state as Sun becomes the state as Machine, something neither religious nor inspiring worship. A disenchanted, sober world, Marx and Weber were to say, later, in their capacity as heirs. Soon, Hegel came out against Fichte: the modern state, he said, was more complex than 'a machine with a single spring which imparts movement to all the rest of the infinite wheel-work'. He substituted for the image of the machine that of the living organism. Fichte himself turned his machine into a tree, with the state uniting its various parts as roots, trunk and leaves. We have not stopped cultivating these refinements – O cybernetics! They cannot hide the primary agreement between all the metaphors: to speak of the state as a tree or as a machine is to speak of it prosaically.

In France, if we are to believe Paul Valéry, civilization has known since the war of 1914 that it is mortal. In Germany the states, and, consequently, the master thinkers, civilization, have known it since 1789. The special position accorded by Marx to Persia, the only historical people of the East, comes from Hegel's *Philosophy of History*: 'The Persians are the first historical people; Persia was the first empire that passed away. While China and India remain stationary, and perpetuate a natural vegetative existence even to the present time, this land has been subject to those developments and revolutions which alone manifest a historical condition ... In Persia first arises that light which shines itself, and illuminates what is around; for Zoroaster's "Light" belongs to the world of consciousness – to spirit as a relation to something distinct from itself.' *Ergo Zarathustra.*

The state is a machine because it is mortal. It is a good machine when it knows itself to be mortal. This is why 'the history of Persia ... constitutes strictly the beginning of world history; for the grand interest of spirit in history is to attain an unlimited immanence of subjectivity – by an absolute antithesis to attain complete harmony'.

Our own antithesis, that of the living, is death. We conscious beings have our own death, whereby the antithesis becomes 'absolute'. The state is the living machine wherein each element of a people knows that it is mortal and renders itself mortal to other peoples – one dies for one's country by experiencing it as something mortal. The modern, rational state is a machine consciously organized on the basis of permanent awareness that the fatherland, that is, the state itself, is in danger.

Machiavelli, three centuries before Hegel, advised the modern Prince, the state, to employ, in order to establish his authority, methods that were as strong as could be, even bloody, and also methods that were hypocritical and underhand. Commentators have often pointed to the irony of Machiavelli *publicly* calling on the Prince to remain *secretive*. The book tells the Prince of a thousand and one ways to oppress the people, and publication of the book informs the peoples of the thousand and one machinations resorted to by the Prince. When young, and very probably revolutionary in outlook, Hegel did not appreciate the paradox. He approved of Machiavelli ('gangrenous limbs cannot be cured with lavender water'), understanding him with a seriousness that was thenceforth to be characteristically German: Machiavelli had one interlocutor only, the Prince, and political science was not merely *about* the state but *for* the state. The latter, being mortal, must become mortal to everything around it. 'To engineer anarchy is the supreme or perhaps the only crime against a state.'

A disciplinary machine

Whatever the complexity attributed to it, the modern rational state is characterized by two features: it has a centre, and it is visible.

For the Germans to escape from their dispersed condition, the army and the public finances must be in the hands of an indivisible authority: 'the public authority must be concentrated in one centre'. This centralism is to be achieved by force – none of the thinkers is naïve enough to believe in the peaceful birth of states. The violence required is not solely or necessarily physical, 'if this centre is secure on its own account in virtue of the awe of the masses' (Hegel). The state machine allows a certain amount of play, leaving its subordinates a field for independent action and initiative in which freedom of property and freedom of thought are exercised. The rational state takes account of realities, of particular liberties; it does not *determine* its subjects' lives, but supervises them: 'The highest public authority must carry the supreme oversight of these aforementioned aspects of the domestic relationships of a people and their organization (which has been settled by chance and ancient arbitrary decisions); equally obvious is it that these aspects may not hinder the chief activity of the state, since on the contrary this activity must secure itself before all else, and to this end it is not to spare the subordinate systems of rights and privileges.'

The regime of supreme oversight can be conceived in a variety of ways, but its principle is a simple one: the state abandons the 'beyond' to the various religions and keeps for itself the realm of the visible, of the 'phenomena', of that which is apparent. In his first work, allegedly 'libertarian' in character, Fichte states the general equation between the separation of church and state and the division between the visible and the invisible: 'Domination by the state is not uncertain, like that which the church exercises over men's consciences: it commands actions which are expressed in the visible world ... It needs to be able to count for certain on the result of every action that it has ordered, just as in a well-arranged machine one can be sure of the interlocking of one wheel with another ... A state that walks leaning on the crutches of religion only reveals its own weakness.'

Hegel blames Fichte for developing a too mechanistic and police-like conception of oversight by the state: he adds the element of tragedy. The Antigone of Hegel is guilty even though her intentions are pure, for the truth of intention lies in the deed, and the deed takes place, together with its consequences, in the visible and centred space of the supreme oversight. Antigone appeals to ancestral tradition in honouring the corpse of one of her brothers (a rebel against the state) equally with that of her other brother (who has died in the service of the city). By doing this she flouts the authority of the ruler, Creon, setting up the laws of the beyond against the government of this world: the equality of the dead challenges the inequality of life. She plots, she cultivates her family's clan, she founds a 'party', she subverts the ruler's own son ... Her femininity becomes an 'enemy within'.

Hegel's analyses of Sophocles' tragedy are original, depicting as they do an Antigone who is symmetrical with Creon, equally guilty and guilty in the same way: both of them are breaking a law. Tragedy becomes politics, with Hegel reversing Napoleon's formula: the Emperor is said to have told Goethe that, in modern times, politics is our tragedy. For the philosopher, the tragedy of the ancients is already modern politics. While Antigone challenges the centralism of the state, Creon interferes with the cult of the dead, thereby coming into conflict with freedom of opinion: in the world of the modern state, both sides must perish.

By way of detour through Greece, the regime of 'supreme oversight' is strengthened with the mechanisms of mutual surveillance.

The panoptic apparatus

Every modern citizen may share the fate of Antigone. Each of his actions has to be read in that political and centred setting in which he could be challenging the central, mortal state: 'only the stones are innocent.' The implications of a deed may not be apparent to him, but nevertheless they assume significance in the deed's relation to the centre, and are visible to others – the individual, who is always one-sided in this way or that, lets more of himself be seen than he can see for himself.

In other words, the law of suspects, though transcended, is never abolished; the drama of the Jacobin terror, put before us by Hegel, introduces the citizen to wisdom in so far as it threatens to be reproduced, which constitutes it the permanent lesson. The transition from the Ancien Régime to the state of reason takes place precisely there: 'Suspicion attained a terrible power and brought to the scaffold the Monarch ...' From the moment that the state is obliged to concern itself with the freedom of its subjects, the reign of Reason advances, that reign in which the master thinkers inaugurate their own.

There appear straight away:

(1) the person subject to surveillance (Antigone does more of this than she realizes; everyone is in danger of escaping from self-surveillance, for he may do something which affects the state centre without realizing it);

(2) mutual surveillance (other people see what the individual may miss);

(3) the central headquarters of surveillance (the state) that is: the area of visibility – (1) and (2) – and the centripetal warden-ship which together form the elementary structures of the panoptic prison.

The prisoners (Antigone and Creon) in their ('ideological') cells are seen (by the public or by the author) without them-selves seeing (they do not know their own one-sidedness). Reciprocally, at the centre, *the state sees without being seen.*

This formula provides the key to an apparent monstrosity, which is so striking that Marx makes it his knock-down criticism of the Hegelian state. At the summit of his rational construc-tion Hegel places the most irrational creature possible – a monarch who is hereditary, therefore chosen by the chance of nature, a monarch who may sometimes be perverse, weak-minded, paranoiac, or a congenital idiot. Examples are plentiful, and embarrass not only the monarchies. This problem did not escape Hegel's attention. He pointed to it not as a weakness but as a proof of the excellence of his construction, concluding that, the more perfect the state, the more a matter of indifference is the personality of the monarch: 'The government rests with the official world, and the personal decision of the monarch consti-tutes its apex ... Yet, with firmly established laws, and a settled organization of the state, what is left to the sole arbitrament of the monarch is, in point of substance, no great matter.'

It matters little whether there is a warder in the central observatory of the panoptic prison: if it has been constructed according to the rules ('with firmly established laws and a settled organization of the state') it provides the feeling that we are perpetually under surveillance (always and at any moment), in so far as we cannot turn round towards our warders, nor they towards the central warder. The latter can be away as much as he likes: the structure is sufficient and we all sense his gaze upon the backs of our necks, whether his eyes are actually open or shut.

Hegel places *anyone at all* at the centre of the monarchy: 'A monarch ... has only to say "yes" and dot the "i".' Here there can be no failure or mistake due to inattention, insuperable irrationality, compromise with reaction. With a single stroke of genius the philosopher has defined the height of (disciplinary) rationality: with the most utter idiot at its head, the prison goes on functioning.

There is no contradiction here: Hegel defines his ruler as he who sees without being seen. If Marx perceives a contradiction, he does not perceive the modern state.

The high places

Thinking that they were giving a lesson to the states of their time, instructing the peoples in how to build modern states, claiming that they were teaching everything to the state, in reality they learnt everything from it.

The history of world civilization is merely the history of states. They die, to be sure, but only in each other's arms. In the world's course they form a chain, passing from hand to hand the torch of culture. The historical distinction possessed by Persia is that she it was that, in the Hegelian manner, effected the first transfer of the torch, bowing out in favour of her successor: 'China and India ... have remained – Persia has not. The transition to Greece ... here ... shows itself also externally, as a transmission of sovereignty – an occurrence which from this time forward is ever and anon repeated. For the Greeks surrender the sceptre of dominion and of civilization to the Romans and the Romans are subdued by the Germans.' War, death and submission: philosophically, the history of states becomes worldwide in scope

The lesson of history is accompanied by practical sociological work. Hegel divides the population into three classes which are needed for the proper functioning of the modern state. The first of these is a military and bureaucratic nobility, indifferent to private interest and to death, defending the general interests of the state in peace as in war. The Marxist sees in this a proof of Hegel's chimerical 'idealism': a more naïve observer fancies he sees in it a cunning but too optimistic prefiguration of what was to become the '*nomenklatura*' of the Soviet Union and the various bureaucracies in the socialist countries. This 'nobility' is open to all competent persons and is recruited by examination: inspired by Napoleon's 'Imperial nobility' and the reforms in Prussia, it foretells the French administrative corps, its E.N.A. and the machinery of the national educational system.

The intermediate class functions in the world of labour, need, private interest – it is bourgeois civil society as a whole, the people of the towns safeguarded from death; bourgeois craftsmen, journeymen, all mixed together (at that time it was difficult to single out the workers from the rest). The third class, the peasants, is 'substantial' because attached to the soil. It is regarded as lacking 'self-consciousness'. (Marx was to say the same, equating peasants with barbarians.) Supplying its own substance to the rest of society, in the form of bread for every day and blood for great occasions, the Hegelian peasant constitutes the strength of the army and the soundness of the state: die and hold your tongue.

In this panoptic view of history and society, the state can take upon itself the relation of dominated dominance which was identified at the outset as the Jewish ugliness. The state, dominating everything, also dominates its bourgeois Jewry. Though Hegel did not invent the dictatorship of the proletariat, he gave a foretaste of it, defining by service to the state the new nobility of functionaries, the proletariat of the dictatorship.

Who climbs on whose shoulders ?

At first sight the state is a Mount Everest. Perched on its summit, the master thinker estimates the extent of the modern planet and gauges its depths. This 'roof of the world' exists, however, only under the skull of the aforesaid thinker, who, having clambered on to his own shoulders, brandishes ever higher the placard of the modern state, and his pick-handle.

The master thinkers were not the inventors of the modern state, even if they became its sandwich-men or its recruiting sergeants. They explored, in the modern state's alarming cavities, a new solidarity between knowledge and power, the experts and the disciplinary society, the new intellectuals and the new state formed on the model of the European revolutions They were not so 'idealist' as all that!

I think, therefore the state is

The inner drama and the intellectual itinerary of the young European have hardly changed in two centuries. Hegel began his thinking with the contrast between the love of domination (the Jew) and the domination of love (in turn, Greek patriotic love and Christian love). By way of a crisis lasting several years which he called his 'neurasthenia', he learnt to get his hands dirty, like Sartre's hero, exchanging his 'beautiful soul' for a worldly commitment.

'To think, to conceive, is to dominate' (*begreifen ist beherr-schen*) was the happy thought upon which he built up his science. (If you remove the word 'concept' from his *Great Logic*, the text drains away.) At first, Hegel recoiled from the idea in horror, proclaiming it to be 'Jewish'. Then he got used to it. And the Jew, no longer polarizing all the horror of 'abstraction', lost his importance. Modern society does not get rid of its bourgeois abstraction, but dominates it by means of a state which is still more 'abstract' and which causes to hover over everyone the terror of the supreme abstraction, the risk of death that is run by a fatherland always in danger.

World history, the 'old' Hegel tells us, was born in the states of the East where moral freedom was lacking but where 'abstraction was the supreme principle' – where the bureaucrats calculated to a sufficiently elaborate degree, consolidating great empires. Consciousness of the world-wide nature of this history no longer begins with the 'abstractly' universal history of the Jews or with Greek philosophy. It is to Rome, in the end, that

Hegel points: 'In the history of the world, it is with the Roman world that politics effectively enters the scene as abstract universal destiny.' The Greek ideal, still held in honour, is now carefully wedged between Persia and Rome, two administrations that were universal because imperial. Hegel's horror of the Jew and his nostalgia for Greece have been transcended, because the world's course moves towards universal domination: 'It is not in time that everything comes to be and passes away, rather time itself is the *becoming*, this coming-to-be and passing away, *the actually existent abstraction*, Chronos (Time, Saturn) from whom everything real is born and by whom its offspring is destroyed.'

Philosophy of the state, philosophy of the bureaucracy and philosophy of imperialism all cultivate the same garden: 'To conceive is to dominate.' Descartes summed up the whole of his metaphysical itinerary in the formula: I think, therefore God is. Let us listen, over the course of two centuries, to the militants of the various states which had been realized, affirming, in low voices: I think, therefore the state is. Let us listen to ourselves.

The beggars of Europe

The concept 'Jew' is not to be explained by way of the reality of the Jew but by the need for the concept. Understand by this: reason of state. That will to dominate which was described as Abraham's destiny has turned out to be the law of the modern state. Once his neurasthenia was over, when the hour of reconciliation between concept and reality sounded, Hegel projected universal abstraction no longer upon the ugly 'other one' but into the so-much-admired history of the world.

The circle was closed. It was as the internal enemy of the state that the Jew had been aimed at. In doing this the German intellectuals were not in the least original. Sometimes the Jews form a 'state within the state', with its own 'organization' and 'particularisms' (Dostoyevsky), sometimes their 'pettiness' makes them capable merely of tavern-keeping and usury, and offers 'proof of their irremediable moral insolvency, their total human bankruptcy' (Dostoyevsky again). Their *pettiness* is to be seen in their absolute misappreciation of the sense of the state. On the left, Proudhon links the two themes: 'A few, strongly emphasized pages on the Jews. A freemasonry throughout Europe. A race incapable of forming a state, ungovernable by itself, is wonderfully in agreement about exploiting the others. Its analogues in the Bohemians, the Polish *émigrés*, the Greeks, and all who wander.'

All who wander: that's the point. Under the name of 'Jew', condemnation is cast upon an entire little world that is liable to escape from the state by crossing its frontiers and, by violating these, to upset the disciplinary society. The Europe of states strives to shut out the 'fringe people': the master thinkers hand over to the master purgers, who, in the Nazi camps, mix Jews with homosexuals, and in the Russian camps herd together everyone who deviates. Liberal Europe has preferred to assimilate and normalize in a calmer way, with cultural instead of physical genocide.

When the Abbé Grégoire called in 1788 for emancipation of the Jews, he said clearly that the problem was not confined to them: 'France embraces perhaps eight million subjects, some of whom can barely stammer a few mispronounced words or a few disjointed phrases in our idiom; others are completely ignorant of it.' Affecting as it did one-third of the population of France at that time, this was a matter of state importance.

Equality of rights must lead to assimilation, and so to the elimination of that 'Teutonic–Hebraic–Rabbinic jargon'. That was how the *patois* of the Alsatian Jews was described, with the modern state naming in this definition what it saw as its principal enemies: the foreigner beyond the Rhine, the most traditional of traditions, and religion (the contempt of Paris for the priests of the Vendée).

The modern state treats as making up all one family Bécassine [the comically stupid Breton; compare the Englishman's 'Paddy' – Trans.], the Yid, the Wog and the Poof – 'for we still live confronted by that murderous trap, the idea that the right to recognized and approved existence – to existence, in short – is confined to those human groups which have at least the aspiration to form a state' (R. Marienstras).

The statesman and his 'other'

Though the state's 'Jew' is not necessarily Jewish, the young states nevertheless did show a marked tendency to try out on the Jews all the treatments destined for every disturbing element. For this purpose it was easy to exploit the ancient accumulation of Christian hatred for the 'deicide people'. Even though states tend to follow lines of least resistance, it is risky to explain in terms of religion alone a racial hatred which exploded more and more catastrophically in societies that were less and less religious, among thinkers for whom God had long been dead, and in political circles which proclaimed themselves pagan or material-ist.

The formula of the Jew as 'a state within the state' was put forward by Schiller, who used it long before the Great Leap Forward of antisemitism. The poet pointed to the situation of the Jews in Egypt, nomads who 'camped' in the empire of the Pharaohs, without being allowed to participate in the life of the cities, and thereby preserved their tribal independence. This population was ready to take collective action to free itself when there came into effect 'the mission of Moses' (the title of a work by Schiller which was to seem far too democratic and philosemitic to those who made play with his formula). The epithet 'Jewish' was to be applied to every form of community outside the state, every form of collective life outside oversight by the central administration, every subversive possibility whereby the individual escaped from the alternative between private life and public service. Here is an example: 'Once, when passing through the Inner City, I suddenly encountered a phenomenon in a long caftan and wearing black sidelocks. My first thought was: Is this a Jew? They certainly did not have this appearance in Linz. I watched the man stealthily and cauti-ously; but the longer I gazed at that strange countenance and examined it feature by feature, the more the question shaped itself in my brain: Is this a German?'

It is the story of a revelation. Before that moment, Hitler had not understood antisemitism. Thenceforth, with the help of a few pamphlets, he turned it into his banner. Something struck him about the man in the long caftan. Was it that he was a Jew? No. First and foremost, that he was a non-German – who, through Hitler's care and attention, would become a non-human-being. From then onward Hitler set himself a task: to spot the Jew wherever he might be, and disassimilate the assimilated, for the truth of the Jew lay in that unassimilable caftan. Unassimilable to what? To religion? He had none. 'Is this a German?' With black sidelocks like that? Unassimilable to the state-nation!

When hatred is focused upon the Jew, who is looking, if not the state? And whom does the state attack, killing two birds with one stone, if not all the tramps, all the lousy creatures who in one way or another escape from its control, the likely bearers of some anti-state subversion?

The ideological multiplier

The master thinkers disarm before racism. It is not that they are under Christian influence – still today suspected of atheism, they are too independent to honour any dogmas but their own – nor that they have psychological or psycho-pathological difficulties: who hasn't? In so far as they all take the state as point of departure in their thinking, they arrive at legitimization of the racist surveillance that the state establishes over its territory. The Jew is the concentrate of what has to be destroyed. Either because he lacks, through pettiness of spirit, the sense of the state (and along with him so many others, like those Negroes whose enslavement Hegel justifies because their 'condition is capable of no development or culture, and as we see them today, such have they always been'), or because, as a state within the state, the Jew functions as a foreign agent.

This state racism is not only the root of the quasi-universal antisemitism of nineteenth-century thought, it provides the key to the racist mass movements which burst forth in the same period. The 'Hep! Hep!' (*Hierosolyma est perdita*, 'Jerusalem is lost') of the German students setting out on Jew-hunts in 1819 was the cry of *nationalist* students. They dreamt of erecting over the corpse of the Yid, not a church but a state. All historical interpretations fail if they confine themselves to explaining these well-dated phenomena by a mere sum of traditional religious antisemitism and individual pathological phenomena. The coincidence between emergence of modern states and revival of racism is always to be found.

In 1915 the genocide of the Armenians by the Young Turks shows that the religious pretexts invoked are eminently variable in this sort of affair. What does *not* vary is the cult of the state. The Young Turks – secularist, nationalist, democratic – wanted to build a modern state on the ruins of the old Ottoman Empire. The Armenians could not be assimilated culturally, for they were literate in their own language. Nor could they be assimilated on the plane of religion or economics, for they were Christians and they possessed their own bourgeois mercantile élite. Though they never challenged the power of the Young Turks, their very presence constituted an opaque zone in the transparent space subject to the 'supreme oversight'. The other countries of Europe were discreet, well understanding the 'reason of state' for the slaughter of millions. Pierre Loti celebrated it in France. Lenin cultivated the friendship of Young Turkey and Hitler openly appealed to the example it had given, when he imposed his final solution of the Jewish problem.

Every rule calls for an exception. The Italian people provides one in this case. It rejected antisemitism when its Fascist state adopted racism as official doctrine. Yet 'religious roots' were not lacking in the country which initiated the shutting-up of the Jews, giving the world both the word 'ghetto' and the thing itself. The so-called 'economic causes' of antisemitism did not operate, despite the existence of an Italian Jewish bourgeoisie. It is therefore necessary in this case to explain the Italian's attitude to his Jew by the general attitude of the Italian to his state. Italy was not carried away with enthusiasm by the antisemitic crusade, and the Italians were also the ones who broke ranks like no other nation in Europe during the war of 1914–18. At present they are refusing to let themselves be disciplined even by a Left which, headed by the trade unions, calls on them to roll up their sleeves ... The Italians are difficult to *mobilize.*

They are not antisemitic and they lack the cult of the state. The latter circumstance explains the former.

One can distinguish – pejoratively – as *ideologies* the conglomeration of simple ideas which fostered the great massacres of the twentieth century by serving as agents of transmission, as resonators, as justifications – in short, by oiling the wheels and tensing the springs of the machinery of extermination. Ideology is thus that without which crimes can be counted on one's fingers, on the scale of Macbeth – that force thanks to which crimes can multiply to the scale of a 'final solution' or of a Gulag Archipelago.

It is easy to see that the lever of ideology has a fulcrum: the power of the state. All ideologies channel through the state the transformation of the world that they plan to effect. The master thinkers were the fathers of the reigning ideologies, in that they provided the state with their reasons of state.

2 Why I Am So Revolutionary
(Fichte, to Start With)

'For the hour hath come, thou knowest it forsooth, for the great, evil, long, slow mob-and-slave-insurrection: it extendeth and extendeth!'

NIETZSCHE, *Thus Spake Zarathustra*

'I think that I feel the World Spirit like a friend's warm hand in my own; when I wake up, I wonder if I have clasped only my own fingers.'

HÖLDERLIN, *Hyperion*

Apologia for the masters who lead nowhere

Demosthenes, who chewed stones so as to be able the better to speak to the people, fascinates them, as also does Moses – not in his capacity as guide to a Promised Land about which they have nothing to say, but because he gathered the people together and led them out of Pharaoh's Egypt. Also Bonaparte in his speeches to the army in Italy: an image that still excites their admiration after he had become a monarch – 'I saw the Emperor, that World-Soul, leaving the town to go on reconnaissance. It is indeed a wonderful feeling when one sees an individual like this who, concentrated here in one place, on horseback, extends himself over the world and dominates it' (Hegel, at the Battle of Jena, 1806).

At eighteen they want to be preachers rather than scholars or philosophers but it is down here, on this earth, that they aim to exert influence over the masses. A century after their deaths we still wonder whether all the honours of the most speculative philosophy sheltered, rather than extinguished, the fire of the revolutions that they promoted, perhaps consciously. Generation after generation – this was the only place in the world and in history, since Athens, where one generation of philosophers succeeds another – they begin afresh. Büchner distributes his

Christian-Left tracts ('War to the castles, peace to the cottages') and pioneers a new kind of drama, only to die at the age of twenty-three; then comes 'Young Germany'; then the friends Wagner and Bakunin, on the Dresden barricades; then Nietzsche, who knows, sitting in his corner, that 'I am dynamite'. His corner is the world – 'passing between past and future like a heavy cloud'.

Not all of them were to be master thinkers. Hölderlin broke away, and also Büchner, Heine and others. Not all of them caressed the Emperors of the world with their astonished gaze, though they discovered many other wonderful sensations, but they all saw and felt. The Emperor was seated on his horse, surrounded by blood, by the dead and dying: individuals, in moving themselves, moved the world, and they were legion. These are details that are hidden by the tons of incense burned for the modern personality cults of the twentieth century, in whose eyes Hegel's admiration for Napoleon seems a miracle of intelligence, sense of proportion and clearsightedness: 'Thanks to the bath of revolution it took, not only did the French nation free itself from many institutions which the human mind, having emerged from infancy, had outgrown ... but also the individual shook off the fear of death and the habitual way of life, which the changed circumstances deprived of all solidity.'

Compared with our own, their mode of thought appears deficient: in 1976 the almost undisputed beacon-light of French Marxism caused his best pupil to give utterance to a new and shattering truth, namely, that it would perhaps be proper to open up Marxist theory to the problem presented by the millions who died in the socialist concentration camps. A life spent in singing the glory of the Marx who 'made the continent of history surface into scientific theory', and not one word so far about the archipelagoes of *our* history: that tormented flesh had, for this man who had read all the books, deserved no more than a single 'Alas!'. A thought for those who forgive the thinkers for not thinking over their own history: when theory pontificates about the History of the Labour Movement (don't forget the capital letters) while keeping silent about those generations of workers, peasants and intellectuals who moved, under strong escort, into the death-camps, it nevertheless does not debar itself from referring to real history. Since this is not the history of actual bodies, it becomes merely the history of the world-wide petition campaigns launched from the Kremlin, the 'harsh and protracted struggle that was to force back on to the horizon of the Cold War the shadow of catastrophe, repulsed by numberless human arms' (Althusser). The beauty of the image is proportionate to the elevation of the thought: the Marxist 'philosopher' speaks here of the signatures against the atomic bomb (the Stockholm Appeal) that the world's masses were called upon to give at a time when Russia was in a position of some inferiority where that type of weapon was concerned. In the period of that political fraud, the Gulag Archipelago was swallowing ten million fresh victims (probably the fourth such holocaust) – a little detail that would not have been missed by any German thinker of the previous century (Marx included), or by any 'labour movement' of that century.

If 'concrete analysis of a concrete situation is the living soul of Marxism' (Lenin), we can divine what the concrete analysis just mentioned tells us regarding its truly living soul. And this powerful theoretician and subtle politician presumes that his Marxist science equips him to diagnose the 'absolute delirium' of Hegel! And this lesson of his is given with a serious air equalled only by the solemnity of those (the best of the university and political worlds) who listen to it.

'Here is the rose, dance here' (Hegel). Here they pluck you. Reality will, in any case, put its flowers into our hands, whether these flowers be dug up from mud and blood or whether they be made of paper and rhetoric.

From their masters of last century the little masters of today have retained only the art of arranging bouquets – the manner, not the matter, which is henceforth cultivated by the Great Responsible Organizations. Everything has been borrowed from the master thinkers except the courage to go and examine the monster's jaws, even at the risk of getting one's head bitten off. 'Not the courage before witnesses but anchorite and eagle courage, which not even a God any longer beholdeth' (Nietzsche). It is for us to spell out the monstrous truth, the truth about monsters, that we read on their pale lips: to conceive is to dominate.

Extraordinary

All through the nineteenth century, German thinkers thought in terms of the French Revolution, and, according to Fichte and Hegel, their thinking ceased to be philosophy and became science. The science of revolution: 'Hegel's philosophy is the algebra of revolution,' observed the Russian revolutionary Herzen, one of whose faithful readers (Lenin) borrowed this formula, eighty years later, to define his own Marxism.

A discovery was made in the 1960s, on the premises of the École Normale Supérieure in the Rue d'Ulm, in Paris: an attempt was to be made at 'trying to appreciate that quite *extraordinary*, because unprecedented reality: Marxist theory as a *revolutionary* theory, Marxist science as a *revolutionary* science' (Althusser). Underlined as many times as you like, the word seems poorly chosen for describing the thing: 'that quite *unheard-of* reality' was for nineteenth-century Germany the commonest of commonplaces – what was *The* theory or *The* science, whether Marxist or other, that did not claim to be an unprecedented 'algebra', and the algebra 'of revolution'?

The linkage of science and revolution proclaimed to be extraordinary in 1973 (because it 'brings about a decisive "shift" in our conception of science') was encountered by Fichte when he took his first steps in philosophy. The encounter was indeed 'decisive' in 1774, not in 1973: 'Just as this nation delivered mankind from material chains, so my system delivered it from the yoke of the thing-in-itself, from outside influences, and its first principles make man an independent being. The doctrine of Science was born during the years in which the French nation through its energy, was bringing political liberty to triumph . . . I owe it to the valour of the French nation that I was lifted up still higher . . .'

From the French Revolution onward, knowledge was no longer *loved*, because now one *knew*: more than a philosopher, one was a scientist. Already on the third page of the introduction to his first major work, *The Phenomenology of Spirit*, Hegel plays upon these words (Philo-sophy, love of knowing, science, etc.) and takes the opportunity to date the birth of his science from the events in France to which he alludes discreetly as 'the present time'. 'To show that now is the time for philosophy to be raised to the status of a science would therefore be the only true justification of any effort that has this aim, for to do so would demonstrate the necessity of the aim, would indeed at the same time be the accomplishing of it.' The thesis is that henceforth a science is possible which answers the questions that formerly philosophers used to ask. The position from which this thesis is put forward is that our time is the time of revolution, and not just *'inter alia'*, but essentially. Here we perceive the point around which all the thinking of revolutionary intellectuals was to revolve for two centuries: a pivot of enthusiasm but also of delusion, the point of 'fusion' between scientific theory and the movement of the popular revolutions, the point of confusion between the theoretician's pretensions and the requirements of the petty leader of men. This two-centuries-old discovery must have been discreet in its ageing, since it is still possible today to discover it as something 'extraordinary'.

From 1800 onward the master thinkers hand the torch from one to another. For Fichte the last of the philosophers was Kant: after him began science, with himself, Fichte. For Hegel, Fichte was still a philosopher – the last of his line. For Marx the last philosopher was Hegel. But at the Hallowmas of the philosophers it is always Christmas carols that are sung: 'And if great things have been a failure with you, have ye yourselves therefore – been a failure? And if ye yourselves have been a failure, hath man therefore – been a failure? If man, however, hath been a failure: well then! never mind! The higher its type, always the seldomer doth a thing succeed. Ye higher men here, have ye not all – been failures? ... What wonder even that ye have failed and only half-succeeded, ye half-shattered ones! Doth not – man's *future* strive and struggle in you?' (*Thus Spake Zarathustra*).

With, behind them, a revolt that settled accounts with the past, armed with knowledge that dominates the present, builders of the programme that masters the future, each one surpassing his predecessor until Peking is reached, each one presupposing the truth of his predecessor, all announcing what lies ahead, like Nietzsche, in his capacity as spokesman for Zarathustra, the spokesman of the Superman who rises above himself in the affirmation of the eternal recurrence: 'Forward!' there they are erecting in the Valhalla of Western Reason great galleries of mirrors in which the most radical Revolution and the most definitive science reflect each other.

The adventures of Copernicus

The claim to be able to govern revolutions is common to all the master thinkers, even if they do not all assign the same relative weight to the critical masses of 'revolution' and 'science' out of which they make their spiritual atomic bombs.

The encounter of the French Revolution in reality with the German Revolution in thought was celebrated as a 'Copernican revolution' (the formula furnished by Kant, whose principal ideas antedated 1789). By Copernicus was meant the attempt to reduce the physical universe to mathematics which, at the beginning of modern times brought about a redistribution of the spheres of science and mastery (Copernicus, Galileo, Descartes, Newton). Kant meant that this was *the* event which enabled him to escape from what he called 'scepticism' (English empiricism) and 'dogmatism' (reason based upon God), the Scylla and Charybdis negotiated by the smart sailing vessel of the *independence* of reason which knows (scientifically), of will which makes itself (morally) and art (which judges aesthetically). To reveal the functioning, in its independence, of a reason which is slave to nothing, which dictates its own laws, this is Kant's aim, and the grand style of all the master thinkers: 'To become master of the chaos within, to compel one's own chaos to take shape, to act simply, categorically, mathematically, to make oneself *law* ... all the arts know this ambition of the grand style' (Nietzsche).

Copernican science proves that mastery of the physical universe is possible. The French Revolution overthrows the most deeply rooted traditions and the strongest prejudices, 'all

fictions vanish before truth, all follies collapse before Reason'
(Robespierre). It puts mastery of the social and political universe
on the agenda. The situations seem perfectly analogous, and the
young Fichte humbly explains (in cryptic words) to his vener-
ated master Kant that he means to do for the political sciences
what Kant did for the natural sciences, by delimiting, aggres-
sively, the powers possessed by reason in this sphere. The old
philosopher was kind to his brilliant disciple, whose existence he
supported financially though he did not support his project
philosophically. He probably thought the comparison defective,
and perhaps even sensed that a final fillip had just been given to
that formidable continental drift by which there came to be
attached to the human (too human) sciences everything which
formerly had been art, destiny, history, religion, sex, heroism,
thought, life and death. Perhaps the old man of Könisberg-
Kaliningrad understood nothing of what was still 'extraordinary' in the Paris of the 1970s. These were the most twisted
ambiguities of the slogan of the 'Copernican revolution', which
bore the future within themselves as the cloud bears the storm.

The relation between Kant's philosophy and the science of
nature was clear from the outset. Science existed in history,
outside of and separately from critical philosophy. It had been
formed over the centuries and existed as a fact for the thinker
who merely wanted to take its measure. Kant and Copernicus
were two different thinkers. But, in the confrontation of German
Reason with the French Revolution, where did Copernicus
stand?

A game of hide-and-seek then began which has gone on being
played to this day. Sometimes Copernicus is concealed within
the revolution, the historical moment of reason when the masses
'walk on their heads' and when politics is everywhere 'in command' (Mao). Sometimes, before he has taken hold of the
masses and become a material force, he has to be sought in
knowledge that lies outside. 'The proletariat finds its spiritual
weapons in philosophy. And once the lightning of thought has
squarely struck this ingenuous soil of the people ...', we shall
see what we shall see (Marx). Sometimes Copernicus remains
within science, which, by itself, revolutionizes reality: the

peoples are summoned to the 'take-off' conceived by the American experts, or to the technological and scientific revolution of the Russian experts. Sometimes Copernicus moves over completely into the revolution, as, for example, into that of 1848: 'As soon as it has risen up, a class in which the revolutionary interests of society are concentrated finds the content and the material for its revolutionary activity directly in its own situation ... It makes no theoretical inquiries into its own task' (Marx).

Sometimes the science in which Copernicus has again hidden himself is defined as a particular human science – political economy or sociology – and sometimes as scientific method 'in general', the dialectics of nature, for example: sometimes, on the side not now of the scientific object but of the *savant* himself, as the theory of theoretical practice, the old Russian 'gnoseology' or the new French epistemology: or else as a preliminary which anticipates all possible science, a theoretical criticism accompanied by a critical theory: or, again, as a mixture of the variants of all the foregoing possibilities: sometimes even as the 'scientific' analysis of the faults of these possible forms, by means of which one builds a reputation as a *savant* through scratching at the reputations of others: or else, again, it is taken over by a discipline which has hitherto been indifferent to it and about which no one can be sure that it will keep its promises, since it remains precisely at the stage of promises.

Contrary to what peevish souls might suggest, the difficulties do not arise from the impossible encounter of science with revolution: there are only rendezvous, that take place everywhere, with mutual effusions and promises. Copernicus, suffering among us not from want but from an overdose, doesn't know which way to turn. If he is at ease neither in science nor in the revolution, he ends by declaring himself to be wherever he may appear. This is the solution normally settled for in universities, enterprises, organizations and states. It is called a 'personality cult' only when things go wrong, and even then, preferably, in retrospect. Not everyone claims to be a 'corypheus of science' as exclusive as Stalin was, and for the common-or-garden new-style Copernicus the necessary encounter between science and revolution takes place at the mercy of the postal service.

The new universal and university gravity

Sociology, philosophy, epistemology – it matters little which locomotive draws the human sciences, since the general organization of the circulation of knowledge accepts as invariable the project of mastery that was originally conceived as the new 'Copernican revolution'. The thousand-and-one ways of linking science and revolution are all so many variations on that single theme. 'The planets as seen from the earth seem also to go now forward, now backward, and now to stand still. But if we try, with Copernicus, to take our stand on the sun, which Reason only can do, they go their regular courses ... But, and this is just the trouble, we cannot place ourselves at that standpoint when what is involved is the forecasting of free actions. For that would be the standpoint of Providence, which stands outside all human wisdom.' There, still, we have Kant's opinion and his 'trouble'. After him, it was discovered – oh, good! – that the needed 'standpoint' could be the revolution, that sun around which reason would make everything revolve.

Animated by a will to emancipation which does not fail to charm even if it somewhat lacks clarity, the new human sciences have repudiated from the heights of their objectivity the 'subjectivism' of the philosophies which gave them, if not life, then at least the hope of living one day. The Copernican revolution does not consist in making objects revolve around the subject-who-knows, whatever various handbooks of philosophy may say. As the revolution of reason, it kills off, and twice rather than once, the subjective subject, the 'perceptive judgement' (Fichte), the empirical opinion (Hegel), the spontaneous, the immediate: it is not from the standpoint of the earth that the movement of the stars is ordered scientifically, but rather by considering them from a perch upon the sun!

A polemic against common sense, the Copernican revolution is no less a polemic against theological 'other worlds': the cradle of the future human sciences was to be carefully protected both above and below. The enlightenment brought 'from without' to the masses was sought by science nowhere but within its own sphere of mastery. Thereby, Fichte points out, the Copernican revolution causes to revolve around the subject-who-knows not so much things as the philosophizing subject himself: in naming as his philosophic hero Prometheus, 'who wrests fire from the gods', Marx was already lagging behind the *savant* as conceived by Fichte, who lights his fire all by himself.

Hegel carefully stresses that 'everything depends on the essential point: apprehending and expressing the True . . . as subject'. But objectivist, materialist or theoretico-epistemological refutations regularly come along to strike their blows at the subject, because Hegel relates, three paragraphs further on, his subject to the 'unmoving mover' of Aristotle – that divinity which is not God but around which everything revolves. If the game of references back had been followed with greater attention we should have been spared the contents of many Althusserian inkwells devoted to denigrating the alleged 'subjectivism' or religiosity of the philosopher, contrasted with a scientific process proceeding 'without a subject'. Hegel sacrifices nothing to the alleged religious finalism of Aristotle, any more than a Copernican *savant* does who sees the planets revolving around the subject-sun, another unmoving mover. Hegel merely has the decency to know and quote his sources, something that the epistemological *savants* who came after have forgiven him all the less because they often don't know these sources. By calling the class struggle the 'driving-force', the *mover* of history, Marx incurred the guilt for all the sins with which his epigones reproach his predecessors. As for the humble and amiable researcher, whose science is foreign to these problems, he is nevertheless exposed to one question, one only but quite enough: however humble he may have been, the passenger intended to travel in the vehicles of the human sciences, and however 'self-moving' they may be, the question of what moves them must arise, even if one doesn't know how to answer it. The original automobilization of the human sciences around the event of 1789 may explain why their successive claims give such a strong impression of movement in a circle.

This is, of course, an old story for the modern researcher who is anxious to establish 'the facts and the laws', that is, who remains at the point of arrival of the Copernican revolution according to Fichte: *seeing* human relationships as governed by laws comparable to those of natural necessities. Perhaps these necessities are found to be excessively mechanical? One will never manage to *refine* them as much as Hegel did ...

Let treatises of methodology pile up as they may, what is not known is always new, and (another of Fichte's precepts), 'he who has climbed up no longer bothers about the ladder'.

Between brackets, for the academics

What are called the human sciences were not engendered all of a sudden to cope with something which had been overlooked. Nature was carefully studied, then it was observed that there was something else, and eventually some educational establishments were given the title: 'Faculty of Letters and Human Sciences', until more exotic descriptions should come along. Learning theorized about gravity, but also classified species, constructed grammars and reflected upon the circulation of wealth, long before the revolution appeared on the scene. In this extremely close-woven fabric, reference to the French events seems to have added only a few new disciplines. In France, apart from History, Sociology, with its children and grandchildren, derives directly from reflection upon the upheaval of 1789 (Henri de Saint-Simon, and later Auguste Comte). In Germany there was no such explicit filiation. It was through philosophy that the 'sciences of culture' came into relation with the Event. The nineteenth century was ending when German sociology won its letters of nobility: the operation was no longer conscious, so automatic was it. When Max Weber brought out the religious factors in the origin of capitalism, in opposition to the Marxist doctrine of the 'economic mechanisms' and the 'revolutionary spirit' of the young bourgeoisie, he re-performed, as though by cultural automatism, Hegel's operation making the sun of modern reason rise sometimes in 1789 and sometimes with the Reformation. Philosophical reflection on the revolution, when it entered into academic practice, seems merely to have given rise to some school subjects.

Nevertheless, the entry of the revolution into science meant not adding but rending: it rearranged the old faculties and added others only in order to consolidate their re-centring. It made a tear in the fabric of learning, digging a continental divide between the sciences of nature and the sciences of ... culture? society? civilization? the Spirit? Man? In effecting this division, it put on the agenda the question of reunion, of that unity of science which would not have caused so much ink to flow if it had not had to re-absorb so formidable and novel a drift.

There would be no point in referring back directly to a 'theological' influence in order to explain this contrast between man and nature in the sphere of learning. It would still need to be explained how it was that this alleged influence had never taken effect in the days when theology ruled the university, whereas it cut through the whole of learning as soon as the door had been shut upon theology.

All the universities of the West, whatever their implicit theologies, have striven for two centuries to advance abreast the physical sciences and the moral sciences, the sciences of nature and the sciences of humanity: they all gravitate within the sphere of that 'Copernican revolution' brought about by the entry of 1789 into the scientific orbit. From then onward, two projects of mastery have been intermingled. Descartes invites us to find in man, with his capacity for mathematical physics, 'the lord and possessor of nature'. Man capable of revolution comes in, according to the new learning, as the lord and possessor of society. What are the ardent and doctrinal disputes about the human sciences, even reaching the stage of taking up 'the party standpoints', if not disputes over lordship and possession? 'Religion is only the illusory sun which revolves round man as long as he does not revolve round himself': thus did the young Marx hail the new way of going round in circles.

The eternal three phases of revolution

'Anaxagoras had been the first to say that *nous* governs the World; but not until now had man advanced to the recognition of the principle that thought ought to govern spiritual reality.' Greeting thus the 'glorious dawn' of the French Revolution,

Hegel transforms it into a mere curtain-raiser, by an irony which has eluded both those who revere in him the hidden revolutionary and those who denounce him as a renegade. For Anaxagoras did not keep his promises. 'What expectations I had formed, and how grievously was I disappointed! As I proceeded (in my reading), I found my philosopher altogether forsaking mind or any other principle of order, but having recourse to air, and ether, and water, and other eccentricities.' So Socrates tells us, in a passage in the *Phaedo* which Hegel quotes. Similarly, the French Revolution disconcerted and disappointed: it was the dawn of reason, and not that noontide which 'broods on itself – a self-sufficient theme' (Valéry).

This position of spiritual retreat before the Event is not a withdrawal – on the contrary. By presenting the revolution as imperfect, as ailing, the master thinkers won for themselves a dominant position which they still hold. The higher they extolled the exemplary significance of the revolution, the more impressive were their lessons and remedies. Whether they summoned to a second revolution, or to a stabilization that would avoid a revolution's to-ings and fro-ings, or whether they gave their support to counter-revolution, is not decisive: if the revolution was the sunrise, then the sun must be that science which disciplines revolutions, the common programme of these masters.

The lessons of the revolution have been drawn once for all: they are three in number, like the phases making up the Idea of Revolution celebrated thenceforth by all the apologias of the revolutionaries and the apologues of the counter-revolutionaries – when the latter have not confined themselves to massacring, without bothering to offer any justification for their massacres.

(i) *The ideological preparation.* Whether or not this is appreciated, revolution provides proof of the effectiveness of thought. Before governing the world, reason overturns it. 'All important and striking revolutions must be preceded, in the mind of their time, by a secret revolution which is not apparent to everyone ...' This law, here associated by Hegel with Jesus, and drawn from the example of the early Christians, was shown by Engels to be relevant to the cause of socialism. Hegel found it, as though by chance, applying in the period that led up to 1789: 'It has been said that the French Revolution resulted from Philosophy, and it is not without reason that philosophy has been called "*Weltweisheit*" (world wisdom).'

Did the *philosophes* 'programme,' all through the eighteenth century, the Revolution which brought it to an end? The assumption seems to honest historians rather forced, but it has prospered: for two centuries now we have carried our ideas around with the precautions of firework-makers and spied out the best place in which to leave our sticks of dynamite. 'In order to overthrow a political authority one always begins by preparing public opinion and doing ideological work' (Mao Tse-tung). The retrospective illusion is stubborn, although, as is noted on the occasion of every revolution, the 'one' who has been assigned the task of preparing opinion is the first to be surprised by it, and finds himself ill-prepared when the storm begins to blow. Voltaire, Diderot, even Rousseau, advisers all to the enlightened despots, did not have 1789 on their programme. Nor did Lenin, at any rate before 1917, have October 1917 on his. And if Mao was prepared by Marxism, he was probably prepared for anything except for consorting with beggars and revolutionizing the countryside. He had to find some strange signposts: trees whose bark had been gnawed by starving peasants. That doesn't stop anyone from subsequently writing the programme of world revolutions in accordance with the best tradition.

(ii) *Terrorism, or rising to extremes.* The radiation of minds is mortal, and not only for the Ancien Régime, cast into ruins, but for the minds as well. If they turn against each other we have the reign of the law of suspects. Since everyone is carrying dynamite-like ideas around in his head, it is understandable that the Revolution should cause heads to fall, 'like cabbage-heads', as Hegel puts it – his gravestone for those guillotined in 1793.

All the master thinkers have this second phase in mind when they theorize about the struggle to the death, whether this is the struggle between consciousnesses (Hegel) or alienation and class struggle (Marx), or generalized nihilism in the era of resentment (Nietzsche). In any case, the master is not the one who triumphs *in* this struggle but the one who triumphs *by* this struggle, establishing his new order.

(iii) *Knowing how to end a revolution.* 'The river returns to its bed' (Trotsky) and stabilization asserts itself. The basic themes of stabilization were listed by Hegel (with Napoleon in mind): union against danger from without, end of storms and civil peace within, an official redivision of society in respect of functions, jurisdiction and possessions. Hence the great tasks laid down for the state by Hegelian 'Reason', the 'Dictatorship of the Proletariat', or Nietzschean 'mastery': war, political domination of the economy, order, and educating the majority of the population.

The relation between the last two phases is even closer than between the first and the second. The fight, though spoken of as a fight to the death, has to end. All the ostentatious radicalism of the Maoist Cultural Revolutions does not prevent normaliz-ation from being heralded straightaway in every mass mobil-ization. 'Prepare yourselves to face war or natural catastrophes, and do everything in the interest of the people' (Mao) means, already, appealing to the recognized essential functions of the state in order to fill in the gulf dug by the blows that were struck in the fight to the death. He who has conceived at the beginning of any revolution the omnipotence of ideological preparation, who has lived through it not as a gala banquet but as the de-vouring of some by others, must inevitably come in the end to the Directory, the Empire or the N.E.P., those transient figur-ations of an eternal 'third phase'. Malraux applies this schema to the Spanish Revolution: Days of Hope, the Apocalypse, and the Organization of the Apocalypse (in this case the order established by the Communist Party and the Russian policemen in Madrid).

The history of revolutions can thus be related as the history of the masses who cultivate their minds (phase one), become educated through dread (phase two), and discipline themselves (phase three). Or as the Iliad of the state which loses its Ancien

Régime (i), and sinks into a crisis (ii) the depth of which will make it rebound more rational and implacable than ever (iii). Or as the Odyssey of the intellectuals who think freely and anarchically (i: 'the spiritual animal kingdom'), whose anarchy takes bloody forms (ii), and to whom dread restores their reason, the principle of order (iii). Or as the rectification of an idealist right-wing deviation (i) by an adventurist left-wing deviation (ii), to the ultimate advantage of an authority which keeps its guard up against right and left alike. Or as the misadventures of the young generations who think that everything is permitted (i), and end up badly (ii), unless they make an end of it (iii).

One can no longer get out of the sun

The great book of the world whose leaves Descartes turned over has become the account-book of the revolution, perused with no less respect: 'People do not make revolution eagerly any more than they do war. There is this difference, however, that in war compulsion plays the decisive role, in revolution there is no compulsion except that of circumstances.' When he propounded this axiom, Trotsky, fallen and in exile, was no longer a naïve optimist, but was still a scientific revolutionary. As a critic, he still thought of Stalin as a 'circumstance' of the revolutionary process in a backward or illiterate peasant Russia. There are no grounds for accusing him of a naïvely fatalistic or mechanistic belief. Trotsky did not rule out the hypothesis that history can, in certain circumstances, turn round on itself: 'the film of the revolution was running backwards', and Stalin's part in it was that of Kerensky in reverse. In short, he did not think it inconceivable that things would end with a 'restoration of capitalism' (as the Chinese Communists say has happened).

Running backwards or forwards, the film is still the film, and it is not possible to get out of the great pedagogical experiment of the revolution: there are the masses and there are the circumstances, and they transform and educate each other reciprocally. Even evoking the idea of a return journey means that we have to tread the same path twice and leave the revolution by the way we entered it. Once inside the revolution, either we advance in a revolutionary way, or the film goes into reverse. The attachment of the revolutionary to a series of events which ends in a bloodbath is not so much fatalistic as rational. If conceiving the revolutionary 'series' amounts to conceiving that the only compulsion is that imposed by circumstances, the fighter is usually led to refrain from opposing the leadership, however murderous it may become. If he agrees that 'in revolution there is no compulsion except that of circumstances', he finds himself disarmed in face of a compulsion which justifies itself by revolutionary circumstances. Unable to wage a battle which is for him ruled out from the start, he confines himself to criticizing, as an ill-fated adviser, a prince who has made a wrong estimate of the circumstances.

These famous 'circumstances' are witnesses to a past that has not yet been eliminated: Lenin, after 1920, then Trotsky, but Stalin as well, and the Communists of today explain the misfortunes of the revolution by 'backwardness' (preferably that of the masses). When struggles for power become too flagrant to be ignored any longer, they are revised and corrected as so many struggles between the *old* and the *new*, between those who are trying to restore the past and those who want to build the future; in short, between supporters of the film 'running forwards' and advocates of the film 'running backwards': it is accepted by everyone that there can be no change in the scenario which links the future with the past through the 'experience of the masses' alone.

Every revolution is thus seen as a thoroughgoing test of popular sovereignty, in which the masses clash only with themselves and with circumstances, the thousand-years-old war that counterposes them to the 'powers of this world' being suddenly put between brackets: in the camp of revolution there are only, interchangeably, those who are educated while educating and those who educate while being educated, but no hostile compulsion. In other words, every theory of the Revolution assumes that there can be a Chinese wall separating the relations of authority and real compulsion that exist within from those that exist without the camp of revolution. This claim is upheld when there is argument about the thousand-and-one ways of drawing the line between good and bad authority. The history of the world is 'broken in two' (Mao), and what is found in this break is the science of that history.

Since it sets the masses, essentially speaking, only face to face with themselves, the revolution can be reckoned to serve as an all-round pedagogical experiment. In matters which concern it fundamentally, a people cannot be deceived (by a priest-party or by wicked bureaucrats), for we should have to assume that the people *are deceiving themselves*, says (before Trotsky) a Hegel who was strong in the experience of 1789. In the first phase, the people shake off all authority which does not stem from themselves (Ancien Régime). In the second they come face to face with themselves, in the third they impose an order upon themselves, taking into account the abyss that they have glimpsed, and the weight of circumstances. The revolution is thus seen as a process of education without educators, in which the masses carry out 'their own experiment', without any pedagogue having set up the experimental apparatus and organized the circumstances, which to the pupils seem so natural. That is, unless, as in Rousseau's *Émile* and Marivaux's *La Dispute*, there are, behind the scenes, some masters hidden. This last hypothesis is excluded by the thinkers for whom a science, namely, their own, is born from the experience of revolutions.

As in every good laboratory of human science, the master who carries out the experiment claims not to be part of the experiment which checks the correctness of his hypotheses: 'The fundamental political process of the revolution consists in the gradual comprehension by a class of the problems arising from the social crisis – the active orientation of the masses by a method of successive approximations. The different stages of a revolutionary process, certified by a change of parties in which the more extreme always supersedes the less, express the growing pressure to the left of the masses – so long as the swing of the movement does not run into objective obstacles. When it does, there begins a reaction: disappointments... Such, at least, is the general outline of the old revolutions' (Trotsky).

The new revolutions do not differ from the old. Here we find the manner in which, a few years later, Trotsky was to explain that a revolution which has been 'falsified' and then 'betrayed' is still a revolution, and there is a lesson to be learnt from defeat no less than from victory. Was the edifying revolution which has been conceived in the course of two centuries ever anything but the geometrical *locus* of all the lessons addressed to humble mortals? Object lessons? No, master classes!

More rigorous than mathematics

Modern thought conceives the revolution as a scientific experiment. Thereby it basically avoids the objections (or the blandishments) of utopianism, fatalism or millenarianism, which affect only its laxities. It even ducks the political question of where it stands, for or against any concrete revolution: a scientific experiment is never final, however successful it may be, and if it fails it is none the less scientific and rich in lessons – 'from setback to setback until ultimate victory'. Mao places this ultimate victory 'tens of thousands of years' ahead, that is to say, nowhere. Whatever the virulence with which the master thinkers contend amongst themselves, it is on the common basis of the theorization of this scientific experiment that they present objections to each other's ideas.

The revolution is a *scientific* experiment, in the first place, because it is supposed to introduce science into the affairs not just of nature but also of humanity. The 'Enlightenment' prepared the way for 1789, Hegel assumes, by breaking the natural relations maintained by a people with their environment, their traditions, their Ancien Régime rulers. The science of socialism breaks with spontaneity, coming as it does from without (Lenin). The revolution follows the impetus thus given, and reduces the past to 'dust' (Lenin): it uproots the four outmoded things – old thought, old culture, old manners and customs (Mao).

From Hegel to Mao, 'ideological preparation' is recognized as the first phase of the revolution only if it does a great deal more than replace one ('reactionary') ideology by another ('revolutionary'). The destruction of the ideology of the past is quite the contrary of an operation with communicating vessels, in which

the 'good' morality is poured in to replace the 'bad': along with
the old morality the old vessel is also destroyed. Tales and leg-
ends, theatre, families, all are either noisily smashed or discreetly relegated to the museum. This dawn has to 'transform
man in his deepest self' (Mao), creating a new depth for him.
'One cannot construct without destroying. Destroying means
criticizing, that is, making the revolution. In order to destroy
one has to reason, and reasoning means constructing. Thus,
first of all comes destruction, which bears construction within
itself' (Mao). The revolutionaries replace the old morality not
with a new morality but with a science – the 'Enlightenment' as
seen by Hegel, or 'Marxism–Leninism', which for Mao is both
binoculars and microscope. This science will be capable of
everything, even of subsequently diffusing a new morality: hence
the mistake made by outside observers who put the moral cart
before the scientific horse.

Shattering with a hammer-blow all the old attachments,
planting its science in the newly cleared depths, the revolution
introduces the man of the future to universal knowledge. Not,
though, by cramming his head with general, dogmatic truths
(which it will do, also, with the secondary advantages that are
well-known) but by inducing in the revolutionary a scientific
mode of behaviour, transforming him into 'the arrow and the
target of the revolution' (Lin Piao), the subject and the object
alike of this history turned into a scientific experiment. Bukharin, at the Moscow trial, are you guilty? Yes! As target, as
object. But are you innocent? More than that, I am the arrow,
the subject, the prosecutor, the *savant*: 'unprecedented *self-
knowledge*: becoming conscious of oneself not as an individual
but as mankind' (Nietzsche).

The new sun of science is already shining high on the horizon
when the second phase is foreseen, the phase of terror and the
fight to the death. The revolution does not merely settle the
historical problems of an *ancien régime* that is worm-eaten in all
respects, it 'breaks history in two'. Introducing its own science,
it not only sweeps away the dust of ages, it makes a clean sheet
in order to build: the *Realm of the spirit*, the *Empire* of the world,
Organization – it is with these words that conclude, with the

great adventure of the spirit that they claim to reconstruct, the last pages of the *Phenomenology of Spirit*, the Master's masterpiece.

Every Hegelian consciousness 'wills the death of the other', – not because it is assumed to be naturally wicked, or too good to the point of not wanting to let anyone else do good in its place. Nor just because it 'sees' the other: there are soft looks that have the charm of murky skies. Nor directly because it transforms the other into a thing, for the contradiction is apparent to the most obstinate: one gets no joy from torturing a stone. Torture is used in order to obtain 'important' information, the Generals explain, and we rejoice when we make the other person yield up his truth. On the horizon of the fight to the death there is always a certain idea of truth: the consciousnesses enter the lists, and do not stare at each other like china dogs – each wants to be the 'subject' for the other, whom it sees as 'object'; but subject and object of what, if not of this scientific experiment in which the mastery of the world is being decided? Every struggle assumes that something is at stake: it is fought out to the death only for a very high stake, and what could be higher than this science which masters the world? 'Spirit, in the absolute certainty of itself, is lord and master over every deed and actuality, and can cast them off and make them as if they had never happened' (Hegel). Stalin clipped historical photographs so as to eliminate in the past those whom he caused to be murdered in the present. His scissors, his ice-pick and his not very 'scientific' hired killers have been mocked – at the risk of forgetting that these little instruments proved effective to the extent that everyone, opponents, supporters, the 'coryphaeus of science' himself, all acknowledged that dialectical knowledge which splits history in two, to the point, as its promoter warns us, that it can make 'every deed and actuality ... as if they had never happened'. And this was duly done, with the help of scissors and bullets. The dogs do not continue to be mere china dogs when they start to sniff the science of power.

The science of revolution always plays on two tables: it arms the revolutionaries with a theory ('all-powerful because true': Lenin) and it arms the *savants* with a revolution. Without it, the

former might perhaps make revolutions, but would never undertake to make *the* revolution, and the latter would probably conceive events as historical experiments, but never as the Experiment of history after which history assumes its status as the
history of peoples, of the mind, of democracy, of classes, etc.
Called upon to play a role similar to that of the 'Copernican'
mathematicizing of nature, the science *of* revolution implies the
twofold linking of revolution with science and science with
revolution (its genitive is both objective and subjective). The
master thinkers all show themselves more rigorous than the
mathematicians in that, in the history that they cause to be
conceived, the conditions of domination of experience are at the
same time conditions of experience of domination.

Revolution around a crown

Dominating means knowing how to dominate: the master is the
one who knows. The enlightenment of science prepares the way
for revolution by emancipating the future citizen from that
which surrounds him (according to Hegel, 'the natural', according to Mao, 'the four outmoded things'), hurling him into a
struggle which then becomes mortal in so far as it is science that
defines as the prize the rigorous mastery of the world: everything for the one who possesses this science, nothing for the one
who is subjected to it. On the horizon of this science, the encounter becomes a struggle, and the struggle a battle in which
all and everything are committed. By conferring letters of
philosophico-scientific nobility upon the modern practice of
power, the master thinkers clearly showed the deadly consequences of this 'Copernican revolution'. The struggle for
power – scientific, and therefore a fight to the death – spreads
its metastases everywhere. Hegel sees terror as only political
(1793) and he identifies it everywhere a science of domination is
manipulated (among 'liberated' ideologists this produced 'the
spiritual animal kingdom'): which, ultimately, means *everywhere*, for anyone who conceives the struggle between master
and slave together with sensation, perception, understanding

and, in short, all the faculties in which a traditional philosophy is pleased to imagine the eternity of what it calls Man.

What does the master know? To dominate is to know. To know is to dominate. A circle. The circles are vicious, viciousness is what thought must escape from, and there is never any lack of escape-routes. The masters are masters of steel and rails, sellers of guns, hoarders of butter: they rule by means of money and the police. That's the final full stop. In the ultimate struggle, 'we' shall take the money and the police from them, 'we' shall rule – president of all Frenchmen and dictators of the proletariat. Who are 'we'? The principle of modern domination is 'one lord and no serfs', says Hegel: a lord who says 'we' on behalf of everyone, and would otherwise find some difficulty in accumulating capital, whether as guns or as butter. I accumulate for all, I say 'we' for everybody. Who are 'we'? All of us who could say 'I say "we" for everybody.' Again a circle. This could be nationalized: the nation says 'I' for me. Or made world-wide: the international market says 'I' for you. To dominate means to nationalize? For a long time now, to nationalize has meant to dominate! Examples of this are the Bretons of Lower Brittany, the Provençal-speakers of Upper Provence, the immigrant workers, and the soldiers of the two world wars. It is not for being vicious that a circle fails to encircle.

The master is the one who knows, but what does he know? Nothing, perhaps, so vicious is the circle. Nevertheless, it is useless to turn away, as quickly as possible, a startled gaze that is much happier when serenely evaluating tons of steel, mountains of butter and wads of shares. With them we touch something solid, the 'real foundations' of the master's power. The masters follow one another, wresting or handing over these solid realities. Steel rusts, butter goes rancid, papers burn or are given new dockets, but the masters remain. Even if the master's knowledge is nothing, the 'real' foundation of his power is not, on that account, something: as is witnessed, even better than by the 'idealist' Hegel, by the 'materialist' Marx, who urges us not to conceive as relations between things what is in reality a social relation of exploitation. To dominate is to know, to know is to dominate. We go round in a circle, but around the master, and the master goes round too, round about power. The fact that, in the end, everything seems to revolve around power means nothing if this power is clothed or inhabited by a Nothingness:

> ... for within the hollow crown
> That rounds the mortal temples of a king
> Keeps Death his court, and there the antick sits,
> Scoffing his state and grinning at his pomp;
> Allowing him a breath, a little scene,
> To monarchize, be feared, and kill with looks.
>
> SHAKESPEARE, *Richard II*

Master through dread

The master has a way all his own of marking out the vicious circle. He shuts others up therein. He has a way of his own of knowing nothing about it: he knows what Nothingness is. 'Better to want Nothingness than to want nothing,' says Nietzsche, defining the creative Master, the hammer that smashes and sculpts (contrasting this 'active nihilism' with the 'passive' nihilism of the slave who suffers, who wants nothing). Better to know Nothingness than to know nothing might similarly be the conclusion of the highly Hegelian 'struggle' between Master and Slave.

Knowledge does not merely begin the fight to the death, it brings the solution to this conflict. At the end of the battle, the master is the one who knows how to die, while the slave is the one who gives in, because he is too fond of life. Then there comes, or is supposed to come, the fable related by the Sons of the People when in power, after their hard day's work, to the children of the toilers: the master enjoys the fruits of the labour of others and becomes idiotic, the slave of his slave, whereas the latter gives human shape to the world, and in shaping it shapes himself, masters nature, and, in so doing, masters himself, to the point of no longer fearing the master, and overthrowing him.

The master thinker sets out this pious legend in clear-cut terms. The slave's work, in so far as it is simple labour, certainly implies a measure of knowledge. Marx sticks on it the label of 'craft idiocy', following the lead given by Hegel, with his scorn for the 'brutalization', the 'self-will ... still enmeshed in slavery'. The particular knowledge possessed by the slave is the knowledge of a particular slave, and by Hegelian logic is therefore in every case particularly servile. The slave cannot attain to general knowledge otherwise than by adopting the general point of view, that of his master: one leaves slavery by the master's door.

Does this mean that the slave will violently overthrow the master, inverting the violence which oppresses him into a violence which frees him? Sartre explored this path, showing that revolutionary violence revives within its own organization the relation of domination and servitude which it began by tearing itself away from: when the group being formed wants to master the situation, it structures itself in that same relationship. We thus remain within the framework of Hegel's analyses of the Jacobin Terror. Does this mean a return to the starting-point?

Liberation by labour is ruled out. The operation carried on by the slave escapes from him, it is work that is wholly *subject to command*, with its fruits, its purpose and its design all alien to the mere executant: 'What the bondsman does is really the action of the lord.' Marx goes further, describing as *abstract* the labour (that of a tailor, for example) which produces an exchange-value under modern conditions of exploitation: 'The exchange-value is produced by it not as tailoring as such but as abstract universal labour, and this belongs to a social framework not devised by the tailor.' Only the needle of the universal, the abstraction, the master-exploiter, sews the social fabric. As for the labour of the slave, it produces the slave – 'self-willed', brutalized.

The slavery of labour liberates not the slave but the master! Having come back to real history, Hegel judges that the *gradual* abolition of slavery would be 'wiser and more equitable than its sudden removal'. To be sure, slavery is unjust, 'for the essence of humanity is freedom' ... *but* ... 'but for this, man must be matured'. Slavery thus asserts itself as a (general) principle of maturation for freedom. Feudal serfdom, together with the 'iron rods' of the Inquisition, anticipate Nietzsche's *Genealogy of Morals*: 'It was not so much *from* slavery as *through* slavery that man was emancipated' (Hegel's own emphasis). Does this apologia for discipline merely take account of the past? We ought to examine closely this curious way of accounting. Or does it programme the future? Does science use two weights and two measures for what it imagines behind itself and what it foresees lying ahead?

Through the work of the slave, the barbarian master can give way to the cultured master. The former enjoyed and gorged himself in crude fashion, becoming 'the slave of his slave'. The latter 'does to himself what he does to his slave': he does, in the sphere of the universal, and clear-sightedly, what the slave does in the sphere of the particular and of his own self-will. Whereas the slave *works* 'in some particular dread', the master *cultivates* dread ('universal dissolution *in general*'). It is he who emerges first from the relation of domination and servitude – as a Stoic, says Hegel: this fanciful interpretation of philosophy is of interest because it shows symptomatically that one can escape here from the dead-end of the Master and the Slave only upward. It is the master who thinks far ahead, and in order to continue along the same track the slave must imitate him by mastering himself.

The slave emerges from slavery by becoming a master, not by overthrowing the masters. He joins their community by participating in what constitutes their mastery, by sharing their dread. He has to 'experience absolute dread'. He has to transcend 'particular dreads', such as dreads of losing this or that thing, or even his life. He has not to glorify his labour as a liberator but to discover it 'in fragments' and to reduce it to fragments: 'Since the entire contents of its natural consciousness have not been jeopardized, . . . having a "mind of one's own" is self-will, a freedom which is still enmeshed in servitude.' In order to become a master, the slave must know how to lose his labour just as he must know how to lose his life: he emerges from slavery by the way he entered it. He had refused 'to destroy in himself every immediate being', he had interrupted the fight to the death because he was too much attached to life. Having become a citizen he proves himself capable of being a soldier, of rising to extremes, of accomplishing 'the movement of absolute abstraction', of applying 'the supreme test by means of death' – in short, of dying for his country. Thereafter, he is in the picture.

For the slave, 'the fear of the lord is the beginning of wisdom'. And what is the culmination of wisdom? Liberation through labour? No, indeed. The overthrow of the master? No, again! The highest point of wisdom, which, in the rational state, means that no one is a slave, is that everybody has only one master, the absolute master: death. Wanting and knowing Nothingness means knowing and wanting death.

Necro-logical

He is master who knows and wants mastery, which means death. What is the source of this equation? Apparently, it is a mere observation. If things are to be mastered they have to be taken objectively: 'This disappearance, this vanishing of the finite is not a mere possibility which may or may not be realized: the nature of finite things is that they contain the germ of their own disappearance. The moment of their birth is at the same time the moment of their death.' Mastery becomes objective by taking hold of things from the angle of their death, even when what is involved is living things: the anatomy lesson is given on a corpse, and all medicine proclaimed itself scientific in the nineteenth century by studying the body *in vitro*, dead (Foucault, *La Naissance de la clinique*). By measuring creatures on the basis of their condition in death, Hegel does more than merely observe, he expounds the project of mastery which begins to furnish the setting for the sciences and techniques described as 'human' in the modern world.

The idea that we are mortal is not new, nor is the will to transform one's life into a destiny, placing it within some 'Thing' with a larger life than one's own – country, religion, art, philosophy, or simply the family – or just another person. Traditionally, these 'things' which give an air of eternity to what is finite are not mastered: one touches but does not embrace them, or if one embraces them one does not hug them, and if one hugs them one cannot extinguish them. One's country may break one's family ties, the philosopher may cavalierly break with respect for his country (Socrates), he may make off with art and subordinate religion (Plato): there nevertheless remains 'something' that cannot be got round, a truth which possesses him without his ever possessing it – the mania itself for philosophizing.

At first sight, Hegel seems to be saying no more than this, and it is even his favourite way of advancing his ideas: he 'transcends' art in religion and religion in absolute knowledge. Does the dispute among the master thinkers amount to tapping up one's neighbour's ultimate 'things' so as to place one's own still higher? The True, says Hegel. Art, 'so as not to perish from truth', objects Nietzsche. And Marx? The Good, perhaps, that which will be realized by the 'associated producers' in those stewpots of the future which only the fire of revolution will bring to the boil? Here we perceive the almost imperceptible difference which digs an insuperable chasm between the old thinkers and the modern ones. In order to know and to write *Capital*, says Marx, you don't need to be able to boil the stewpots of the future. Art . . . But, Nietzsche warns, precisely not in order to escape from death or the finite condition and claim to find 'the whole certain Gospel in the gaze of Raphael's Madonnas'. Beauty makes us 'superficial through depth': instead of opening a door on the invisible and the eternal, it brings us back to earth. 'When power makes itself mild and condescends to the visible, I call this beauty condescension.' Far from resting all mastery upon what is beyond mastery (the 'Good', the 'Beautiful', the 'True'), the master thinker finds power in the Beautiful, and in what it was thought could not be mastered, the supreme force of mastery.

If one masters things from the angle of their death, it is appropriate, in order to master everything, to have done with immortal or infinite things and impose upon them as upon the rest the 'absolute master', death. Hegelian transcendence does not mean denying in order to end up somewhere, in solid reality. 'The finite is perishable and disappears.' The master does not console himself for this despair, he despairs of it. 'Disappearance, nothingness, far from constituting the ultimate end, are perishable and disappear in their turn.' What is the ultimate end? While usually reproaching Hegel for having conceived history on the basis of an end to history, at which he is said to have presumptuously placed himself, commentators have never exactly defined where this end was. The Prussian state? North America, which, according to a saying of Napoleon's, repeated by the philosopher, was taking over from a 'too narrow' Europe? Or the empire of the Slavs, Russia? For Hegel, the latter had not said her last word, but in smashing Napoleon had spoken her first. The end of history is that history never ceases to end, it is in a continual count-down: there is no need to be present at the Last Judgement to know how the ages will end, if none of the things on which one counts can bring either surprise or disappointment, if while living they already master themselves as though dead, if their birth certificate also serves as their death certificate.

Death in labour

Since life is no longer the hour of birth and not yet the hour of death, there are many different ways of being squeezed between those two dates – happy ones, sad ones, some that are oblivious, and others that are very careful, or carefully unaware. Ethnologists and folk-lore specialists have listed a lot of them; missing, no doubt, some which writers collect in the night, or sculptors read in men's eyes. The master thinkers, however, know only three, all of which superimpose the hour of birth upon the hour of death. There is the way followed by the man who just gets born, without acknowledging that he will die, like the animals according to Hegel – the person who, instead of 'me', says 'my family', 'my land', 'my gods'. The peasant is supposed to embody this state of unconsciousness – 'substance' without self-consciousness (Hegel), a 'barbarian' (Marx). There is the way followed by the man who lives already in the hour of his death, the soldier who risks everything, the statesman who (like all officials) sacrifices his private life to the public service, all those who devote themselves to their country or to some still loftier idea and whose social status depends on so doing: guardians of the fatherland, representatives of order and of the people, professional revolutionaries, depending on the panoplies offered for clothing the master.

Between the peasant and the statesman, between the one who is put lowest, on the grounds that he is unaware of death, and the one who stands on the summit because he is said to face the 'highest' dangers – war, revolution, atomic apocalypse or oil crisis – there are those who constitute the originality of modern society, a pair who are sometimes united (Hegel) and sometimes separated (Marx): the bourgeois and his workman. They do not spend their time either in getting born or in dying, but in working, in the modern sense of the word: 'Labour is an act of annihilation bridled by a sad necessity.' As an 'act of annihilation' modern labour dominates nature, it belongs to the master in that it wrests from the (traditional) world of (agricultural) life a second world which is fabricated, manageable, 'human', that is, not 'natural' – the labour of the peasant, being considered less inventive, more subordinate, by a prejudice not confined to the nineteenth century. From another angle, labour is not an act of the master in that one does not allow oneself to enjoy life while working – it is a bridled, repressed act which is carried out in division: between production and the product, which eludes the producer, between the manual and the mental sides, between the concrete skill that a task presupposes and the abstract, money value which it is accorded. Contrasts between dead labour and living labour, between the individual and the social, the tangible and the abstract: whether they are deplored or glorified (and all the master thinkers do both, either at the same time or successively), the very fact that such divisions can be made shows the formidable effectiveness of modern labour.

Labour is a 'deferred death', both for the disciplined worker, who, in order to go to work each morning, has to 'kill his destiny', and for the bourgeois who does not accumulate in order to live but lives in order to accumulate. The worker–employer pair thus provide *proof* that mastery of the world is not obtained by edifying speeches, nor by good feelings, nor by enlightening this earth with some other-wordly truth. Hegel and Marx, like Nietzsche, show us in labour the effectiveness of modern mastery, the power of 'abstraction', of that 'life which bears death within itself', of discipline. If the master is master because he faces death, modern labour shows that this is no pious claptrap, but the most everyday and effective way of earning one's bread and changing the world – by losing a life about which, apart from labour, one must know nothing except that one is losing it.

Actually, the position of the worker–employer pair at the centre of the schema of mastery set up by the master thinkers is entirely theoretical. Society includes many other classes. Neither the worker nor the property-owner are, spontaneously, up to the role assigned to them: hence the need for a body of theoreticians who come along to teach them 'from without' concerning the power that they embody without knowing it. The present state will educate the employers, the future state, the Party, will select the future masters – while the master thinkers will educate the educators even as they themselves are educated by the masses, that is, by the secret that the latter bear but that they alone know: production. Science of the state, science of the revolution, science of setting to work – three variants of a single body of knowledge. That of Master Ubu, who knew how to begin at the end, by saying, 'on the trap-door': 'The finite, in perishing, attains its being-in-itself by this negation of itself, by striking at itself it re-joins itself.'

From persuasion to dissuasion

The American strategists imagined that they possessed, with the thermo-nuclear weapon, the principle of a new order, based on the prospect of a suicidal right-and-left. Being capable of a 'second strike', each having the power to smash the other even though itself mortally wounded, the two super-powers no longer had to reach agreement around more or less dubious common interests – their most selfishly solitary interest became supremely common to them both. Were they to die separately or to live together, that was the question. And the only question, the strategists added: any and every clash, however limited (and even if it brought the Big Two into conflict only through inter-posed small states), involved the danger of starting the final

conflagration. If this danger was not obvious, the Big Two
might enlarge it by their alternating interventions, 'escalating'
a scale of violence which would proceed from an infinitely
minor dispute to the Apocalypse. The choice between order and
chaos, peace and the end of the world, was translated into every
local conflict that was thus over-determined, fixed and appeased
in the shadow of the supreme threat. Is not the Open-Sesame
which inaugurates peace for all, under the tutelary and pre-
fectoral guarantee of the super-powers, to be found in the
reign of 'dissuasion'?

Formerly, people explained themselves through sermons,
arguments or guns. And the strongest, in respect of the chosen
instrument, was the winner. Today there is nothing to be
explained, and it is enough to explain this nothing: if you go on
like that you are heading for catastrophe – stop, or there will be
a disaster. Formerly, people persuaded, exchanging arguments
that were positive – morally or physically, brutally or cunningly
– in order to reach a decision. Today we are content to dissuade,
sending each other negative arguments: all are equal in death,
even if some have made themselves a bit more equal than others,
because, so they claim, they have exclusive control of the threat
of death.

This nascent order of reciprocal terror was a feature of Western culture long before the invention of nuclear weapons. The
era of persuasion ended for the master thinkers with the appearance of the portents of a revolution whose first phase, still a
'silent' one, of 'ideological preparation' cuts through all
'natural' links with the environment and brings the definitive
departure. The fact that this act of detachment was subsequently
put further back signified an earlier end to that era of persuasion
(of the 'morality' of morals, of 'positive religion', of 'the relations of man with man'). It matters little whether the moment
of the Copernican caesura be interpreted as the Protestant
Reformation (Hegel), or the origin of capitalism (Marx), or even
Copernicus himself: 'Since Copernicus, man seems to have
fallen on to a steep plane – he rolls faster and faster away from
the centre – whither? into nothingness? into the thrilling sensation of his own nothingness?' (Nietzsche, *The Genealogy of*

Morals). The bomb was not yet regulating the diplomatic ballet when the earth was already having to be lived in and governed dissuasively.

At the outset, nature is what we consume. 'The feeling of separation is need, the feeling that separation has ended is enjoyment.' Desire devours, enjoyment is devouring, and if satiety never ceases it is because it is more natural to devour the satiety itself – the spiritualization of the animal starting-point is only a devouring of the devouring. Another person who is satiated revives his hunger when you look at him, or *vice versa*. Labour is only enjoyment hindered, bridled and re-pressed, that is, devoured by the other one, the master. Culture is self-control, self-devouring, transition from the particular to the universal, sacrifice of one's life to one's idea: in the state, art, religion or the world of learning, the citizen, the artist, the believer or the philosopher all agree that 'to be recognized and to be suppressed is, immediately, the same thing'.

Everything subtle, profound, definitive and rigorous that has been said about nuclear weapons – which means not much – was said already a century before. The strategists of nuclear war are not the discoverers of gunpowder in its scientifico-philosophico-historico-apocalyptic usage. It was Hegel who introduced us to modern war: 'This war is not a war of families against families but of peoples against peoples, and consequently hatred itself is undifferentiated, free from all personal elements. Death enters the realm of the universal from which it came, and it is without anger: this is produced sometimes but is suppressed just as easily. The firearm is the invention of general death, indifferent and impersonal . . .'

Replace 'families' by nations and 'peoples' by super-powers, and you save a considerable slice of the expenditure on strategic research, producing cheaply the essence of the discourse main-tained by these powers. The dimensions of the countries have shrunk to 'family' size, which means that any will to resist the Imperium of the Big Two has become a thing of the past. The scale has altered, but not the argument: 'death – general, indiffer-ent, impersonal', propels henceforth no longer 'national honour' but the discipline of the 'camp of freedom' in the West and the 'camp of peace ' in the East. Whether guns or missiles be used, the highest argument is still the 'test by means of death'.

Whatever the political limits he imposes upon his mind, any-body can see, given the magnitude of the American débâcle in Vietnam, that neither information about a situation nor oper-ational effectiveness constitutes the strength of the argument of the new strategists. The theories of dissuasion are universally diffused and generally accepted because they are less new than the weapons that they commend. That order relies upon force is a very old truth. That this force can only be persuasive and coercive if it asserts itself as destructive and dissuasive is an opinion that did not wait for the Pentagon experts before being cultivated in the gardens of modern thought: 'Nihilism, the ideal of the highest power of the spirit, of the richest life, now destructive, now ironic.' It is an opinion too fine for them, and the Pentagon experts will wait long for a Nietzsche to tell them what they are.

The final duel

Dissuasive distrust: we must agree on anything at all, since each is capable of anything, even of the worst. Dissuasive mastery: we must agree on everything, since anything can happen: above all, the Apocalypse. The dissuasive order does not subordinate an anarchy to a superior order which is positive (assumed, in the old way, to entail conviction on the part of everyone). It sub-jects a lower anarchy in the name of a higher one: its scale of values piles one upon another abysses that are more and more bottomless. Order reigns in the first circle of Hell, because it is encased in a second which is more frightening: 'Successful wars have checked domestic unrest and consolidated the power of the state at home' (Hegel).

Modern states have not abolished the contradictions between town and country, workers and employers, rich and poor; they have subjected them to other contradictions which they have presented as being more immediately mortal, turning themselves into 'a besieged fortress' (Stalin), practising 'brinkmanship' (U.S.A.), preparing for world wars as for natural disasters

(Mao), fixing the gaze of a whole people upon 'the blue line of the Vosges' or on the need to occupy '*Lebensraum*' – in other words, cultivating what Hegel distinguished prophetically as 'the ethical moment in war'.

It is enough to socialize men on the basis of their freedom, said Fichte, first witness of the revolution. Hegel improved on this: 'The organic principle is freedom: let the governor himself be the governed.' The word 'organic' emphasizes that men do not allow themselves to be arranged like things or animals, and that it is necessary to refine the rationalist principles of Fichte. The duel of war here receives its speculative decorations: pure liberties which maintain a terroristic commerce with each other do not discipline and mobilize men *for* but *against*. State against state, class against class, party against party. The modern world has to crystallize itself entirely into a dual symmetry.

Revolutions were themselves to be theorized in Europe in accordance with the mirror-principle. When Engels commented on the 'proletarian' insurrection of June 1848, he admired the strategic skill of the Parisians and explained by discipline their achievements which 'would be quite inexplicable if in the national workshops the workers had not been already to a certain extent organized on military lines, ... so that they only needed to apply their industrial organization to their military enterprise'. Later it was 'factory discipline' that Lenin saw as the basis of the capacity for organization possessed by the working class, in accordance with the universal principle of increasing levels of discipline: the Party must be more authoritarian than the state which it undertakes to combat, more secretive than any secret police, more highly militarized than the enemy army, and more strictly hierarchical than all the existing hierarchies. Someone who devotes all his attention to aping the authority that he seeks to overthrow should not be surprised to find that he has set up in its place a caricatural double of that same authority.

Science of revolution? Science of the state? Science of organization? Strategy of dissuasion? Nietzsche summed up this great programme in sober terms: educating the species through war and for war.

The masters who set themselves the task of conceiving the

nascent order of the modern revolutions obviously have political differences amongst themselves regarding these revolutions. But they all, from Hegel onward, profess great admiration for the one who felt the necessity and secured the means . . . to end the revolution. 'We owe it to Napoleon (and not at all to the French Revolution, which had in view the "fraternity" of the nations, and the florid interchange of good graces among people generally) that several warlike centuries, which have not had their like in past history, may now follow one another – in short, that we have now entered the classical age of war, war at the same time scientific and popular, on the grandest scale (as regards means, talents and discipline), to which all coming millenniums will look back with envy and awe as a work of perfection' (Nietzsche). This fragment is so perfect that perhaps the coming millennia will look at it neither with nor without envy, for there will be nobody left to indulge in retrospective reflections. Meanwhile one can quote without either envy or respect this clear exposition of a programme in process of accomplishment, a futurology including the means for its own realization, and its *scientific* realization.

3 Why I Am So Clever
(Hegel and His Followers)

'It is the most important point, you know, that the tutor should be *dignified* and at a distance from the pupil . . .

'So I sit at the further end of the room: outside the door (*which is shut*) sits the scout: outside the outer door (*also shut*) sits the sub-scout: half-way downstairs sits the sub-sub-scout: and down in the yard sits the *pupil*.

'The questions are shouted from one to the other, and the answers come back in the same way . . .

'*Tutor*: What is twice three?

'*Scout*: What's a rice tree?

'*Sub-scout*: When is ice free?

'*Sub-sub-scout*: What's a nice fee?

'*Pupil* (*timidly*): Half a guinea!

'*Sub-sub-scout*: Can't forge any!

'*Sub-scout*: Ho for Jinny!

'*Scout*: Don't be a ninny! . . .'

LEWIS CARROLL, *to Henrietta and Edwin Dodgson*

Paris time

The game of hide-and-seek between the revolution and the science of revolution has gone on for two centuries now. I have everything to learn from the revolution, says science, modestly, as in the case of Marx when confronted by the Paris Commune. I have everything to teach the revolution, suggest at the same time the forty volumes of the scientific works of Marx and Engels, which can be understood, says Lenin (in forty-five further volumes), only by those who have mastered Hegel's *Science of Logic* (two volumes only, but referring to the entire history of Western thought and opening several long shelves in the library).

With the revolution of 1789 'Heaven came down to earth' (Hegel). Each of the master thinkers contributes his share here: Marx by making Prometheus, who wrested fire from the gods, the hero of his philosophy. Nietzsche himself, though far from being a 'revolutionist' in his approach, is no exception: when he says that Wagner brings the German people the opportunity for a new Greek tragedy he is making a double allusion to the French Revolution. A direct allusion, because Wagner, after participating actively in the revolution of 1848 in Germany, resolved to raise his barricade on the aristocratic stage of the Opera (and said so, in *Art and Revolution*). An indirect allusion, because, since Hölderlin and Hegel, the German intellectual has always set out towards an ideal Greece whenever he wanted to encounter the actual French Revolution. *The Origin of Tragedy*, while turning its back on the French uproar, yet replies to the eternal question of the master thinkers: how are the Germans to complete properly what the Parisians have only begun?

This question has become one of world-wide application as a result of the amazing feats of theoretical tight-rope-walking performed by the great Marxist leaders of the twentieth century. That the 'proletarian revolution' should follow a 'bourgeois revolution' as naturally as the month of October follows the month of February was not self-evident to the orthodox Marxists, who had formed the habit of interposing between the two a bourgeois epoch estimated in centuries rather than days. Lenin explained to them that the exception proved the rule, since Russia was 'the weakest link', not in Marxist reasoning but in the European order. After Lenin, Mao was to make the exception the rule for the century, proclaiming that in our epoch the 'revolutions of new democracy' launch the bourgeois and proletarian revolutions in a single process. Thus, theory ascribes to the evolution of reality the reality of its own convolutions. If Peking finds itself suddenly switched to Paris time, is this not because for a long period now science has been commenting on one and the same revolution?

'This was ... a glorious mental dawn. All thinking beings shared in the jubilation of this epoch. Emotions of a lofty character stirred men's minds at that time; a spiritual enthusiasm thrilled through the world ...' (Hegel).

The world's clock

The flatterer lives at the expense of his listener. The 'greater' the revolution, the more enormous the science that explains its greatness. What more persuasive than a doctrine which assures the revolutionary that he is not making revolutions but *one* revolution, and not just one but *the* revolution? All the more so because every revolutionary tends to persuade himself that this is the case, just as every artist sets to work in the hope that he will create a masterpiece – perhaps *the* masterpiece. The science of the masterpiece produces academism in its various forms: what does the science of revolution produce?

The Jacobins clutched the works of Jean-Jacques Rousseau, which gave universal significance to their deeds, with each of Paris's eventful 'days' rivalling the others for the privilege of marking Year One of the world's liberty. In the nineteenth century the French historians took over and, whether glorifying or condemning it, made *the* revolution their favourite world event. France long remained closed to the influence of the master thinkers, with Hegel as impossible to find there as Marxism, which Sartre noted. The fact was that their place had been taken: the work done by the German philosophers became in France the work done by the historians. With history on this side of the Rhine and philosophy on the other, on both banks the world's clock was set by the event of 1789.

This delicate work had nothing innocent about it. The major histories of the Revolution coincide closely with the major trends in French politics: the Radicals were Dantonists, like Michelet, and the historian Mathiez rehabilitated Robespierre like the good Leninist that he was. Similarly, the German thinkers started out in their reasoning with the Revolution as their zero point and developed their thoughts not as 'antiquaries' but as 'builders of the future', working out the programme of the new state: under the pretext of commenting on the Revolution, they constructed their science of governing the masses, and, before or with Nietzsche, discovered the 'utility' of historical studies, 'under the guidance of life making use of the past'.

The plebs

Authority is not to be taken for granted: the distinction between rulers and ruled does not constitute a natural, and still less an eternal, 'datum'. To all conservatives who appeal to the experience of the centuries, Fichte counterposes the Revolution: 'The state has not asked any of us for our consent, but it ought to have.'

Fichte was the first to lift the stone which thereafter the master thinkers handed on from one to another, and he described it with unequalled precision: 'The community cannot exercise the right of coercion directly upon itself . . . It is therefore obliged to delegate the execution of this right to one person, or to an entire constituted body, and by making this separation it becomes a people (*Plebs*).' Fichte, who was not unaware that the word *plebs* is used in German in a pejorative sense, considered it necessary to use this word in order to specify the people as an entity separate from authority (that of the Prince, of the rulers), and he designates all the ruled, as a whole, as the people-*plebs*. He deliberately revived the way the word had been used by Machiavelli.

The first task of the state is to convince the *plebs* that it must let itself be ruled, by making it acknowledge that it governs *itself*, through delegation of powers. The state is not merely *modern* in that it claims a monopoly of physical coercion and the exercise of force, it becomes *rational* by 'scientifically' justifying its existence in the eyes of the peoples of whose general interests it claims to be the sole defender. 'The truth is that if "people" means a particular section of the citizens, then it means precisely that section which does not know what it wills' (Hegel). The monopoly of force is coupled with a monopoly of knowledge.

And what if the people have no use for the state? Then the people become that *plebs* which Hegel, unlike Fichte, distinguishes from the people: 'To regard the will of the executive as bad . . . is a presupposition characteristic of the rabble (*Plebs*) or of the negative outlook generally.' Confidence in the higher powers is popular, suspicion of them is plebeian. Hegel designates, pejoratively, as *plebs* that section of the people which may become ungovernable. 'If a large mass of persons sinks below the minimum standard that seems normally necessary for the members of a given society, if it thus loses the feeling of the rightness, legitimacy and honour of existing through its own activity and its own labour, then we get the formation of a *plebs* ...' With his pupils the older Hegel was more explicit, stating that the economic pauperism of bourgeois society created the objective conditions for a *plebs*-populace, and that the supplementary subjective condition was a question of mentality: 'Poverty in itself does not make men into a rabble; a rabble is created only when there is joined to poverty a disposition of mind, an inner indignation against the rich, against society, against the government, etc. A further consequence of this attitude is that, through their dependence on chance, men become frivolous and idle, like the Neapolitan *lazzaroni*, for example.' The British workman, though poor, remains respectful of good morals and of the government. Hegel does not include him in his *plebs*, unlike the *lazzaroni* – not to mention the 'hippy' workmen of our own day.

Fichte grasped the problem at its point of origin. The *plebs* means the people by whom the state has to legitimize itself: 'I must submit myself in perfect freedom.' The same view was taken by Hegel. The modern state is rational only in so far as it makes itself understood and accepted by free subjects, by a people. He grasps the same problem by its end-point, assuming it to have been solved: the *plebs*-populace is then that unassimilated residue upon which all the winds of revolt are likely to blow. If this *residue* is kept in minority status, it is a problem for the police: if it attains majority status, numerically or ideologically, then the result is revolution.

Sandwiched between the people and the riff-raff, the concept of the *plebs* thus points to the principal snag that the master thinkers encounter in their approach to revolutions. The task they all take upon themselves is that of strengthening the relation between the *plebs* and the state. A rough note written by Nietzsche formulates it bluntly:

The great revolt of the *plebs* and the slaves
– the mediocrities who no longer believe in the saints or men of great worth (e.g., in Christ or Luther)
– the bourgeois who no longer believe in the superiority of the ruling classes (hence revolutions).
– the labourers of science who no longer believe in the philosophers.
– the women who no longer believe in the superiority of men.

As usual, Nietzsche sets out frankly what the other master thinkers mention only in veiled terms: Heaven no longer rules the earth, bourgeois civil society is prey to the anarchy of the market, and ideas are hardly less anarchical. Now, under such conditions, can one govern the *plebs*?

The strategy of enforcing literacy

No one refuses to learn to read without acting the child or the madman, putting himself among those who are forced to learn to read on pain of being sent to prison. In a calm period the literate are the good workmen of civilization, the happy foot-soldiers of the European and world wars, the valiant sugar-cane-cutters of the proletarian revolutions in the tropics. In a difficult situation, revolutions end in the combined deluges of baths of culture and of blood. When the town undertakes to discipline the countryside, so as to ensure that it will be fed, the conflagrations started by its expeditionary columns are taken to represent enlightenment, while peasant resistance is the dark night of obscurantism – the Vendéens of 1793, the Cristeros of the Mexican revolution, the peasants of Northern Portugal. All these friends of the revolution in its opening phases are seen as rebelling not against a new order imposed by the townsmen and the state but against . . . culture.

Having conquered the towns and the machinery of state, the Russian Bolsheviks found themselves isolated in an empire that was ninety per cent peasant: the raft of revolutionary science was being navigated by guesswork over 'the ocean of the small peasantry', and every spring brought its series of plebeian revolts – peasant revolts always, workers' revolts if there were any workers left (Petrograd), or revolts of a mixed character

(Kronstadt). The solution found by Lenin was encapsulated in a slogan: 'Cultural Revolution'. This covered a few simple measures: the entire population to be made literate, primary education to penetrate the countryside, and the latter to be linked with the centres of authority by circuits of commerce both economic and cultural. In *Better Fewer But Better*, Lenin's last article (March 1923), he stressed that these apparently benign measures are the fundamental elements in the great strategic plan of every revolution: 'I think that this has happened in all really great revolutions, for really great revolutions grow out of the contradictions between the old ... and the very abstract striving for the new, which must be so new as not to contain the tiniest particle of the old.'

There was no gulf between the 'humble' tasks of enforcing literacy and the great projects of the revolution's first days ('cleansing the land of Russia of all vermin', as Lenin had written in January 1918). The tactics of cleansing had become more subtle (in theory) and more thoroughgoing (in practice), and all were aimed at the same target, namely, causing every tiniest particle of the old to disappear.

Enforcing literacy is never a mere matter of teaching how to read or to count, it means teaching people afresh how to speak and to behave, that is, making them unlearn that which the state does not have the privilege of teaching. All the world's colonial peoples know a lot about what is meant by this.

It is necessary to know how to end a revolution, whispers the new order: it makes of revolutionary radicalism (not the tiniest particle of the old) a new method for eradicating the resistance of the *plebs* (all resistance is rooted in a past of resistances, and attacking it at the root means wresting from it that past, which is obscure ... and therefore obscurantist). Or one could put it like this: how to end revolutions by means of pedagogy!

Having conceived the emergence of the rational state after the French Revolution, Fichte marketed his new science, the purpose of which he revealed with the innocence of a beginner: 'The Science of Knowledge possesses positive utility: it is pedagogical in the widest sense. It shows, on the basis of the highest principles, precisely because it teaches us to grasp Man in his totality, how one must form men so as to produce in them, lastingly, moral and religious feelings, and so as to make them more and more universal.'

The new state wants a new man – the one promised to us by pedagogy 'in the widest sense'. This terminology becomes that of the great enterprises dealing with human flesh: it is a question of *producing* feelings, of *building*, forming (*bilden*) Man, of *grasping* his totality. The following century was to be that of the pedagogues. Stalin called them 'engineers of souls', and though he is dead, they are not.

One lord and no serfs

'The East knew and to the present day knows only that *one* is free; the Greek and Roman world that *some* are free; the German world knows that *all* are free. The first political form therefore which we observe in history is *despotism*, the second *democracy and aristocracy*, the third *monarchy*.' This seeming paradox of Hegel's sums up the general lesson of revolution: precisely because *all* are free, they delegate the power of coercion to a particular organ, distinct from the community, namely, the rational state. The Hegelian 'monarchy' is a mere recognition of this split between the dominators and the dominated and does not signify the despotism of a single person. If he were to return amongst us, Hegel would translate 'monarchy' into more fashionable terms: personalization of authority, presidential regime, cult of personality. 'In monarchy ... there is one lord and no serfs,' the master thinker adds, giving us the key to modern discipline. No one is a serf because the lord's eye is inside every head: every prisoner keeps permanent watch upon himself, he is his own warder, and 800 million Chinese are 800 million Maos.

The vocation of the scholar

On the pretext of educating the subjects and turning each one into a statesman, the eye of the state is installed within each head. Revolutions reveal the mortality of governments, and philosophers like Plato no longer ask to be kings. Modestly, they place themselves between the peoples and the state, that is, above both of them: we move from the philosopher-king to the learned theoretician who has taken upon himself the mission of 'surveying as from on high the actual advancement of the human race in general' (Fichte, *The Vocation of the Scholar*).

Fichte's 'on high' is the same as Lenin's 'without', from which he claimed to be bringing science to the working class. The 'scholar,' like the professional revolutionary, puts forward a claim to be 'the teacher of the human race'. In a deeper kinship, these thinkers no longer aspire merely to give scientific guidance to the state, from near or far, they intend to lead it to its own death. Fichte, even in his most authoritarian and nationalist phases, spoke of the ultimate disappearance of the state, just as Lenin did, before he took power. In this anarchism of the Last Days is expressed the triumph of a good education: every statesman will 'self-manage' himself in a self-discipline that realizes the idea of the society of supreme oversight – a prison without warders.

It is enough to acquire 'knowledge of the faculties and wants of man' and along with this to have 'acquaintance with the means of developing and satisfying them' – the rest is a mere matter of public education.

The vocation of the scholar means electrification plus the power of the alphabet.

To everyone his own plebs

The master thinkers refute one another violently, and each cries victory when he discovers those whom his predecessor has left on the shelf: these 'residues' become fresh masses to be mobilized.

Hegel had placed on the fringe of his rational state a *plebs* which he carefully distinguished from the people by its wretched condition and the spirit of revolt which might animate it. This is the starting-point of Marx's critique, which requires 'the formation of a class with radical chains, a class of civil society which is not a class of civil society, an estate which is the dis-

solution of all estates . . .; which, in a word, is the complete loss
of man and hence can win itself only through the complete re-
winning of man. This dissolution of society as a particular estate
is the proletariat.'

The master thinkers thus overtake each other . . . in the *plebs*.
They expand, to be sure, the 'people' which is to be the foundation of the state, but they do not all deal with it in the same
way. Marx distinguishes between the good working class, which
is a people in Hegel's sense, and the bad riff-raff, the *lumpen-
proletariat*, which is a mere re-issue of the *plebs* according to
Hegel. Bakunin, in his turn, reproaches Marx, and appeals to
'that great popular rabble which, being almost untouched by
any bourgeois civilization, bears within itself, in its passions,
. . . all the seeds of future socialism . . .'

Bakunin initiates the Leninist critique of 'the aristocracy of
labour', sold to the bourgeoisie, and the all-embracing denunci-
ation of the 'developed' proletariats by the 'Third-World'
school and the Chinese-style communists, in their 'radical'
moments.

The different leaders speak in the same terms of the different
masses to which they refer: in 'dissolution', in 'complete loss of
itself', the mass in question, 'almost untouched by any bourgeois civilization', has value by virtue of this very virginity. It
will be the sheet whose blankness is its defence, the sheet on
which the master thinker will freely inscribe his finest poem, it
will be the fallow land that the state will freely plough up in
order to give itself rational foundations.

What defines the radical class is its presumed rootlessness: it
gives promise of a solution by virtue of its apparent utter dissolution. If it is to re-educate us, is this not so precisely to the
extent that the master thinker takes it over as being totally
uneducated, and therefore completely educable by him?

By summoning masses that are supposed to be more and more
radical, meaning virgin and mute, the master thinker perfects
his fantastic ventriloquy performance. Before he takes our breath
away, he takes the power of speech from these masses, who are
perhaps not so inarticulate as he dreams them to be.

Fidelity to the State and to the Revolution

Successive generations have striven to isolate out from Hegel's work a body of left-wing thought, a revolutionary method which they contrast with the right-wing system of the alleged 'official philosopher' of the Prussian state. They are victims of optical illusions: whether his left or his right profile be looked at, one and the same Hegel appears to our view. Heine – the poet, German and Jew – was to note this, at the end of his life. Ill and ironic, the poet advised his former Left-Hegelian friends, Feuerbach, Ruge, Marx and Bauer, to re-read the story of that 'bluestocking without feet' who, wound around its Biblical tree, murmured all the promises of Hegelianism 6,000 years before the Battle of Jena, while listening Eve licked her lips in the shadow of the Tree of Knowledge.

One may, with Marcuse, claim that Hegel 'freed philosophic approaches to reality from the powerful religious and theological influences that were operative even upon secular forms of eighteenth-century thought', and thus provided 'a preliminary enunciation of the decisive passages in which Marx later revolutionized Western thought'. But Hegel, like Marx, derived this liberation from the French Revolution, 'which caused Heaven to come down upon earth', and he took it over in the very special fashion of the master thinkers, linking knowledge and power, freedom of the people *and* rationality of the state.

Contrary to what Marcuse goes on to say, the older Hegel was *not* guilty of 'betraying his highest philosophical ideas' when he concluded that 'the people "is that part of the state which does not know what it wants"'. For the young Hegel a people is a people only if it has a state – otherwise, like the inhabitants of Germany, it is nothing but a 'mass' (*Menge*). And if Marx distinguishes only two great classes, polarizing the bourgeois system, this is not because he is unaware of the others' existence but because, according to him, these two alone are capable of rivalling each other for power through taking control of the state.

Peoples and classes capable of having a state of their own – or else, nothing. This choice is found in all the master thinkers, young and old, right and left. In other words: outside of the state (either the present or the future one), one doesn't know what one wants. On this point they all turn out to be Hegelians, and Marcuse's argument is seen to be futile.

It will perhaps be suggested that the Right hopes to build its rational society 'from above' whereas the Left promises to build it 'from below'. Actually, the master thinkers proceed neither from above nor from below, but from themselves and their science. They expect one thing only – to be listened to, which presupposes, above, a rational state (either existing or to be built), and, below, a *plebs* that is educable, that is, virginal.

Education for life and for death

Saying that, outside the state, the people 'does not know what it wants' (Hegel) signifies shutting up the *plebs* within socially defined positions – those of the child or the lunatic. While the state shows little hesitation in locking up, or even treating, 'in the Soviet way', as a sufferer from mental illness, anyone who expresses opposition to it, it makes use, more generally, of the first way out of the problem: the people, that big child, has never had too much education.

Where methods of education are concerned, the master thinkers are divided. For Fichte, a premature Leninist, the state, with its arsenal of means of coercion, needs to be understood as an 'educative institution': the roads to freedom will be hedged with the barbed wire of constraints, for 'programme of government and plan of education are one and the same thing'. Hegel criticized this mechanical and administrative aspect of Fichtean education, and proposed a more strategic method – education by struggle, in the Maoist manner. Nietzsche was to find every method good, in so far as the aim assigned by all of them to education was the same: *training* and *selection*.

Educating, says Hegel, the advocate of the complex method, means, in the first place, teaching to speak. There lies the implicit relation with the state, for 'the barbarians do not know what they want to say', deprived as they are of civilization. If language already contains reason of state, this is because it has been conceived as an instrument of power: 'The first act by which Adam instituted his authority over the animals was when he named them.' Naming something means taking possession of it and attributing to it a 'soul'. Education is, from the outset, apprenticeship to mastery of things and animals. In relation to human beings, this apprenticeship to domination reveals itself through a struggle for domination.

Children are 'the death of their parents'. Hegel's formulation has often been taken as anticipating Freud and psychoanalysis. It would have been useful to inquire *what* form of psychoanalysis can be recognized in the educative conflict projected by Hegel. It is a game in which what one side wins the other must lose. It is a strictly limited game, played behind closed doors between parents and children. At the start, the child is nothing and the parents everything: 'The inorganic nature of the child is the knowledge of the parents.' At the end, the child is everything, that is, everything that his parents were, and all that remains for them is to disappear. 'What they give to him they themselves lose; they die in him; in fact, what they give him is their own consciousness.'

Here Hegel meets not Freud but Mao. He shows how the struggle for power can become the best means of preserving power. Hegelian education amounts to the mere transfer of an unchanged power from generation to generation: the parents die in their children, but not without having passed on to them, in the fire of struggle, 'their own consciousness'. Everyone dies in the family except the family itself: the King is dead, long live the King.

Perfectly conservative although wholly made up of conflicts, this model education shows how one can try to perpetuate the state as the state and the *plebs* as the *plebs* without recoiling in horror before class struggles, wars and revolutions.

Shrouding the night in darkness

For the absolute educator, the child and the *plebs* are virgin lands, to be colonized freely: nothing stands in the way of the *conquistador*, there is not a vestige of civilization. Outside his relation with authority, the child, like the *plebs*, does not know what he wants. He will, it is promised, become everything on condition that, at the outset, he lets it be impressed upon him that he is nothing. In order to conclude the game between the child and his parents, between the *plebs* and the state, in order to reproduce power by power, untouched and untouchable, the whole business has to start from scratch.

In the beginning was the blank page. Or the page made blank? Or the palimpsest?

When the educator requires the child to act like a child he is telling him to make himself empty, so as to receive a soul: 'The education of the child consists in the fact that the consciousness deposited in him, as something other than what he is himself, becomes his own consciousness'. The child was 'other' than the consciousness which is deposited in him, and educating him means making sure that he forgets that fact. This 'other' might look into the eyes of his educator and find there a darkness akin to his own: it is necessary that the forgetting be complete and final. The enlightenment of education drives out, burns up, consumes a night of which Hegel once said, before he confined himself to stirring its ashes: 'Man is this night, this empty Nothingness which contains everything in its undivided simplicity ... Here a bleeding head suddenly arises, there another apparition, all in white – and they disappear just as suddenly ... It is this night that we perceive if we look into a man's eyes: we plunge our gaze into a night which becomes terrible: it is the night of the world that is then showing itself to us.'

Hegel places that night at the very beginning of the educative development of man which he calls 'experience of consciousness', dialectics, phenomenology of the spirit. The night is situated beforehand, it is what he starts from, but that depth which he evokes does not let itself be reduced to a point, even if this be the starting-point he indicates subsequently, the dead-end of a night in which darkness reigns and all cats are grey. This second night, of inky darkness, he lays over the first one as though to efface the frightening discovery.

Education is a putting to death. One starts to speak, saying that there is nothing to be said about the original night except that, in it, Being and Nothingness are the same, in the greyness ascribed to cats. In saying that, one has already put forward something other than that night, one has departed from it: this 'flight forward' is called progress in the experience of the consciousness, this progressive epic gives us the dialectical becoming. Tomorrow you will be a man, and free, on condition that you do not turn back towards that from which education turns you away, and on condition that it does not return to you: 'Enjoying, however, an absolute liberty, the idea does not merely pass over into life, or as finite cognition allow life to show in it: in its own absolute truth it resolves to let the "moment" of its particularity, or of the first characterization and other-being, the immediate idea, as its reflected mirage, go forth freely as Nature.'

In the state of the master thinkers there is one lord and no serfs because all the subjects have received a good education: their most absolute freedom being to dismiss themselves, they think with their master and like their master – or, more precisely, the master thinks in them, while they strive to get rid of that part of their own night which might have been able to feel itself enslaved, and to resist. Hegel in Year 01 of the age of brainwashing.

Burn your boats !

'Bring your problems out into the open. Don't criticize from behind.' Mao launches mass campaigns in order that nothing may remain hidden, either in the consciousness of the masses or in the corridors of the bureaucracy. Conflicts break out, heads roll, the official framework changes somewhat, but at the same time the supreme oversight is strengthened, visibility is increased, the centre remains immune from attack, incarnate in the person of the Chairman (Hegel would have said 'the monarch'). Whether Mao or somebody else, the name no longer signifies anything but a position, the watchman's post which emerges firmer than ever from this operation.

These 'cultural revolutions' in the Chinese style reproduce, after all, the schema of Hegel's system of education. Through wall-posters, statements of grievances, protests and even acts of violence, the people is called upon to *pour out its heart*. Having brought everything out into the open, the people finds itself, like the Hegelian child, standing before the Educator who holds the monopoly of transmission of news and ideas (printed newspapers, radio, television), of interpretation of doctrine (circulation of selected quotations), and of knowledge of the mechanisms of power (such-and-such a leader became a traitor ten years ago ...). Everyone has turned out his bag, and the child or the *plebs* thus 'emptied' stands face to face with the educator who is armed with what Hegel calls 'the knowledge of the parents', whereas the Chinese Communist Party calls its power-cum-knowledge 'Marxism-Leninism'.

This struggle for power makes possible the selection and renewal of the élites. The *cadres* move around but the principle of *encadrement* remains untouchable: all of those who fight *for* power place power itself beyond challenge, confirming and preserving it. The child is the death of his parents, and he accomplishes this death only by himself becoming a parent. The state and the Party are kept alive by this struggle which Mao compares to a metabolism: 'A proletarian Party must reject whatever has gone bad, and absorb the new so as to be full of dynamism. Unless it rejects the waste-products and absorbs new blood the Party cannot be dynamic.'

The procedure is effective only in so far as it takes place within a limited space. The *plebs* is called upon to burn its boats: having everything to win, it must be allowed nothing to hang on to. It uproots its own past; it makes public revelation of its private conversations; its long underground galleries dug out over centuries in order to resist those on high have now to be laid open to the sky, by means of the heavy bulldozers of struggle–criticism–reform. 'If problems exist but are not brought into the open, they will long remain unsolved and may even drag on for years' (Mao). Nothing must be left dragging when zero hour comes for the struggle for power, that moment when the proletariat is called upon to 'wield its power in every sphere'. Everything has already been fixed, the field of battle is marked off, the state and the Party have cut off the *plebs* from its rear.

There were three thousand plays in the repertory of the classical Chinese theatre. In them the people gave itself the spectacle of the men of power – looking at them, envying them, mocking them. At the end of the Cultural Revolution only three were left, each one more edifying than the rest. Edifying in a vacuum. From that stage which had been thoroughly cleared there had been eliminated not so much the Emperors and Empresses, the young ladies and gentlemen, as the resistance put up, laughingly and through centuries, to these mighty ones of a passing day.

Mao, following Clausewitz, analysed well the reasons why a people at war can get the better of an opponent whose material and economic power is greatly superior. A people defending itself on its own territory can protract its defensive war, withdraw into the depths of the country, leaving the invader to conquer the towns and centres, and then encircling him with the campaigns and storms of a whole population. Contrariwise to the schema of the people's war, the scenario of the struggle for power has this struggle starting with the centre, and aims at besieging this centre, the fascination of which remains permanent ('bombard the headquarters'). Above all, the people should be deprived of any possibility of strategic retreat, by obliging it to let go of its bases of resistance – cultural, political and moral – and risk everything at once. A succession 'over a thousand years' of 'cultural revolutions' of this sort would alter nothing in this game decided in advance, since the state machine retains the privilege of starting and stopping the said 'cultural revolutions'. The privilege of the people in protracted wars was that they could put off the 'decisive battle', taking time to mobilize themselves in depth and to wear the enemy down. On the fallacious pretext of bringing everything out into the open, the struggle for power strives to dynamite this ultimate, strategic resource possessed by the *plebs*.

Making the heart the heart's grave

The child enters the order of the family as the *plebs* enters reason of state, saying farewell to its inner night: the voices of reason resound better in the echo of the void. Family, moral and political education postulates that the initial exclusion is definitive, that is, can be repeated *ad infinitum*: the citizen tears himself away from private life, the revolutionary refrains from all 'sentimentality', and when an earthquake occurs, the good Maoist Chinese saves the Communist district officer rather than his own children, because 'the Communists always and everywhere represent the interests of the movement as a whole' (Marx, in the *Communist Manifesto*).

Education brings everyone out of the night in order to expose him to the sun of reason of state: this goes back to Plato's *Republic*. Strictly modern, though, is the emptying of the interior by which it is not so much the one being educated who comes out of the night as the night that is expelled from within him. Strictly modern is the 'zero level' at which education leaves its patient, with nothing but the skin on the hollow bones of his consciousness. To be sure, man has instincts, interests, purposes by which he relates to the world and to other people: 'External existence has its roots in what is inward.' 'But,' Hegel adds, 'the roots belong to his inner life, they are his; he can tear them out of his heart; his will, his freedom represent that power of abstraction from everything whereby the heart can make itself the grave of the heart.'

His heart having become a crypt, the child dreams only of becoming a parent, the militant dreams only of power, the intellectual turns himself into a master thinker and the *plebs* conceives the state.

The theory then celebrates its apotheosis by applying to everything that is not itself – its 'residue' – the pejorative epithets of sentimentality, subjectivism, disorder, night; where would it celebrate its triumph better than in the brain of the practical man, pure of any theoretical spark, attached to what is solid, concrete and serious, that is, to the only toys that the theory leaves him to play with? One has the right to dream, said Lenin, provided one dreams 'seriously'.

The mortuary

The master thinkers are guilty of no negligence; it is useless to refer to their supposed 'forgettings' in order to clean up their theory, saving their science by means of a little additive. The white night to which the educator condemns his child and his *plebs* is a night without secrets. Let us free ourselves of the notion that something is hidden away in what Hegel rejects – Existence, Matter, Feeling, Democracy – some little thing which was only waiting for us (Left Marxists, Existentialist Hegelians, or what have you) to come along and save the whole thing. What is twisted cannot be straightened in a theory in which nothing exists except for the purpose of twisting and tearing out.

The night that the thinker eliminates at the start of his educational process, the night which is not yet locked up in a dream of reason, these images that associate, speak and give us to think outside the limits of the family and the state – Hegel will never again speak of this night, which means that he will do nothing but speak of it. This night accompanies the long road of the consciousness which is educating itself. This consciousness becomes self-consciousness, or cultivated consciousness, by constantly tearing itself away from its nocturnal double (called by Hegel 'natural consciousness'). At every one of the stages of its education (*figures of the spirit*) the consciousness transforms its heart into a grave, and harshly abstracts from itself. 'What Hegel calls natural consciousness is not congruent at all with the sensitive consciousness, natural knowledge is alive in all figures of the spirit.' Education is in danger of seeing its work disintegrated every time that the one being educated lets himself go towards whatever fascinates him, and that he establishes with it a direct, immediate relationship which is night because it has not been whitened by the death of the heart and the mediation of the theory. Art is 'a thing of the past' in Hegel's view, because it is still immersed in this night of natural consciousness

– and, along with it, religion. Not that these two no longer exist: they exist as a past to be transcended by a knowledge of today. This operation is topical, if we remember that 'transcend' means for Hegel to annihilate, to set aside, to preserve, to recover, and to supervise from a higher position: art and religion, owing to their nocturnal appearance, need to be dominated by the great reason of the master thinkers.

The nocturnal face of art or of religion does not consist in what they may signify that is irrational or mystical: Hegelian reason makes a point of explaining these mysteries to us more prosaically and, so it claims, more clearly. The night is not in what is seen but in the way of seeing. Hegel defines this way as that of opinion (*Meinung*) and he contrasts it with his science. Defining his 'natural consciousness' as the 'system of opinion', he revives the old Platonic contrast between vulgar opinion and learned science. He adds a new meaning which Heidegger hears with a well-turned ear: opinion means 'the immediate focusing upon something, the trusting acceptance of what is given (*Minne*)', with, furthermore, the sense of 'something we receive, hold, and assert as our own'.   There thus belongs to the sphere of nocturnal opinion everything which has not remained in the mortuary of the heart's death and control by theory. This meant for Hegel feeling, art and religion, and was to mean for Lenin 'spontaneity' and 'economism', and for Mao Tse-tung 'putting oneself first'.

These truths which transcend artistic communication were perhaps set forth earlier and more truly in the theatre (that lower level of Hegelian knowledge) by Shakespeare (that target of the Chinese Cultural Revolution):

Lady Anne: No beast so fierce but knows some touch of pity.
Gloucester: But I know none, and therefore am no beast.

(*Richard III*)

The terrorist theory

Reason has never finished excluding that which it excludes, says Hegel, as if it were precisely the exclusive task of his reason to exclude. The hunting down of natural consciousness never ceases: this is perhaps because the passion of reason is to drive out rather than to take. Making the child childish, making the people a miserable *plebs* confronted by a state that is more and more learned and therefore haughty, therefore distant, and therefore superior – is this an unexpected and, so to speak, involuntary consequence of the work done by the theory of the master thinkers, or is this the most *consequent* part of its work?

Whitening the night, preventing 'bloody heads' and 'ghosts' that vanish from breaking the thread of learned discourses (I am a Marxist, therefore I do not read *The Gulag Archipelago*), protecting the state from the manifold and scattered voices that it aims to conceal, protecting families from desires and constituted bodies from families, the state from the egoism of institutions, the empires from the independence of nations – the exorcisms carried out by the powers of the modern world are exploits of reason and science.

In face of the child deprived of his night and the *plebs* cut off from its means of resistance, it is precisely with science and reason that the master thinkers intend to robe the rulers. Hegel condensed all the vaguely materialistic philosophy of the Enlightenment in the formula: 'The being of Spirit is a bone'. His epic of the consciousness conquering itself could equally well be summed up in a call: 'The hunt is up.' And if such naïve persons as ourselves ask what hunt is meant here, the children and the *plebs* are not authorized to answer. The hunters, having devastated their hunting-ground long since, are quite unaware of what they are pursuing. What does that matter? Shoot at sight at anything you don't know.

4   Why We Are So Metaphysical

' Whereupon Panurge said that the leaf of paper was written on,
but in such a subtle way that no one could see the writing.'

RABELAIS

A Hiroshima love

That everything whirls around in the struggle for power, that
the world is a battlefield – O.K.! The ancient Greeks already
told us so. But that the power in question is power to destroy,
and the battle one of annihilation – that's what sounds modern to
a modern ear. Did the master thinkers compose the Requiem for
the twentieth century, and sing it *in extenso,* even before the
death-pits were filled? Why not? Their programme was to take
history as though from zero-level and write it out rationally on
a blank sheet. An iron ideology, the fire of machine-guns and
lead can sweep the lands clean, a hundred thousand suns can
wipe out a city, and the terrorized earth will recover its virginal
pallor. A *tabula rasa* for the promoters of the future: a round
table for the compilers of blueprints. The plans of authority do
not 'correspond' to reality and still less do they reflect it, since
authority's business is, precisely, to make reality bend until it
fits the plans. They did not invent this future dedicated to mastery of nature and domination of the planet: it had been waiting
for a long time, crouched behind them. They thought it out
rigorously and systematically, anticipating it as nobody had done
before them. 'The deserts grow: woe him who doth them hide!'
(*Thus Spake Zarathustra*).

He who says 'desert' (in German, *Wüste*) says 'destruction',
'devastation' (*Verwüstung*), that is, war and death (Hegel uses
this term to describe the efficacity of Tamerlane and Genghis
Khan, 'the brooms of God'). The desert thus announced is not
a feature of the landscape, an interesting item of geography, an
unexpected discovery by a tourist among ideas. Not at all.
Devastation, ravaging, the action of *creating a desert before one-*

self constitutes the most intimate secret of our history, what it has produced that is most historically our own. At least, if we are to believe Hegel, who is regarded by the learned as being less 'irresponsible' than Nietzsche: at least, if we read his most frequently quoted remark, the one most commented on, and ultimately, the most secret: 'Lacking strength, Beauty hates the Understanding for asking of it what it cannot do. But the life of the Spirit is not the life that shrinks from death and keeps itself untouched by devastation (*Verwüstung*), but rather the life that endures it and maintains itself in it.' The desert of which Hegel and Nietzsche speak is not a natural desert, but neither is it a 'spiritual' one. Reason does not go into the desert as anchorites do: it thrusts the desert before it, devastating things and men, driving Beauty to desperation in order to subject everything to its *force*: 'Spirit is this power only by looking the negative in the face, and tarrying with it.' This tarrying, this *time spent (Verweilt)*, is precisely the spirit-of-the-desert, a desert which is time and not space. 'This tarrying with the negative is the magical power that converts it into being. This power is identical with what we earlier called the subject.'

The True is the Subject, says Hegel: so we are told by every textbook of philosophy. He hints also that the Subject is the Desert, that the Desert is the Subject. Nietzsche saw that. Let us be fashionable and replace 'Subject' by 'driving-force of history', or whatever phrase may be preferred that is even more fashionable. We then get: Devastation is the driving force of history (or anything else that may be named instead of 'the Desert').

Could it be that the truth of the master thinkers is a desert truth? That it contains and hides the deserts that are to come?

What is German idealism?

Mother of sciences, arms and laws – what shall we call this thought which circulates between Fichte's *Science of Knowledge*, Hegel's *Logic*, Marx's *Critique* and Nietzsche's *Genealogies*? It is a knowledge that is anterior to the sciences which it thrusts before it; a philosophy which refuses to let itself be called one philosophy among others, resembling, as it does, no other philosophy; a metaphysics that proclaims the end of metaphysics; a theology of the death of God, an ontology that will not accept that a being (*ontos*) may be other than this same ontology, since it aims to be the logic that makes the world our world. Let us call it 'German idealism', so as to pin it down between the cross-fire of ignorance with a historico-geographical veneer and stupidity cultivating its mumblings in the textbooks.

German? This thinking in terms of mastery is found all over our planet, it issues forth from Washington and Peking just as from Moscow! Idealism? Reducing things, the world, to ideas, and ideas to things in one's head (unless the head is also just an idea) – there's a quaint notion! Quaint enough for cutting history as with a knife: on my right the 'idealists', on my left the 'materialists', decrees Lenin, whetting his penknife of orthodoxy that would soon have real heads rolling, while penetrating hearts.

Condemning Hegel's idealism, Lenin took care to preserve its 'active side' – the penknife, precisely! In his innocence, he carried off the whole lot, for it was just the active side of their thought that the German masters had called 'idealism'. Every inactive form of idealism was condemned by the German idealists with unequalled violence: the modern materialists derive all their striking arguments from this source. Who but Fichte killed (speculatively) the inactive consciousness? Who, before Hegel, launched upon the 'beautiful soul' and the 'unhappy consciousness' such a cartload of reprimands that they are still raining down a century later? Who did more than Nietzsche to pillory every form of *passive* nihilism? Who, better than these, sided with the world's course against all inward virtue?

Nietzsche summed up the way in which they were idealistic: 'Let us rid ourselves of a prejudice here: idealizing does not consist, as it is generally believed, in a suppression or elimination of detail or of inessential features. A stupendous *accentuation* of the principle characteristics is by far the most decisive factor at work, and in consequence the minor characteristics vanish.'

O.K., 'German idealism', then – provided that we add that the

world of today is 'Germany', and that we give the name 'idealism' to the various projects for mastery of the world which confront each other, 'bringing out from what has been extracted'
and 'causing to disappear' by means of very material forms of
extraction and no less materialist disappearances.

Very homely

The question which the 'German idealists' applied their minds
to in the French Revolution was older than them, and more
European than German. 'There is only one indivisible point
which is the true *locus* ... In painting, the perspective determines this. But who is to determine it in truth and morality?'
asks Pascal. The question is older than him, too, assuming as
acquired that placing in perspective which masters mathematically both landscape and physical nature.

Descartes is the hero closest to us, says Hegel, in his history
of philosophy. ('It is not until Descartes is arrived at that we
really enter upon a philosophy which is, properly speaking,
independent ... Here, we may say, we are at home, and like the
mariner after a long voyage in a tempestuous sea, we may now
hail the sight of land.') Descartes was the first to set out method-
ically the scheme for domination of the world designed to make
us 'lords and possessors of nature'. He was also the first to
formulate a *morality for the meantime*, that is, a provisional
morality, 'conditional upon inventory', with the inventory here
consisting in securing the assurance of one's reason: 'My whole
object was always to achieve certainty and to probe beneath the
shifting soil and the sands to find the underlying rock ...'

Of little significance are the maxims – convenient? prudent?
with double meanings? – which Descartes sets forth, since he
formulates them as only provisional. Though he advises the
reader that one should let oneself be ruled by the laws and customs of one's country, he has already broken decisively with the
most ancestral of laws and the deepest-rooted of customs, submitting them to the tribunal of his mastery: 'I should not have
thought that I ought to content myself with the opinions of
others for a single moment, had I not made up my mind to

exercise my judgement on them at the proper time ...' That *proper time* arrived a century and a half later, in Germany.

An 'indivisible point' in morality was called for by Pascal, himself already a post-Cartesian. Far from retreating, as though out of Christian humility, on the contrary, he advanced into the universe of mastery. Until when will it be necessary to rest content with the provisional in matters of behaviour? When shall we reach *terra firma*? Frequently formulating his apologia for Christianity in terms of mastery – even though of a difficult mastery, one not to be mastered except through a wager – he already brought up the questions of a Great Helmsman: 'The harbour is the judge of those aboard ship but where are we going to find a harbour in morals?' Whom does he mean by 'we'? Those who are piloting the ship? Those who are judging how it is being steered? We, the lords and possessors of nature, are called upon to become lords and possessors of 'morality' as well – that is, of human as well as of physical matters.

To this appeal the master thinkers reply – and, in their shadow, a whole procession of human sciences. Does this mean that the proper time has come, as Descartes wished it would, or that our ship has reached Pascal's port? The fact that an appeal has been more widely heard does not necessarily mean that it has been better understood.

On the bill-board

The Golden Age is not 'behind us' but 'ahead of us', wrote the young Fichte, in the glow of the revolutionary dawn. History was only beginning: this pamphleteer wrote on the flyleaf of his *Demand for Freedom of Thought*: 'At Heliopolis, in the last year of the age of darkness.' Ninety years later the tone had changed: 'The deserts grow: woe him who doth them hide!' (*Thus Spake Zarathustra*). A different mood, a different accent, for one and the same attitude. Still on the agenda was the great task of governing the future: the project of mastery was being deployed as a programme of action.

All looking backward, even though it take us to the very origins of mankind, becomes for the master thinkers, looking forward and futurology. 'We have, in traversing the past, ... only to do with what is *present*' (Hegel). Not that it is a matter of seeing, through a retrospective illusion, our present existence as something eternal, by imagining it in the past: that permanent risk goes along with a deeper design – to grasp in the past the force of the future, to find in history the driving force of history. Hegel calls 'the Spirit' the locomotive of the future, in the sense in which one speaks of the spirit of the age or of a civilization ('the present form of spirit comprehends within it all earlier steps'). Marx sees this locomotive as 'class struggle' ('the history of all hitherto existing society is the history of class struggles' – that opening phrase of the *Manifesto* which embarrassed Engels, already, when he acquired some serious knowledge of ethnology).

The presumptuous emphasis placed by the men of the nineteenth century upon the past may seem to us out-of-date (for example: 'Human anatomy contains a key to the anatomy of the ape' – Marx). When we indulge ourselves by criticizing their erroneous reconstructions we run the risk of clearing away only the crude side-aspects of a scheme which is still predominant. The essential feature of the historical work of the master thinkers does not consist in superimposing their present upon the past of mankind, launching two moments of time. Their grander ambition is not satisfied with moving *in* time, but plans to coincide with the movement *of* time. Whereas the ordinary understanding rests content with 'contemplating facts (*facta*) in time', Fichte's doctrine of science proposes to reflect upon the action of time itself: 'If you consider the origin of time, you thereby consider the origin of everything.' The master thinker studies history only in order to make history. If he goes back to the origins of mankind, it is in order to make mankind capable of mastering that origin, in other words, of programming the future: 'I love him who justifieth the future ones and redeemeth the past ones ... I love all who are like heavy drops falling one by one out of the dark cloud that lowereth over man: they herald the coming of the lightning, and succumb as heralds' (*Thus Spake Zarathustra*).

There has been a division of labour: German idealism set

forth a programme, and our very materialistic century is putting this programme into practice.

There and back

In the days when France was collapsing in its 'strange defeat' (Marc Bloch) by the Nazi forces, the greatest of contemporary German thinkers, Heidegger, was conducting a seminar on Nietzsche. He revealed what was derived from Descartes, the pioneer by whom 'was formed for the first time that resolute approach through which the modern technology of mechanical energy has become possible, and with it, metaphysically speaking, the world of today and its mankind'. The war of Nietzsche against Descartes would not take place.

Heidegger added, bringing the loftiest metaphysics into relation to the most burning topicality, just after June 1940: 'At the present time we have recently witnessed the working of a mysterious law of history, namely, that it can happen one day to a people (meaning the French) that they are no longer up to the level of the metaphysics issuing from their own history, and this at this very moment when this metaphysics has been transformed into an absolute.'

'No longer up to the level'? France served as illustration, with her defeat seen as not due to lack of equipment or poor organization, as not physical but metaphysical: 'It is not enough to possess armoured cars, aeroplanes and signals apparatus, nor is it enough to have individuals who are able to operate such engines and instruments: it is not even enough for man to be able merely to master technology as though this were something neutral in itself...'

What was needed in order to be 'up to the level'? A mankind in conformity with the metaphysical truth of modern technology, 'that is, which allows itself to be totally dominated by the essence of technology, so as thereby to be capable, precisely, of directing and utilizing for itself the various processes and possibilities of technology'. What was here proved by June 1940, others were later to prove by 'Stalin organs' or Patton's tanks, and so on, down to the B52s.

Heidegger made pro-Nazi speeches during a few months of 1933. In this fact the problem of the German intelligentsia of our century is circumscribed – that intelligentsia which cannot conceive 'revolution' or 'nation' without taking up absolute positions, either for or against, but almost always frenzied ones. Let us leave to those learned men who are so fortunate as to have avoided this wretchedness the task of showing that it is exclusively a German wretchedness – that we ought to burn Heidegger at the stake for his six months' sympathy with National-Socialism, while glossing over the fifty years spent by others in hailing the (national) socialism of the fatherland of the Gulag Archipelago.

More generally: when he says that the defeated French were not sufficiently 'up to the level' of the demands of technological mastery of the world, Heidegger does not seem to be 'Nazi'. Judging the French to be 'not sufficiently up to the level', instead of finding the Germans too much up to that level, amounts to sharing the opinions inculcated to the man in the street. The American in his giant bomber is up to that level, over Vietnam. The Russian despot firing off his satellites in clusters can equally claim to be up to the level of what he calls the 'technical and scientific revolution'. That 'metaphysics transformed into an absolute', after having filled the heads of thinking men, is now spread all over the front page, sustaining the large-scale circulation of newsprint and of conflagrations.

Heidegger did not remain settled in those ideas, which he had the honesty to publish, and which the admirers of the various ruling powers, established or to be established, could take up as they wished. Long before him, the master thinkers had proclaimed that being 'up to the level' means being up to the level of the tank, or higher, flying in an aeroplane, or higher, at the level of the Kremlin and the Pentagon, or higher still, at 6,000 feet above any inhabited locality ... The dominant point of view of the dominator.

And what if the 'strange defeat' resulted not from failing to be up to that level but from *trying* to be? By which the France of 1940 was not so much lagging behind history as ahead of the 'great powers' of today, which appear great because they are *overwhelming* – even more so one over the other than one by the other.

And what if the 'strange defeat' could be, in its turn, undone by those alone who renounce all 'levels', those who – at the very moment when that metaphysics was transformed into an absolute – 'dreamed', as Marc Bloch tells us, 'of a modern type of warfare waged by guerillas against tanks and motorized detachments'. That dream, more out-of-date than any idea of a master thinker ever was, is unspeakably vulgar, it amounts to no longer thinking in terms of domination, but of resisting the structures of domination, blowing them to pieces, rediscovering the foot-soldier beneath the motorized one, and beneath the foot-soldier the guerilla – outside the master, the free mortal. A dream, extremely mean from the standpoint of metaphysics, in which the historian from the Sorbonne who had suffered the 'strange defeat' began to think like a guerilla of the antipodes before becoming 'Narbonne', the executed Resistance fighter: 'In Rennes I saw a German column, composed for the most part of motorcyclists, moving unopposed down the Boulevard Sévigné, and all the old instincts of the footslogger stirred in me ... I was badly tempted ... to lie in wait for that damned column at the corner of some spinney of the Breton countryside, which is so admirably suited by nature for the mounting of ambushes ... I am quite certain that three-quarters of the men would have jumped at the chance of playing a game like that. But, alas, the regulations had never envisaged such a possibility.'

The great Western

How does one make a desert? By mobilizing all the forces of destruction: we should be ungracious not to agree to that, we children born grey-haired in the epoch called by Lenin the epoch of 'wars and revolutions'.

With men who stake everything at the heart of the storm, because at that centre they escape from the 'quicksand' of common uncertainties and touch Descartes's rock of self-certainty. Even if this be in the greatest objective uncertainty of the moment which, scientifically and in solitude, they master. *On s'engage, et puis on voit* (one joins battle, and then one gets a clear view), says Lenin, quoting Napoleon. Then he joins battle with the mob, and beats them down.

In a game in which everything is at stake, a game in which we are torn away from our 'petty problems', from our sentimental or even religious ties, from 'spontaneity', economism and aestheticism – in short, from every interest that is immediately our own. In order to see ourselves raised to the level of the great problems of world domination, in order to transcend ourselves, *en bloc*, in the man of the future, either Hegel's god (who affirms himself by negating the world) or the Superman of Nietzsche. 'Say there must be no such passage (from the finite to the infinite), and you say there is to be no thinking. And, in sooth, animals make no such transition' (Hegel).

In a radical and final division, wherein mankind is both player and stake, called upon to decide for itself, once for all, between the spirit and the animal, the elevation of the master and the servile crowd, socialism and barbarism.

And this in the full brightness of a Noon where nothing has been played but everything is being played. Among freedmen, in the frankness of a philosophical language which ends by stating things as they will be: 'The time of the struggle for world domination draws near: it will be fought out in the name of basic philosophical doctrines' (Nietzsche).

I can, therefore I am

At the end of the Second World War, two French intellectuals set about finding where they stood in the world's course. One, Maurice Merleau-Ponty, examined the stenographic record of the great trials which Stalin organized in Moscow. The other, Jean-Paul Sartre, found in Hegel's *Phenomenology of the Spirit* the same intellectual passions which caused the Bolshevik leaders to become filled with dread, to kill themselves, or to be put to death. In a century and a half nothing had changed, except that the esoteric treatise had been re-written as the stenographic record of world events. The 'subjects' endeavour once more to discard all 'subjectivism', so as the better to coincide with the 'rock', the driving-force of history (known in those days as 'the socialist fatherland'). The thoughts and works of Sartre and Merleau-Ponty were catalogued under the heading 'existentialism', and as such they were promptly 'refuted'. The scenery has varied, refutations have followed refutations, but the same play has now been performed for two centuries: the subject is still running, pursued by the shadow of his subjectivism, trying to leap into the central fire that governs all things. With the improvement in means of communication, he sets off to the antipodes, teaching, on his outward journey, progress, historical take-off or revolution to peoples whom he does not know, and being taught himself on his return. He proclaims yet again the final world conflict, changing its geography only to tell the same story. If the subject can't change, perhaps he has to find a new public?

Unchanged beneath the sun of Asia or of America is that mental theatre in which the 'ego' which has been modern for several centuries in Europe assigns himself the task of coinciding with the centre of the world. The most meticulous of scholars still argue about who it is that Descartes means when he prepares the banner of 'I doubt, therefore I think: I think, therefore I am'. On the pretext of making it more precise, or of refuting it, speculative minds have sometimes refined the formulation and sometimes made it cruder: 'The concept of reality is equivalent to the concept of activity ... To say that everything in the self is reality is to say that the self is *solely* active; it is self merely insofar as it is active ...' (Fichte). At the root of all radicalisms we still find the *Cogito* ('I think'), if it is true that being radical means grasping things by the root, and that 'for man the root is man himself' (Marx).

'I doubt' has been translated as 'I kill', 'I make war', 'I break away', 'I make revolution'. 'I think' has been dialecticized into 'you think better than I do, on my behalf'. A world dimension has been given to 'I am': 'All the beauty, all the sublimity that we have attributed to things real or imaginary, I want to claim as the property and product of Man, as his finest apologia. Man as poet, thinker, god, love, power: the kingly munificence with which he has endowed everything, so as to impoverish and

sadden himself! That was, until that time, his greatest abnega-
tion – the fact that he admired and adored, and had been able to
hide from himself that it was he who had created the very
object of his admiration' (Nietzsche).

For all the abstractors of quintessences who think they have
long since gone beyond that – have they not also refuted humanism? – Nietzsche lays it on the line: 'To "humanize" the world
means to feel ourselves ever more and more masters upon
earth.' The hypnotist refutes humanism or anti-humanism,
objectivism or subjectivism, hurling one pebble after another
into the same pool of the *Cogito*: the rings that he makes are all
just as prettily concentric, and the point which is the centre of
the world still preoccupies minds forgetful of ephemeral residues.

The promised wealth

The manners change, but the claim to coincide with the centre
of the world remains – that claim to cast in the bronze of history
an 'I think' that shall be the absolute and unshakeable foundation of the truth, whether or not there be graven on the
pedestal the original Cartesian formula: *fundamentum absolutum
inconcussum veritatis*. There are those who cast themselves in the
mould and those who worship the one and only beneficiary,
there are leaders who turn their souls to bronze and sub-
leaders who lend bronze a soul – all chase the same hare released
by the master thinkers, a pretty mechanical device whose fore-
paws beat out 'I think' while its followers master the globe.

'Why I am so wise', 'Why I am so clever', 'why I write such
excellent books', 'why I am a fatality'. By choosing such unseemly titles for the chapters of his *Ecce Homo*, Nietzsche gave
warning, say his biographers, of the madness that was soon to
take him in its grip. Unless Nietzsche was the only one who
dared to express a passion which, for all that it comes out less
directly in their case, is no less insistent in the other master
thinkers. All of them considered, with Fichte, that, 'if the word
"philosophy" is to designate anything specific, it must designate
precisely this science' – that is, *their* science. All of them explained in their books why they wrote such good ones and,

placing themselves historically, analysed why they were a fatality for the world. Hegel did not claim to be situated at the end of history, and if he has naïvely been accused of so doing it is because, where history was concerned, he prided himself not on saying the last word but the most subtle.

Raphael was 'a painter': he was dependent on the division of labour, 'shut up within the limits of a particular art', whereas 'in a communist society, there are no painters but only people who engage in painting among other activities' (Marx). The idea seems straightforward enough: who wants the dreariness of working alone? Who would not be willing to call 'alienation' the corner where he is wilting? From where, though, do we get the notion that it was Mozart's 'limitation' to be, not a sculptor or a tight-rope walker, but 'only' a musician? From what standpoint does it seem self-evident that the ideal 'communist organization of society' must break down the 'limitation' that causes there to be 'painters, sculptors, etc., who are only that and nothing more'? Who tells us that these limitations are to be compared to the 'local barriers' and 'national frontiers' which, so Marx wagers, will be lifted by future mankind?

Didn't Mozart have eyes to see the work of Raphael? And wouldn't Raphael have had ears to hear plainchant? Why must it absolutely be the case that *listening* to music is *less* than making it: isn't it composed while one listens to it and in order that it may be listened to? Doesn't the listener recompose it in his turn? No, Mozart has to be, as well as a musician, also an architect, a novelist, a film-maker, a plumber, a peasant, and, maybe, a People's Commissar, or else he remains a 'victim' of the division of labour. Not because his rich protectors eventually left him to die of hunger, but because it was not given unto him to be a poly-artist or total man. It was not so much of money – that false wealth of the bourgeoisie – that he was deprived, but of that true promised wealth of Marx's communism: 'The rich human being is ... the human being *in need* of a totality of human manifestations of life – the man in whom his own realization exists as an inner necessity ...'

In so far as Raphael was 'only' a painter, all other human activities 'limited' him. Perhaps he appreciated them with great subtlety and sensitivity; that matters little to the master thinker. The true wealth lies in making oneself, in being, everything. By not being a dancer one loses one's legs, by not appearing on the stage one erases one's face, by not painting one sacrifices one's right arm, and the 'division of labour' threatens to leave us with only ten fingers and two ears, like that poor musician who was 'only' Mozart.

What is the immense difference between making music and listening to it (in which case it is supposed to elude us)? It is usual to present Mozart as the absolute and unshakable foundation of music, or at least of Mozartian music. Let Marx be seen as a philosopher of praxis, a dialectical materialist, a phenomenologist, a scholar. Fine! But let it be acknowledged that he thinks like all the other master thinkers in the domain of 'I-think-therefore-I-am': I make music, therefore it does not elude me. I will manifest the human totality of life, therefore nothing will elude me. Raphael is so much alienated by the division of labour that he fails to paint 'why I am such a good painter', that he does not explain in verse 'why I am so clever', and that he does not enclose a statue of 'myself as fatality' in a temple he has designed as his finest 'apologia'.

The division of labour is a wretched business because it divides the mastery of 'I-think-therefore-I-am' and is thereby shown to be difficult, if not impossible, to master. This lets us suspect why the anarchy of the capitalist market is denounced by all the master thinkers – not because it is capitalist, but because it is anarchy.

Exclusion-inclusion

The movement in which the subject withdraws into himself, doubting, thinking and being, has been accompanied, since the relation which Descartes deduced from this, by a violent rejection which puts 'outside of me' the madman, soon caught up with, in the seventeenth century, by all those lousinesses of the reason that need to be locked up. The 'gesture that excludes' (Foucault) does not remain forever the discreet and barely expressed accompaniment of the *Cogito*. The master thinkers bring forth the 'you do not think' which dwelt within the dominating act of 'I think': the thing (Fichte's 'non-self'), the other (in Hegel's duel), *Capital*, the nihilistic history of the *plebs* – always, a 'don't think' hurls at 'I think' its 'supreme' challenge.

Thus, we shake 'I think' when we demand that it remain something outside itself. Outside the subject is the object ('if I am to present anything at all, I must oppose it to the presenting self', that is, to myself – Fichte). To one side still are inter-subjectivity, production-relations and the perpetual joy of becoming ... The polemic against the master's idealism ends only in making his idealism more polemical, that is, making his will to dominate more imperial. The successive master thinkers bring to light a 'residue' and throw it in each other's faces as the forgotten factor which cancels out the finest speculative constructions: but it is always a *residue to be conquered*, a 'don't think' which is only a 'not yet thought', something not yet dominated. You have seen the fight against the thing, but you have forgotten other people. You carefully reflect the relation to the other as a relation of domination, but you have missed out the movement of the masses, by supposing that they are passive. You have conceived the revolution, but not the chaos of becoming from which it does not escape ... The problems change their terms, but the solution stays the same: achieve mastery, mastery, this is the Law and the Prophets!

God as vicious circle

The Ego-Master swells up to the size of the universe, while the whole universe is, 'so to speak, back-to-back with this con-sciousness'. The Ego makes itself a 'receptacle for all and every-thing' (Hegel). He who finds this statement too indecently idealist replaces the Ego by a Board of Directors practising a democratic 'round table', that is, a discussion without top or tail, but carried on among bosses. Or by a Central Committee equipped more traditionally with its microscope and binoculars, meaning its short-term and long-term Marxism-Leninism. Was it not discovered, in the second half of the twentieth century, that the 'I think' subject was not necessarily a man? Limited companies, like socialist societies, all argue about the advantages and disadvantages of collective leadership: 'I think' may not be an individual, but remains nevertheless a General Headquarters.

Descartes was, it has been said, that 'French horseman who set off at such a fine pace'. He has never stopped riding – the cowboy continually crossing a 'new frontier', an officer in the Red Cavalry, or a proletarian 'storming Heaven' in Marx's head. The subject of history will not find himself 'in truth' until he has completed his journey round the world and the world has been completely dominated. Thus spake the master thinkers, enclosing all thought in a circle which the young Descartes had mentioned, so to speak, in passing: I think, therefore God exists, *Cogito ergo Deus est*.

Having become lord and possessor of the world, I shall find myself. In order to acquire this possession and lordship I need a method, I need to be, originally, a conqueror. I need to have found myself from the outset. This is circular thinking. For example, Descartes says that God guarantees that those of my ideas that are clear and distinct are true, but God is true for me only because my clear and distinct ideas, the order of my reasoning, lead to him. The true is the subject, the subject is at the beginning, but the true, likewise, is only the result (Hegel). Communism is 'the riddle of history solved', but about communism we know, as it were, nothing, since we don't boil 'the stewpots of the future' (Marx). The subject flees from himself in order to conquer the world, and the world gathers together within the subject. A vicious circle if ever there was one, but this vice is not nothing: both the world and the subject, perpetually hurled from one to the other, bounce back.

It is useless, having reached this point, to deplore the fact that Man is so keen to take himself for God. A tear once shed upon these great illusions and crazy hopes, we think we can now return to a better sort of discretion. Alas, the circle precedes that 'drama of atheistic humanism' which offers merely a vulgarization thereof; the connection stretches a long way farther back than Descartes, even, if we follow the meticulous genealogy that Heidegger gives for it, entitling it the 'onto-theo-logical' circle.

We call 'ontological' our consideration of being in general, as a whole, that being common to the chimera of our dreams, a door-handle, a lark, little Chinese, Mao Tse-tung, and God, whom we say exists, or has existed. 'Theological' applies to our investigation of that which *is* in those beings which, as Aristotle already said, are more or less beings: he calls 'divine', or 'God,' that which in beings *is* the most – any connection with a personal being regarded as creator of heaven and earth constituting an absolute anachronism. (On the contrary, it was this 'creator' to whom it happened that he was conceived in Aristotle's categories.) All of us, Raphael included, will not be truly ourselves except under communism, the communist being thereby showing that he is more perfectly a being than the alienated quasi-non-being of the division of labour and capitalism: this is a statement just as perfectly atheistic as it is theological. It is useless to compel a Christian to discover his own offspring in the so-called Marxist religion: Christian 'philosophy' and Marxist 'philosophy' are essentially the children of one and the same project of mastery, whenever they intermingle to give orders to the world.

Being finds expression in 'many ways,' Aristotle calmly observed. This is said 'in general' of the world, and very 'specially' of the divine. This variety of ways closes in a circle when domination of the world comes on to the agenda. Mastery takes everything as its objective, and is thereby ontological: it recognizes nothing outside itself, staking all on one throw, and is thereby theological: 'Around the hero everything turns to tragedy, around the demi-god everything becomes a satirical game; around the god everything is – how shall we put it – perhaps the world' (Nietzsche).

A vicious circle, the Copernican revolution, the onto-theological circle: the crown of the modern master.

The speculative proposition

Hegel explains that the appearance of a vicious circle enshrines the highest wisdom when he comments on the style of his discourses and the twisting and turning of his approach: 'this course that generates itself, going forth from, and returning into, itself'. By the name of 'dialectical movement' or 'speculative proposition' Hegel defines nothing other than the grand style of modern mastery: it not only dominates things from without (like other branches of knowledge, even mathematics, according to the master thinkers), it wants to possess them from within – a royal road that cannot be followed in the 'dressing-gown' of common sense, because one must agree to lose oneself totally in it in order to win everything.

When I say that the tree is green, the tree is called the *subject* of my proposition and the greenness with which I qualify the tree is its *predicate*. In autumn the tree will be yellow rather than green, so that it is green only by the accident of spring. The leek, too, is green. Therefore, greenness does not belong to the tree, any more than the tree to greenness. Between the subject and the predicate of an ordinary sentence the relation is only accidental: I perceive in this way, but I might see things differently. When I say 'God is being', the contrary is true: the subject (God) passes over entirely into the predicate (being), since, if the predicate were lacking, the subject would no longer exist as the subject. Furthermore, given the 'conditions of mental culture' required, Hegel explains, 'thinking finds the subject immediately in the predicate': in our ontotheological culture, being is not without something divine to it.

One would like to pull up here, noting that there are a few shreds of theology hanging about Hegel: after all, as a young man, he was a theological student! Official theology's hash having been settled implicitly in all our universities, the only thing that might be needed would be to dust those old memories of his off the eternally living, even revolutionary, side of Hegelian dialectics.

Unfortunately for them, though, these trimming operations overlook the fact that Hegel did not restrict to God the use of the speculative proposition. Every village has its 'Frenchmen who died for France', and its memorials erected to that speculative proposition. Hegel would have shown without difficulty that the subject ('Frenchmen') disappears in the predicate ('France'), having himself made 'dying for' . . . the speculative activity par excellence. Whereas Frenchmen die so that France may live, official France, commemorating them, lives by the death of Frenchmen: the subject has passed over into the predicate and the predicate has become the subject. If we replace 'France' by 'the Revolution', and 'Frenchmen' by 'proletarians', we get a fresh lot of soldiers for the speculative proposition.

After a few gymnastic dialectics, one can discover the speculative proposition in a condensed form, with the verb remaining implicit. Thus, the 'dictatorship of the proletariat', in which the initial subject (proletarians exercising dictatorship) quickly disappears in the predicate (dictatorship), which in its turn becomes the subject (dictatorship exercised over the proletariat).

The speculative proposition (the dialectical movement) functions like a logical machine: it can be made to reproduce the modern concepts of 'God', 'fatherland', 'state', 'revolution one and indivisible', etc., which, although generally accepted, allow the hand of the master to show through. The subject has to abolish itself in the predicate so that the predicate may live as the subject: citizens and revolutionaries have to die for the fatherland (in the latter case, the socialist fatherland) because this fatherland lives by their death. The speculative proposition is the logical generalization of the 'supreme test' administered by the master to the slave in our epoch.

'Speculation' sounds antiquated to our chaste ears, so let us say: science. 'Proposition' sounds hardly any better, so let us say: experiment. Did Hegel twirl his tongue seven times too often in the vocabulary of the faculties of logic or theology? Let us hearken to 'the most critical of all questions' when Nietzsche formulates this in modern prose: 'Whether science is in a position to furnish goals for human action, after it has proved that it can take them away and annihilate them – and then would be the time for a process of experimenting in which every kind of heroism could satisfy itself, an experimenting for centuries, which would put into the shade all the great labours and sacrifices of previous history.' What is Hegel getting at when he says that the subject must find itself again in its predicate, its object? Nietzsche goes on: 'Science has not hitherto built its Cyclopic structures; for that also the time will come.'

How a master thinker assembles his ideas

God? Everything depends on what one means by a word that, in itself, is empty. 'For this reason it may be expedient to avoid the name "God".' Hegel, gently here, suggests that the famous atheism which is the pride of the modern thinkers might amount to nothing but a mere matter of words. Is not what signifies, in proofs of the existence of God, more than just a word, that movement of the proof which is at once elevation and demonstration?

Demonstration in the sense in which 'to deal with anything in a speculative or philosophical way simply means to bring into connection thoughts which we already have.' What does 'bringing them into connection' mean, if not mastering them, adopting the unifying standpoint which one may call 'god', but equally well 'fatherland', or 'socialism'? So that in every case there is a geometrical *locus* for all possible questions (the 'positive' definition), that without which no question could be asked (the 'negative' definition – primary, according to Hegel): a Frenchman who does not sacrifice everything for his country sees himself suspected of desertion, for what would a Frenchman be without France? A proletarian who abandons the camp of socialism is a renegade; a man without religion is an animal (Hegel).

Elevation in so far as we do not leave a finite world in order to visit an infinite being: the proofs of the existence of God make, according to Hegel, a movement within, and not a tourist trip. Conceiving things as finite (proofs '*ex contingentia mundi*') amounts to conceiving the necessary as that which defines, not as another world: 'Appearance is the arising and passing away that does not itself arise and pass away, but is "in itself", and constitutes the actuality and the movement of the life of truth.'

The standpoint of God, this 'Appearance', is not that of another world but a different standpoint in relation to the same world: the standpoint of the master. And the master's standpoint does not remain external to what it dominates, but expresses the most internal mastery, that which dominates the circulation of everything in the speculative proposition. What matters in the becoming-predicate of the subject and in the becoming-subject of the predicate is that the movement thus engendered wins everything without ever having to leave itself: the appearance of the world is both mastery of the appearance and appearance of the mastery. And so, elevation.

The speculative proposition was at first described as 'infinite intuition of the world'. What does infinite intuition mean? 'The finite is characterized, for Hegel, by fixity. Fixing means setting, in the sense of setting something aside, and consequently setting it in antagonism ... Thus, for finiteness, all determination, everything determined, is surrounded by what is not determined, by nothingness ... If this is the finite, then the infinite (*Unendliche*) is that position which, on the contrary, does not make the antagonists disappear but retains them in their antagonism within their very unification' (Heidegger). This unifying standpoint masters the antagonisms, not so much like a god dominating from Olympus as like a General Bonaparte sizing up a battlefield. The world is 'unity which has within it all the contradictions' (Heidegger) and the world spirit is the master of the situation.

The standpoint of God consists no longer of seeing everything while being itself locatable nowhere, plumbing all hearts and loins because never itself shut up in one heart. Sartre blamed Mauriac for claiming to see what was going on inside the characters in his novels: he would not be able to make the same objection regarding the master thinkers, who do not undertake to break into everyone's conscience. For them it is enough to say that the world is a battlefield, and that therein anyone at all employs all his weapons, even the most secret. The struggle is fought out to the death, until each camp has brought all its batteries into action, until the humblest combatant has fired his last shot. It is the common principle of domestic 'scenes'.

It is not so much the assumption of the gods as the Flight of the Eagle that governs the plan of action of the master thinkers.

Unseemly questions

The modern master does not reject any of our questions: on the contrary, he helps us to formulate them: more than that, he himself asks them all. He does not let himself be shut up in any prejudice, he rejects the 'local' certainties of common sense in the name of mankind: 'Since the man of common sense makes his appeal to feeling, to an oracle within his breast, he is finished and done with anyone who does not agree ... In other words, he tramples underfoot the roots of humanity' (Hegel). The master will re-establish the contact thus broken off; he leaves no one in his lonely corner, he has something to say to everybody, he takes humanity by the root, what matters is to say everything, and he will not be short of words: 'For it is the nature of humanity to press onward to agreement with others; human nature only really exists in an achieved community of minds.'

If we look more closely, we see that the master thinker asks all the questions except one, the question of the whole that all these questions form together. If, with Hegel, we make God the geometrical (or, more precisely, the speculative) *locus* of all questions we ought not to be surprised when we see him violently reject the suggestion made by Kant that this 'God' might, in his turn, ask himself about himself: 'I am from eternity to eternity, besides me there is nothing, unless what exists by my will; but whence then am I?' This is dread, observes Hegel: 'Here everything sinks under us, and floats without support or foothold.' Our philosopher has long since got over the 'neurasthenia' of his adolescence, and plugs the hole against this dread by forbidding the question: 'There is one thing which speculative reason must above all else "allow to go", and that is the putting of such a question as "Whence am I?" into the mouth of the absolutely necessary and unconditioned. As if that outside of which nothing exists unless through its will, that which is simply infinite, could look beyond itself for an other than itself, and ask about something beyond itself.' If it is I who ask all the questions, I cannot be questioned: the totality of all questions does not question.

We see the same Operation Sealed-Lips when it is Man who questions himself: 'When you ask about the creation of nature and man, you are abstracting, in so doing, from man and nature ... Don't think, don't ask me, for as soon as you think and ask, your *abstraction* from the existence of nature and man has no meaning.' This is obvious to 'a reasonable mind', says Marx, as a good master thinker. To question is, Hegelianly, to 'abstract', that is, to 'conceive', that is, to 'dominate': the last question is asked by the one who is the last to dominate, the one who cannot be questioned in his turn. That, says Marx, would be 'absurd'. I question all the beings, even about their absences and disappearances, even though I could not question them unless they had been at one time 'present' to me in their own way. I can abstract from this presence before every fact, past, present or to come, bar one: I cannot abstract from my power to abstract: in so far as it is I who ask the questions, I no longer question myself ... So speaks the self-conceit of the master.

Let us now assume that it is not we men that have asked the first and last questions, and still less God. In that case we shall have to call 'world' and 'becoming' that which jostles us and questions us, the '*locus*' of all possible questions. A master thinker was to present, in the same way as before, this world as something that cannot be questioned in its turn: without meaning, without value, without purpose – 'the total value of the world cannot be valued' (Nietzsche). There are those who grow desperate in questioning back the one who asks all the questions, such as the 'passive nihilists' who run after a meaning while knowing that it can exist only as the meaning of the course they run: the will to despair. Nietzsche, as an 'active nihilist', assumed the power of the question, which is the power of all the questions, as Hegel assumed God and Marx assumed Man.

God, Man, the World: three sources of all questions which cannot themselves be questioned. It is they that determine 'in the last instance' and reply 'in the last analysis'. Let us pass over the economic, sociological and literary variants; it is always a matter of the supreme mastery held by the master. Actually, the three '*loci*' in which the master thinkers imagined the Ultimate to lie were not accidental. The metaphysics of the eighteenth century divided, scholastically, the last questions which it proposed to deal with into four chapters: ontology (or 'general metaphysics'), cosmology, psychology, and natural theology (these last three chapters, together, forming the metaphysics called 'special', in contrast to 'general').

The science of the master thinkers is a metaphysics in the

sense in which the eighteenth century defined the latter as being both 'the science which includes the first principles of human cognition' and 'the science of the most universal properties (predicates) of all things' (Kant). In this sense, metaphysics is 'general', or, as Heidegger has it, 'catholic' (from the Greek word meaning directed towards the entirety of beings, towards things taken as a whole).

The 'speculative proposition' operation consists in finding the subject of these catholic predicates (properties) which enable us to conceive the world as the world and each thing as something. Hegel was to find his subject in the chapter 'natural theology': Marx was to Marxify the chapter 'psychology', turning it into 'anthropology': Nietzsche was to take over the chapter 'cosmology'. In each case, knowledge was closed off by sticking together the special metaphysics (from which the last subjects were taken) and the general metaphysics (which provided the 'predicates'). This sticking-together was called 'the end of metaphysics', and did not take place without battles between giants, each disputing the other's right to sum up the world's wisdom in this chapter of special metaphysics rather than that one: Hegel was too theological for the neighbouring masters, Marx too humanistic, Nietzsche too naturalistic.

What would the last word be? Though they quarrelled about it, none of them doubted its existence, that last word on the 'nature' of humanity which would enable us to regulate 'mutual agreement' and institute 'the community of minds' – regulate and institute with a master's hand, that goes without saying: 'The anti-human, the merely animal, consists in staying within the sphere of feeling, and being able to communicate only at that level' (Hegel). Come now! Can one communicate through feeling? Outside the range of that rational fist of the speculative proposition which says everything about everything?

The major affirmation

The non-true is a degree, a moment and a one-sided perception of the truth: 'Nor *is* there such a thing as the false, any more than there *is* something evil. The evil and the false, to be sure, are not as bad as the devil...' (Hegel). Something that looks like evil may give rise to good: history progresses through its 'bad side', and, Marx adds cheerfully (he is discussing child labour in factories), 'in history as in nature, corruption is the laboratory of life'. Ugliness itself ought not to be really ugly, whispered Zarathustra: when that which is heavier and blacker than anything else in the world slides into one's throat, one should imitate the shepherd: 'He bit with a strong bite! Far away did he spit the head of the serpent: and sprang up.' The master is master of the true as of the false, of good and evil, of the ugly just as much as of the beautiful, because truer, more beautiful and better than all these contrasts is mastery itself. Being able not to err is by far superior to not being able to err, said Descartes. Being *and* non-being, false *and* true, the masters dominate, not letting themselves be squeezed into the choice but claiming to grasp 'the affirmative aspect of the relationship as a whole' (Hegel).

On the horizon of all the master thinkers is 'the ideal of the most world-approving, exuberant and vivacious man, who has not only learnt to compromise and make arrangement with that which was and is, but wishes to have it again *as it was and is*, for all eternity...'

Nietzsche did not conceal the disturbing side of this ideal. The 'most world-approving' man is followed, as though by his shadow, by the donkey that says 'yea' to everything and takes all burdens on his back. Behind the world approver is there a yes-man? Does our century – more Nietzschean still, perhaps – no longer allow us to distinguish between shadow and reality? Does wanting the master's hay mean acting the donkey?

The minor affirmations

The ideal man is, for the master thinkers, no sweet, unattainable dream but a programme. Their reading of the past provides the basis for this project's feasibility – not that they are content to decipher history 'objectively', with the resources of the age. Much more than that: their objectivity takes for its objective precisely the discovering at each moment of history of the key to that moment, what affirms and produces it. In other words, it is their very 'objectivity' that causes them to recover the historical object *par excellence*, that which affirms 'the riddle solved'. (On the basis of this common method, the riddle will subsequently be revealed as 'self-consciousness', 'communism' or 'the superman').

Historical discussion of the accuracy of the analyses of the past which have been offered will never eliminate the intrinsic power of these analyses, which is not so much to give an account of the past as to programme the future. For example, Hegel's interpretation of the Protestant Reformation. He cuts it to his own measurements, intending to make of it the anticipated German rejoinder to the French Revolution. The latter poses, point-blank, the question of the modern state: the German Reformation is held to have introduced what that state lacks – the cultural, religious and ideological preparation of the masses. Religion and the state: 'It is an enormous mistake either to separate these inseparable opposites or to identify them or to declare that they are indifferent to one another'. Religion affirms the state, the state affirms religion.

How does the Reformation illuminate this problem of problems, the 'monstrous blunder of our times'? In that by it 'the divine spirit introduces itself into actuality'. What does this mean? Three things: instead of *chastity*, marriage of the clergy; instead of the vow of *poverty*, work and 'gainful activity'; instead of monastic withdrawal from the world, or the ecclesiastical hierarchy with the vow of *obedience*, obedience to the law and to the state. In short, the manners and customs needed for the life of the modern state: 'the ethical dignity of *marriage* is devalued by the "higher" institutionalized *chastity* of priests, monks and nuns; the diligence, work and activity by which *property* is acquired is abrogated by the "higher" institutionalized vow of *poverty* ... Instead of *honesty* in transactions and intelligent participation in common concerns of the community, a *blind obedience* to authorities without right or duty is demanded. In summary, the enslavement of conscience inevitably follows'. In short: Family, Labour, Fatherland!

It is more than dubious whether this Hegelian interpretation correctly describes religious life before and after Luther (even though many sociologists have copied it). There is no point in quibbling, what matters is the future: Hegel asks about the conditions needed if the modern world and the modern state are to be affirmed. He determines what our 'religion' must be, in this connection: modern man has to work socially, take a stand politically, and live as a family man. If Hegel's perception of the past is to be taken with a pinch of salt, his anticipation of the standardizations to come is striking.

Between the major affirmation of everything and the minor down-to-earth affirmations, between the true that wishes to be itself and the religion of the family, for the master thinkers things go round and round. Thus, Marx, Engels and Lenin were indeed to see the factory as a 'mitigated prison' (Fourier) and yet to approve of it, with all its military discipline, because it is with military discipline that the proletariat is supposed first to carry out the revolution, and then to exercise its dictatorship. The freest of them all, who puts art highest, was nevertheless to find a still higher level in 'Art as it appears without the artist, i.e., as a body, an organization (the Prussian Officers' Corps, the Order of the Jesuits)' (Nietzsche).

Between the minor disciplines of the major affirmation and the major affirmation of the minor disciplines, as between nineteenth-century thought and twentieth-century standardizations, is it not easy to make out the differences? But who perceives the slippage of these differences, that they cannot be maintained, that the power of the master is not to be shared? The master's power cannot be divided by the master himself: it can be resisted and thereby held back and reduced, but this will not be done by the master or by the thought of the master thinkers.

Why this long way round?

From the standpoint of history, one lifetime is no time at all. And yet I have had several opportunities to see the majority of Frenchmen behave like skunks. Or, where some of them were concerned, like cowardly conniving sheep. I know myself well enough to realize that I share the defects and the dispositions of this majority, and am no better than they are, even if sometimes an accident of birth has deprived me of the possibility to behave shamefully.

On this somewhat mucky ground one beholds with all the greater admiration those who, without being compelled by their particular situation, refused to join in the filthiness. In the resistance to the Nazi occupation and in the resistance to the colonial war in Algeria, with its massacres and tortures, certain priests played a decisive part, often despite the attitude taken by their hierarchy, or flatly in opposition to it. I respect them because I envy their courage, because I owe to them the lives of some who are very close to me, and, in general, because, without them, the air in France would be unbreathable. Rare are the struggles against injustice of one kind or another in which one doesn't come upon them, here or there in the poor districts and out-of-the-way factories.

Society being what it is, an individual has few opportunities to exchange ideas with persons who do not belong to his everyday circle. As for discussion by way of the printed word, that presents more risks of misunderstanding than chances of enlightenment, having regard to the surrounding authoritarianism which makes the atmosphere so academic, learned and pasteurized. Hence these preliminaries.

May 1968 was the occasion for some courageous priests, certain of whom had always taken up a challenging attitude, to meet together and pool their thoughts: 'We need to realize that God does not mean at all lordship, hierarchy, authority, providence, the technocrat who has made a plan which is working out more or less well, but anyway, working out – that God is, precisely, gratuituousness, self-effacement in the night, chaos in the greyness of everyday life . . .'

There is nothing less authoritarian than these two thousand French priests. The platform around which they rally contains three points: 'labour, marriage, political activity', says the newspaper *Le Monde* (18 January 1972). They proclaim three freedoms which break with the tradition (at least with the present tradition . . .) of the church: 'Let us say, indeed: right to work and right to marry, but let us make it plain: these are imperatives of commitment.'

Not having a soul educated in the sacred mysteries, none of these points can offend me, taken separately, but taken as a whole they do, when they are said to sum up the extreme form of present-day opposition to clericalism. The same set of breaks with tradition enabled Hegel to define the 'morality' needed for stabilizing the modern state and standardizing its inhabitants. It is not these breaks in themselves that I am talking about – those who make them are the best judges of the need for them – but their politico-philosophical implications, their contestatory point. Did not these breaks serve, according to Hegel, to integrate society, by making religion the safeguard of public order?

How such a platform eventually reveals its ambiguity, lending itself to authoritarian interpretations and not only to contestatory ones, will perhaps be shown to us by the priests concerned, who are now scattered in various hot spots. The platform itself conforms discreetly to paragraph 552 of the *Encyclopaedia of the Philosophical Sciences*, in which 'the religious spirit and the ethical meaning of the state' (more precisely, what is left of the modernized church and what is preparing to be the rational state) 'are the only firm guarantees of a good life, when they mutually respect each other and co-operate' (Hegel). What, indeed, offers less of a challenge to the authority of the modern state than a religious conception of politics accompanied by a political conception of religion?

The Jerusalem of Western metaphysics

Modern clericalism wishes to be scientific: the believer is to bow down before the God of the philosophers and the scholars, or whatever is left of him after he has been through the mincer of the human sciences. The ontological proof of the existence of God is no longer offered, but only the ontopolitical proof of the existence of the believer: a good Christian is the one who votes as he ought.

Clerically reinforced, ontopolitical election claims ('to change life') are presented as onto-theo-political crusades ('the liberation of man'). And France, voting, becomes the Jerusalem of Western metaphysics. The common programme transforms 'everything', that is, being as such (in general metaphysics), with the unions of university teachers causing its truth to exist, while the Christians manifest its goodness, and the artists glorify its beauty. Thus, the 'cultural workers' have their role to play in *metaphysica specialis* and define the *Verum Unum, Bonum* of the programme. The Christian clergy are needed for the staging of the play and are assured that they will feel at home in it. Sometimes, dialectics will mix the whole lot together in its speculative proposition: God has become a programme and the programme is God. Amen.

And yet, God is God. Exploitation is exploitation. All dictatorship is dictatorship. A camp is a camp. After a hundred years of speculative exploits, it is good to come back to that and allow oneself to be definitively 'transcended' by dialectics. Everything is not in everything, these despised tautologies have the merit of specifying: at the same time, they refer us back to experience, but never to the monologue of the big smarty-boots who knows everything. It would be better to be backward Russian peasants. Those who were brought together in the camps: idealists of every hue, fringe-people, vermin, oppositionists . . . All those who were not in the programme.

Clavel signs, speaks with his own voice. He is an individual, not an organization. He comes into the open, and checks for himself the programme of government. That did not take long. The *Nouvelle Critique*, the review of the French Communist Party's intellectuals, treated him as an Inquisitor in its issue of March 1976. Behold here the petty bargaining of a grand alliance: if you forget Gulag, we'll forget the Inquisition; if you'll leave us to our temporal affairs, we won't cast doubt on your realm of the spirit. This is the policy of 'outstretched dirty hands', was the ironical comment of Paul Thibaud, the editor of *Esprit*. It remains true that the French Communist Party is perfectly sincere: it has a lot to learn from the Churches. They are needed for the consolidation of authority. This general law was illustrated by Stalin already in 1942, in the sudden respect he showed for the power of a Church without which men will not go into battle. The same principle applies to today's elections. With God on our side.

It is so much easier to read *Capital* with piety, even with Christian piety, finding in it the memorial and martyrology of the worker of the nineteenth century – so much easier than to discover the Archipelago, the martyrology of the 'Marxist' worker, or, in the case of those who 'go Chinese' at small cost to themselves, to peruse Pasqualini's book. Clavel's devotion is not of that easy kind.

5 How I Became a Fatality
(Marx Among Others)

> 'If it were done when 'tis done, then 'twere well
> It were done quickly; if the assassination
> Could trammel up the consequence, and catch
> With his surcease success; that but this blow
> Might be the be-all and the end-all here,
> But here, upon this bank and shoal of time,
> We'd jump the life to come.'

SHAKESPEARE, *Macbeth*, I, 7

Ecce Maestro!

Criticism of the 'old' master thinker by his young and disrespectful successor follows a regular pattern: there is something missing from your programme-discourse, and in its name I hereby overthrow your programme. Outside his rational state there was the freedom of the bourgeois and of 'civil society' – that was Hegel's objection to Fichte. Beyond the bourgeois there was still the worker, said Marx, in his turn. Still further beyond, there was the world to be dominated, suggested Nietzsche. And, as though fetched out of a conjuror's hat, what do you see embodied in this 'residue'? Why, your own programme, standing on its hind legs and making a long nose at you with its front ones.

The master thinkers scrutinize each other with formidable lucidity. While granting his elder, Fichte, the merit of having inaugurated the German 'philosophical revolution', the young Hegel denounces all the more vigorously the strange Fichtean rational state in which 'the police know pretty well where every citizen is at any time of day, and what he is doing'. Hegel shows that the 'absolutely perfect self-control' postulated by the Fichtean ego is fulfilled in a generalized suspicion which aims to keep an eye on people rather than to punish them, to dissuade rather than coerce, to safeguard rather than restore. 'In the

Prussian army a foreigner is supervised by only one trustee. In Fichte's state every citizen will keep at least half a dozen people busy with supervision, accounts, etc., each of these supervisors will keep at least another half-dozen busy, and so *ad infinitum*.' In Dostoyevsky's *The Devils*, Shigalyov sums up this speculative 'map of the land of love' in the phrase: 'Starting from unlimited freedom, I arrived at unlimited despotism.'

While Hegel's critique of Fichte anticipated all the challenges to 'Chinese bureaucracy', Marx's critique of Hegel can be taken as being addressed, a century in advance, to the Russian socialist regime: a body of 'rational' officials who operate in the realm of 'the universal' and therein look after their private interests – what better definition for the Soviet *nomenklatura*, that politico-economic apparatus which covers its dachas, private shops and privileges with the red cloak of 'proletarian internationalism'? Premonitory in their turn seem Bakunin's reproaches regarding the 'authoritarianism' and the many 'unscrupulous acts' of Marx as an organizer. The beam in the eye of the neighbouring master thinker is always clearly visible.

This tactic of successive dismantlings passes through two phases. In the first place, you don't deserve your crown: everything you advocate turns out to signify a police state. Quotations and commentaries to prove this are provided. Then, next: you needed to call in the police because you 'forgot' that large section of the population which is still oppressed, and in whose name I speak. On this point it is Bakunin who brings up the rear, with the 'flower of the proletariat' in his button-hole – not that 'higher stratum, the most civilized and comfortable of the workers', whom the Marxists have in mind, but 'that great popular rabble, which, being almost untouched by any bourgeois civilization, bears within itself all the seeds of future socialism'. You cut across the police state, you turn left, and you install yourself, in your turn, as master thinker for an 'extremist' phase.

So, then, Hegel begotten by Fichte, Marx begotten by Hegel, and so on? This linear and Biblical movement goes forward within the enclosed universe of their common programme: for all that it is linear, it still goes round and round, and if it is

Biblical, then this is because it eternally passes on the baton of the same scientific promise. 'Marx is a man of very high intelligence, and, moreover, a scholar in the widest and most serious sense of that word,' says Bakunin at the very height of his quarrel with Marx. Had he not left to Marx the task of defining that 'socialism' of which his rabble bore the 'seeds'? Bakunin's political 'knocking' of Marx left his science, his political economy untouched. By leaving to Marx the task of defining the supreme matters at stake (capitalism and socialism) and claiming merely to improve the methods to be used (anti-authoritarian instead of authoritarian), Bakunin failed to quit the sacred circle of revolutionary science and its authority. Though the settlements of accounts between thinkers are as ruthless as those between the sheriffs of Wild West townships, the enemy brothers still present a united front against the Indians.

Each one noisily overturns his predecessor, each one speaks in the name of the forgotten ... but only in order to advocate the same scientific programming for them. When Marx undertakes to set Hegel's idealism materialistically 'on its feet' he employs the image whereby Hegel hails the French Revolution, in which 'man stands on his head', and claims to set the world to rights in this way, just as Fichte had done. Looked at from this angle or that, upside down or right way up, put back on its feet, it is always the same point of view that each one of the master thinkers discovers to be the other's: the science of the police state. And none of them perceives this in himself. 'Lift up your hearts, my brethren, high, higher! And do not forget your legs! Lift up also your legs, ye good dancers, and better still if you stand upon your heads!' (*Thus Spake Zarathustra*).

The order for mobilization

Generation follows generation among the masters who write out upon a 'virgin' surface the solution to the riddle of a prehistory that is nearing its end – whereas, thanks to them, true history is now starting from scratch. Should we even speak of 'generations' if we did not have in mind the golden legend of those successive 'philosophical revolutions'? Ah, the succession of venerable

heads with beards of varying length, upon the postage-stamps of
the socialist countries . . .

Soon the movement started by the master thinkers proves to
be a whirlwind, and carries them off like wisps of straw, one
after the other, even though none of them *acts*. Not materially
at any rate, on the scale that smaller minds, with the booming
largeness of the twentieth century, have given to the words
'action', 'revolution', 'history'. What does that matter? Any of
them could have written, as Nietzsche did: 'What I am telling is
the history of the next two centuries.' A strategy has its own
logic, which is a logic of action: the masters of the nineteenth
century were carried along by this logic, seizing hold of us by
means of the action which it dictates.

The history related by all the master thinkers, that of the
absolute beginning, of mastery of the world and of society, is
told by Marx, who was the first to do this systematically, as a
story of the times to come (Nietzsche was later to query this
capacity for telling stories which characterizes the 'builders of
the future'). Thereby Marx became the most 'operational' of
the master thinkers, but also the one in whom *all* of them were
operational. It was not, in fact, the details of Marx's 'scientific
predictions' that ensured the success of his doctrine. He forecast capitalist crises, each one sharper and more final, every five
years, so that he was constantly afraid that he would not have
time to finish his great work, *Capital*, owing to the imminence of
the world revolution that must result from these crises. As for
his directives for the conduct of the labour movement, these
were vague and contradictory enough to mobilize the proletarians of all countries against each another – in the European
wars (with the trenches of Verdun besprinkled on both sides
with holy water both Christian and Marxist), in the civil wars,
and in the conflicts between socialist powers. Marx is not operational in 'detail', but neither is he operational merely as a
'prophet': freer and more imaginative spirits are available for
constructing utopias. Marx is operational *on the grand scale*: he
offers a strategic grid for deciphering, and so for organizing, the
major conflicts of the modern world.

All of them had the grid of an apocalyptic finale, a Napoleonic duel between the great principles which polarize the space and time of mankind: Nature and Spirit, Slave and Master, Labour and Capital, Socialism and Barbarism. What remained was to survey the ground, mark off the camps, set out things and arrange men, to the point of making the most secret doctrine of the thinkers quite plain to all, and the daily bread of the combatants: 'Comrades, we love the sun that gives us light, but if the rich and the aggressors were to try to monopolize the sun, we should say: "Let the sun be extinguished, let darkness reign, eternal night . . ."' (Trotsky, 11 September 1918). In order that people might believe that the sun could be monopolized, Marx had to write *Capital*.

A science of great resources

Before figuring in the records of history and crime, the cult of the personality was an eminently academic activity, a normal practice among professors – in relation to one another, and on the part of each one towards himself. Marx's defenders and his critics alike usually accept the highly personalized division which distinguishes as 'good' or 'bad', it doesn't matter which, the revolutionary Marx from a Hegel who is 'the last of the philosophers' . . . not to mention the other masters, who are usually overlooked.

Marx and his friend Engels also sacrificed to this pleasant university tradition which requires that one should study thought within the well-defined limits of the thinker's civil status. How embarrassing that we haven't found the identity card of Shakespeare or Homer! Was each of them one person or several? Marx took care to avoid such confusion: he was the first to add together German philosophy, French revolutionary politics and British political economy, and also the first to deduce therefrom the science of revolution which he bequeathed to Europe's proletariat. With right of primogeniture for the German workers? A sign! The entire operation never takes us out of the framework of 'German idealism', of that 'philosophical revolution' kindled by Fichte with the flames of the French Revolution and of the criticism made thereof by the British (Fichte's first work was a reply to the 'liberal' Burke). The economic doctrines of the British, like the political doctrines of the French, were in fact known and reflected upon by the masters from the outset: Marx 'read' Ricardo in the same way as Hegel 'read' Adam Smith, Steuart, and so on with respect and attention, so as to extract the philosophical 'substantial marrow'. The British were 'vulgar', or, in the case of the greatest among them, 'classical': the German master was to be modern and scientific.

Marx's science receives in its cradle the whole heritage of the *Wissenschaft* – philosophy realized as science – of Fichte and of Hegel. Marx can do no less than the predecessors whom he names himself, and so he puts forward an overall solution for the alleged problems of the French Revolution. How (and so: against what?) to organize a society of men who have learnt to think of themselves as free? How is it possible for the *plebs* to govern themselves? This global character of the question and of the reply was to distinguish scientific socialism from the utopian, dogmatic and partial doctrines which could inspire only an immature proletariat. For example, the proletariat which, after the crushing of the insurrection of June 1848, 'throws itself into doctrinaire experiments, exchange banks and workers' associations, hence into a movement in which it renounces the revolutionizing of the old world by means of the latter's own great, combined resources, and seeks, rather, to achieve its salvation behind society's back, in private fashion, within its limited conditions of existence, and hence necessarily suffers shipwreck.'

When does the proletariat emerge from these limitations? Why, in the revolution, and through the Marxist science of great resources. The absence of a narrow limitation seems, therefore, to be in accordance with the conditions of the non-existence of the proletariat and of the unconditional existence of the masters of theory. They themselves will assume the task of ruling the International by doing away with the 'sects' in the name of what they know: 'The sects ... (are) the infancy of the proletarian movement, just as astrology and alchemy are the infancy of science. If the International were to be founded it was necessary that the proletariat should have gone through this phase.' Thereafter, the working class in power means science in command.

All power to science, for there is a science of power, of the taking of power, of revolution. The post of pilot will fall not to an academic but to the Napoleon of the civil wars to come: 'Industry leads two armies into the field against each other, each of which again carries on a battle within its own ranks, among its own troops. The army whose troops beat each other up the least gains the victory over the opposing host.' Exploiting scientifically the contradictions of *Capital*, organizing no less scientifically the camp of Labour – for a century, experts have been elbowing each other at the gate left ajar by Marx. He himself remains irreplaceable as painter of the battles of the future: 'Is it at all surprising that a society founded on the *opposition* of classes should culminate in brutal *contradiction*, the shock of body against body, as its final dénouement?' (The emphases are Marx's own) He is without peer, too, in the drafts he draws upon a future which, without fulfilling any of his promises, nevertheless ensures him a milliard followers, willing or otherwise. Unless, by an effect of self-anticipation, the promise of the 'final dénouement' is ultimately realized in a 'shock of body against body' conducted under the leadership of Russian and Chinese generals in Marxist contradiction one with the other.

The choosing of the leaders is done on the brink of the abyss, in the shadow of the apocalyptic catastrophe, in the name of the guiding science. On all those points Marx refrains from breaking the thread of 'German idealism', firmly knotted under the evocation of the Revolution's terrors and in meditation upon Napoleon's great battles. The master thinkers spawn Dr Strangeloves all over the planet, even in the remotest townlets of Asia and Africa: 'Paradise is under the shadow of a swordsman – this is also a symbol and a test-word by which souls with noble and warrior-like origin betray and discover themselves' (Nietzsche).

Learning to play the Great Game

In order to mobilize great resources it is necessary to have a great aim; in order to risk everything on one throw, it is necessary that everything shall be at stake. 'Capital comes more and more to the fore as a social power, whose agent is the capitalist. This social power no longer stands in any possible relation to that which the labour of a single individual can create. It becomes an alienated, independent social power, which stands opposed to society . . .'

There is enough to satisfy intellectually the whole of 'society'. The desperate man who wants to find others to share his feelings, through making known the cause of his despair; and also the man full of hope who exorcizes the only thing which stands between his dream and commonplace reality – 'it's the system's fault'. The leader who sounds the call to arms in the war to end war; and the same man when, after the event, he explains why he was defeated: 'Bash capital!' The intellectual who, with one blow, cuts history in two, and the one who quietly adapts himself to it: Capital is the 'old world', and it is *a* world, and therefore everything in the world. Both the bourgeois who thinks he is everything and the worker, whom they want to think himself nothing; both the militants who bring history to childbed and the hero who has impregnated her. By making *Capital* shine with all the lights that German philosophy uses to illuminate its supreme realities, Marx put forward an extraordinarily gratifying object: 'Capital is the all-dominating economic power of bourgeois society. It must form the starting-point as well as the finishing-point.'

The modern world as a whole is under the sway of a single system of domination: Capital is *the master, the vampire*. More soberly put: capital has only one property, that of bringing together the mass of arms and instruments which it finds before it. Capital assembles them all under its command – that is all that it really accumulates. Marx strives to emphasize this universal unity of command. It will be said: he does this the better to overthrow it. Except that, in order to overthrow it, one needs to unite: only unity of command will put an end to unity of command. The state is needed in order to get rid of the state, say both Fichte and Lenin. Good successions take place through struggle and the 'supreme test by means of death' functions once again as a transference of powers.

The power of the separating power

Through its omnipresence, the system of domination reduces to nullity every 'local' attempt at emancipation (described, therefore, as 'partial', 'fragmentary,' 'sectarian'). There can be no salvation other than the central showdown with capital. This strategy at the centre may remain for a long time imprecise and contradictory, but it operates from the outset by asserting its exclusive right to possess the only fulcrum by which the world can be raised up. It rules out any other way. While shouting their irreconcilable opposition to one another, reformist Marxism and revolutionary Marxism agree perfectly on this point, namely that it is the centre that decides everything. Capital is seen as a dual vampire – it exploits, but it also 'absorbs' all the particular struggles waged against it by private persons. Later would come condemnation (in the name of the 'general interests of the movement') of the spontaneously egoistic economism of the workers, or the 'petty bourgeois' nationalism of the peoples fighting for liberation. It is already present in germ in Marx's analysis of the liberties of 1789. His analysis of the 'Rights of Man and of the Citizen' amounts to translating specious and deceptive language into the language of reality: the *formalism* of the rights in question has for its real content the system of domination (the money system, says the young Marx, in *On the Jewish Question*: the system of capital, says the old Marx). The 'icy water' of capitalist calculation determines everything: Liberty, Equality and Property.

One can refine this analysis with many subtleties, methodological, epistemological and pedagogical; between the economic infrastructure and the juridical superstructure one can show, going up and down, the lift of 'dialectical interaction'; or one can discover in law the presence of an 'absent cause' (meaning capital). But whatever the playing with words, one nevertheless finds at the end, 'in the last instance, that which sounds the keynote and speaks the final word, the system of domination, one and indivisible, which appeared openly with 1789: 'The political revolution breaks up bourgeois life into its elements...'

This system of domination, thereafter analysed as bourgeois and capitalist, reproduces, stroke for stroke, the 'reign of the understanding' dear to German philosophy – the picture put forward by Fichte, and then by Hegel, of a world revolutionized politically by the French, and thereby plunged into endless disarray – awaiting the 'philosophical revolution'. Marx, who usually explains that German philosophy presents a miserable reflection of the requirements of the French political situation, suddenly loses his way in this game with mirrors. He upsets chronology, goes back in time, and assumes that the members of the Constituent Assembly had read what Fichte was to write five years later: '*Equality* is nothing but the Ego, that is, the German Ego translated into a French, that is, a political form.' Who is translating whom? What does it matter, if capital is the simultaneous translator who speaks English economically, German philosophically and French politically!

And always says the same thing: 'Money has become a world power (*Weltmacht*) and the practical Jewish spirit has become the practical spirit of the Christian nations.' Even British political economy needs to be given an injection of German philosophy: the system which Smith and Ricardo present as being 'natural' will be exposed as radical and anti-natural, 'Jewish' in the Hegelian sense, entailing the dissolution of every human community and reduction of the individual to atomized solitude in face of the absolute master. Primitive societies know neither capital nor labour (general, abstract labour) because 'the communal system on which (their) mode of production is based prevents the labour of an individual from becoming private labour and his products the private production of a separate individual'. Conversely, the 'prodigious negative power' which Hegel saw in the Jewish religion, and then assumed as 'energy of thought', was rediscovered by Marx manifesting itself above all in the form of money: 'Money is directly the real community of all the individuals ... But the community is, in money, only a pure abstraction, something absolutely fortuitous and external to the individual.' In short, it is 'death' that has to be 'looked in the face'.

Marx interprets Hegelianism by means of political economy (Hegel's logic is 'the money of the spirit, the speculative thought-value of man and nature . . .') Not without having, under the table, rediscovered in the spirit of money that same logic of domination which Hegel was said to have made the money of the spirit.

While undertaking to change the world, German philosophy nevertheless does not cease to interpret it. In presenting his gigantic confrontation, 'Capital versus Labour', did not Marx simply counterpose Hegel to his own double?

Property is rape

Beyond the 'clamorous sphere' of the mutual alienation of commodities lies 'the secret laboratory of production': beneath the circulation of money and its 'universal whoredom' lies exploitation by capital, and rape. Every relationship of domination assumes a dominator and a dominated: this very simple and primary dissymmetry is not apparent *in* the market, where the reciprocity of exchange causes every biter to be bit and every robber to be robbed. Suggesting a relationship of domination in its original dissymmetry, Marx does not echo Proudhon: capitalist property is not theft (*vol*) but rape (*viol*) – rape of the worker's 'labour-power'.

The violence of the worker-employer relationship is neither primitive nor barbarous, but organized and rational. Here the great secret of modern society is at last to be revealed: the exploitation of the worker, how it is that 'surplus-value' is extracted from him, 'not only how capital produces, but how capital is itself produced'.

Like all modern relations of domination, the factory knows only freedoms. Neither slave nor serf, the worker has the right to sell his labour power, and 'this one historical precondition comprises a world's history'. From manufacture to the factory system and large-scale industry, the 'organization of work', meaning the relations of domination and servitude inside the factory, supply the key to the problem of modern times. 'How is it that the *plebs*, knowing that it is free, nevertheless submits to coercion by a government?' asked the other master-thinkers. Look at the factory, Marx replies.

In the beginning, employers and workers come together 'freely', like Hegelian consciousnesses before they fight to the death. Marx does not, of course, present the struggle at the beginning as a struggle between 'consciousnesses', but neither does he present it, strictly speaking, as a class struggle: he makes the formation of 'classes' in the modern sense of the word the *result* of this struggle. 'Primitive' accumulation, the progressive organization of European society following the slow dissolution of feudal relations and the expropriation of the peasants, the disciplining of vagabonds, and the consolidation of the factory system: these are, *inter alia*, the historical prerequisites for the construction of the factory as the 'secret laboratory' of modern society. Marx's descriptions of this sordid and bloody pre-history of contemporary Europe are especially powerful, and a century had to elapse before this systematic examination of the most immediate origins of the modern world was resumed (by Michel Foucault, in his *Madness and Civilization*). Marx bears a share of responsibility for the silence re-established around the historical laboratories of the factory laboratory. He started the hare only to leave it to caper in a 'future' which no longer concerns us. In 'primitive accumulation' the main roles are played by the young modern states (the absolute monarchy) and the new police systems and religions: the episodes are entitled – plunder of the countryside, rural exodus, imprisonment of beggars, colonizing of minds. It is made to appear as though all that forms part not of the present-day structures of the 'mode of production', but of the basely and frivolously historical circumstances of its coming to birth. And *only* of its coming to birth, say the Marxists.

At the end of this martyrology of the producer we are shown the relationship of domination in its true modern form, with the power of capital become an 'immediate autocracy'. We owe to Marx a masterly and prophetic analysis of the strategy of power in large-scale industry. On its 'barracks discipline' side first, with its bosses big and little, 'officers' (managers) and 'N.C.O.s' (foremen, overseers). The fact that these cadres are wage-earners does not mean they are not on the side of power: 'The leadership of industry is an attribute of capital.'

More remarkable still is the picture he gives, in advance, of the intellectual discipline that was to become the grand strategy of the organization of work in the twentieth century. Half a century before Taylor 'rationalized' the production-line, assembling unskilled workers (we-think-for-you), Marx had stressed this tendency to 'separation of manual labour from the intellectual powers of production which it (large-scale industry) transforms into the power of capital over labour'. The promotion of mental work is inversely proportionate to the de-mentalizing of manual work: the detail worker who 'knows nothing' is faced by the cadre who knows and decides everything. This is the logic of the rape which, having been accomplished, produces its own reproduction.

As an utterly isolated individual confronting all the powers of the material and mental order, the modern worker lives in absolute insecurity and works on the brink of the abyss. That, at least, is the situation prescribed for him by the employers' strategy as this is deciphered by Marx – and in which he himself expects to mobilize the worker. It remains to be seen whether anyone is, in fact, situated in that atomized solitude which is the starting-point of all the master thinkers' discourses.

The Hegelian factory

The only material that Marx takes into account when he is writing *Capital* reflects the point of view of the organizers and masters of production (the 'bourgeois'). This is the standpoint of the classical British economists and also of the other sources used by Marx. Even when compiling 'the martyrology of the producers' he relies on the reports of the factory inspectors, those liberal and enlightened counsellors of the despotic princes of the modern factory. Marx was not unaware of the workers' resistance as this was expressed in leaflets, newspapers, speeches, correspondence, songs and poems, as well as in actions, 'wildcat' or otherwise. But it is not on such documents that he bases his great work. He settles the matter once for all. Let no one blame him for this: is it not an unavoidable condition of all more or less scientific research that one has to select one's material, without hope of exhausting all the subjects? By limiting his inquiry in this way Marx decided what he would and *what he would not talk about. Capital*, even when discussing the details of factory life, deals exclusively with the employers' strategy.

Marx's forecasts are certainly brilliant, if we accept that they deal only with large-scale industry conceived as a structure of domination and seen from the angle of the will to dominate, to 'pump out' the 'life force' of the worker. Marx foresees how 'the special skill of each individual machine operator... vanishes as an infinitesimal quantity in the face of the science, the gigantic natural forces, and the mass of social labour embodied in the system of machinery which, together with those three forces, constitutes the power of the "master"'. But with whose eye does he see the 'infinitesimal', ever more 'infinitesimal' worker? Is this not the way of looking that is characteristic of the future master, his will ever more fully accomplished, who is sizing up the infinitesimal future worker?

It will be said: No, not at all. Marx is judging objectively. He sees both sides of the question, he forecasts 'the fragmentation of labour', the de-skilling of the labourer, the misery of the detail workers, the twofold misery of the immigrant worker. Yes, indeed! This picture of absolute hierarchization confirms that his standpoint is that of the master. At the bottom of the modern industrial ladder is the immigrant worker, or the peasant who has just become a worker, who is obliged to perform particularly hard and stupefying work, the hard and stupefying nature of which has often been calculated with a view to straining his strength to the utmost and to destroying so far as possible his capacity for resistance. All that corresponds both to the most cruelly commonplace employers' strategy and to what Marx forecast. To say, though, that this corresponds to *reality* would mean deluding oneself. At the bottom of the ladder, in the most completely de-intellectualized kind of work, modern industry places ... the worker who of all the workers is the most intellectual, an individual who usually speaks several languages, has known several countries, has lived through several historical epochs, who does not let himself be shut up within a narrowly local horizon, and who often possesses a sense of community and solidarity unknown to those around him: namely, the immigrant.

The image of the industrial hierarchy forms part of a strategical conception, not of descriptive truth: its purpose is not to correspond to reality but to make reality correspond to itself, by reducing the workers' resistance to nil. It is not enough to record, thanks to social explosions, that the level of intelligence of the detail worker cannot be reduced to what a lot of stupid petty bosses think it is. The factory never functions with science on the one hand and 'manual' obedience on the other: the science of the cadres can never do without the silent knowledge of the rank-and-file worker, as has been noted by sociologists and other experts when discussing the real profitability of mass-production methods. Every average foreman has to reckon with this silent knowledge possessed by the worker, to which correspond such a lot of possibilities of discreet resistance, 'leaking', braking and so on. The history of the 'organization of work' is nothing but the history of continual strategic readjustments by the bosses' will to dominate (which Marx grasps very well in his plan for the future), at grips with a worker's resistance which is laboriously reinvented at every stage (and which Marx was unable to foresee; because this was not his concern, but also because improvisation and invention are the great resources at the disposal of the proletariat's resistance).

The separation of the workers from each other and from their conditions of work, the dispossession of the individual and his enclosure in a perfectly atomized solitude, the submission of 'living' labour to 'dead' labour which has become 'automatic and autocratic', Capital – these are all familiar features of the Hegelian matrix: the fight to the death, terror, dread on the brink of the abyss, the master. It is also the employers' plan dreaming of its own realization. One might even generalize and perceive in this schema the design of every disciplinary society, in which 'prisons resemble factories, schools, barracks, hospitals, which all resemble prisons' (Foucault). The success achieved is never total, nor the domination complete. Resistance continues. History has a sequence, and the will to dominate always finds something to bite on, not without danger to itself.

Property is rape: Marx carries as far as possible his investigation of the fantasies of the rapist, his examination of the will of
the master he calls Capital – imagining, with all his German
idealism, that a structure of domination can be understood from
the angle of the dominator, that the latter knows the truth about
the dominated, in other words that the rape has proved completely successful. In order to know what has been raped, in
order that nothing may escape him, the rapist says to his victim:
'You have lost everything'. If nothing is left, nothing has
escaped. Defloration becomes the supreme game for the one who
persuades his victim that her virginity is everything: all that is
left is to light a candle to the god of the bigots. Bent over the
victimized *plebs* – either with a murderous leer, or with a cold
medical gaze, or with tears in their eyes, or with all of these
together – the master thinkers never fail to render their verdict:
consummatus est!

Rapist capital is fetishistic, it wants to possess 'everything'.
First of all naïvely, by hoarding money and making a pile. Then
more subtly, by accumulating on an ever more extensive scale,
producing so as to produce more, and so on *ad infinitum*,
'sucking out' from people and from nature, thinking that it
possesses 'everything', no longer in the form of gold but as
machines. Or else as organizer of the workers, stacking men up
and shutting them in as its 'most precious capital' (Stalin). If
we believe that capital possesses everything and everybody, does
not that mean sharing its fetishism? There are the rapists and
the raped, there is difference and struggle: but does that mean
that there are 'successful' rapes?

Capital does not exist

A hundred years later, fervent commentators, austere scholars
and academies in both hemispheres have all failed to get to the
end of Marx's *Capital*, and are still arguing about its table of
contents. It has lost nothing of its mysterious glamour, that
mass of papers left by the dying Marx to his best friend, and by
him to Kautsky, then shared between the two Internationals,
and finally put away in museums. 'I cannot bring myself to send

off anything until I have the whole before me. Whatever short-comings they may have, the merit of my writings is that they are an artistic whole, and that can only be attained by my method of never having them printed until they lie before me as a *whole*' (Marx to Engels, 31 July 1865). Himself the first to be caught in his own trap, Marx nevertheless made of this 'artistic whole' his finest achievement: ever since, admirers, objectors, continuators and freelances of his thought have been carrying forward the task of polishing this complete work which remains perpetually in need of completion: all the mystery of the world in heaps of rough drafts. Did Mallarmé sum up the spiritual history of the next century? He imagined a Book of Books, with leaves movable and removable, which would put us in the situation of being unable finally to turn a single page.

A similar form of equivocal non-existence becomes the fate of Capital when it decorates with its name the title page of a volume which is essentially unfinished and also when it asserts its claims upon the realities of this world; whether gilt-edged or in slices of gold, Capital is no longer to be met with in the world of business any more than in the world of libraries. When, capti-vated by this 'artistic whole' which Marx dreamed of seeing 'whole before me', a Marxist thinks he can point to *The Hand* which governs everything and pulls the strings of the bourgeois world, this discoverer of Dracula gets called to order by his colleagues. We find Lenin denouncing 'ultra-imperialism', the world-wide monocracy imagined by Kautsky: and Stalin taking credit for refuting in practice the one-time Trotskyist argument that 'the world market' dominates everything. 'Capital' with a capital C no more exists as a reality than as a book.

There is indeed a moment when, according to Marx, Capital encounters itself and appears to everyone 'as essentially the *common capital of a class*' (Marx's own emphasis). As though by chance, this is the most superficial, ephemeral and illusory moment, the one when 'interest-bearing' capital operates at the bank and on the stock-exchange, abandoning its links with industry and the factory: the universal and speculative moment of capital is that of speculators' capital. It is then that '*the capital* appears *as a relation to itself*'. Capital in itself and for itself, become something negotiable on the finance market, increasing by itself through bearing interest, producing itself – this is a Hegelian dream! It is the dream related by Keynes to Alice's children, the story of the coin invested at two per cent at the beginning of our era, the income from which, continually reinvested, would be too great today for the world to bear. Capital appears as merely an appearance, a fantasy of a chicken that lays golden eggs, forms of capital bringing profit, 'in which its origin and the secret of its existence are obscured and extinguished'.

With philosophical references added, this critique of the stock-exchange and speculation has nothing specifically Marxist about it, and numerous experts have shown that the serious part of the economy lies in production rather than in the financial mechanisms which are supposed to function independently. What is revealing is that it is here, when he is examining the equalization of the rate of profit, that Marx justifies the use of the singular, here alone that one may speak of *the capital* ('essentially common to a class') and not of *the capitals*. The different capitals acquire a uniform rate of interest on the finance market, assuming that they participate equally in proportion to their respective amounts in the share-out of the average profit: each capital is thus seen as being part of a 'total social capital' and on this basis is admitted to share in the democratic slicing of the cake: 'So long as things go well, competition effects an operating fraternity of the capitalist class, as we have seen in the case of the equalization of the general rate of profit, so that each shares in the common loot in proportion to the size of his respective investment.' As the tone indicates, this is an idyllic situation. Should suspicion and crisis arise, everything becomes a matter of 'strength and cunning', *the capital* bursts into fragments, *the capitals* confront each other, and 'competition then becomes a fight among hostile brothers'. Presenting 'the capital' as an entity implies assuming that the state of war between capitals has ended, which cannot be done without carrying rather far the doctrine of peaceful coexistence. When we speak of 'the capital' we are prisoners of the most superficial of appearances.

It remains the case that Marx has converted the world to the idea of this exclusive and unitary domination which fascinated the master thinkers. Did he not dream of seeing 'before me as a whole' that absolute object which he called Capital, while declaring it to be undiscoverable and showing it, despite himself, to be inexpressible?

Nor does labour

It is impossible to grasp Capital as Capital? Never mind, we shall discover it in that which is supposed to confront it, namely, Labour. 'The whole secret of capital's prolific property of self-valorization lies in the simple fact that it disposes of a certain amount of others' labour for which it does not pay.' But, adds Marx, there's the rub, this 'certain' amount of labour is priced by capital alone, and not by the worker. Capital calculates labour, capital does not calculate itself, labour does not calculate capital: does labour calculate itself?

In itself, 'labour is "not-value"'. The time actually spent in producing something either counts or doesn't count: it may happen that one spends too much time on it, or occupies oneself in producing what is useless or superfluous. The time spent by the worker is not valuable as such (by virtue of its 'use-value') but only when the 'exchange-value' of what he has produced has been recognized. If total capital cannot be grasped except in an illusion, labour in general, for its part, does not let itself be grasped at all: '"The" Labour [Marx's own ironical quotation marks] ... is no more than an abstraction and taken by itself does not exist at all.' Outside the world of commodities, labour is nothing.

Necessarily, labour 'taken by itself does not exist at all': if it were otherwise we should find ourselves in the circle of the biter bit and the founded foundation. Saying that abstract, general, social labour 'produces' capitalism means forgetting that it is just as true that capitalism alone generalizes, abstracts and socializes labour and in its turn produces 'indifference to any specific kind of labour', causing to become real in practice 'labour pure and simple', that 'point of departure of modern economics'. Specific labour produces only specific things.

226   THE FOUR ACES

Labour in general produces capital in general, and *vice versa*
Without any question of priority, the point of departure is the
result and the result is already there at the start: 'The busiest of
all ages – our age – does not know how to make anything out of
its great diligence and wealth, except always more and more
wealth and more and more diligence' (Nietzsche).

Does labour create value? Yes, indeed, but in that case we do
not speak any more of labour as a commodity which is bought
and sold, but of the creative property which 'distinguishes it
from all other commodities and excludes it, as the element that
forms value, from the possibility of having any value of its own'.
Creative labour, 'labour-power', has no price. Reciprocally, in
so far as labour has value (its price, wages) it is not creative:
'It is always some definite labour, it is never labour in general
that is sold and bought'. This would mean falling into that
'vicious circle' of which Marx accused Proudhon (just as
Ricardo objected to it in Adam Smith) – supposing that the
value of labour must be the measure of other values while also
being measured *by* them.

'The' labour can no more be grasped *separately* than can
'the' capital. Neither as value (wages), nor as the effort experienced by the worker. It is not that these realities are not palpable, physiologically tangible, concrete, in present-day society
just as previously. It is not these palpable properties of labour,
however, that constitute the value of things, but a quantitative
estimate of an embodied labour. This 'presupposes that labour
has been equalized by the subordination of man to the machine
or by the extreme division of labour: that men are effaced by
their labour: that the pendulum of the clock has become as
accurate a measure of the relative activity of two workers as it is
of the speed of two locomotives. Therefore, we should not say
that one man's hour is worth another man's hour, but rather that
one man during an hour is worth just as much as another man
during an hour.'

We know that Marxomania and the Boy-Scout outlook have
often sung hymns to the glory of creative labour, which human-
izes nature, naturalizes man and gives promise of that sabbatical
society in which we shall still work, but ... joyously. Despite a

few bugle-calls sounded in this style, what Marx teaches actually points in a quite different direction. When he describes as 'living fire' and 'living time' the labour-power which is the basis of the value of things exchanged, Marx does not claim to be isolating the essence of history, the alpha and omega of humanity, the foundation of all things. It is still the spinner's labour that he is talking about: 'It is by virtue of its general character as expenditure of human labour-power in the abstract that spinning adds new value to the values of the cotton and the spindle.' He shows us here not Prometheus brandishing the living fire, but a capital taking fire from workers. Whether Marxist or not, the medal of labour does not decorate the life of a working man but the man of a working life.

The labour time calculated in the price of commodities is a time spent in overalls, a time passed in the factory (and also, though Marx does not say so, in prison, school and hospital). With 'value-creating' labour no more than with 'interest-bearing capital' does one escape from relations of domination. Is not the fetishizing of 'the' capital or 'the' labour meant as a way of not thinking about domination as such?

Yoke against yoke

In the great family of minds no less than in bourgeois dynasties, successions take place in the Oedipal way: one murders and then burns incense to one's victim, or one flatters and then kills – all that counts is the inheritance. Marx, who was well placed for knowing the scenario, defended himself from his Marxists: 'I sowed dragon's teeth and reaped fleas.' Only fleas? With the original contribution of their respective weaknesses, the Marxists would not have sought so much in Marx for that august and solemn gesture of the sower if they had not found it there. What was asked of Karl was not what he had thought or written, but more than that: what he had 'as a whole' before his eyes, the standpoint of the system of world domination (that world power embodied in money, and subsequently in *the* Capital), with, in addition, apprenticeship to mastership of this mastery (*the* Revolution 'which goes to the root of things').

From beginning to end of the interminable history of Marxism and anti-Marxism, Marx functions as a master thinker. It is assumed that he introduces us to the 'secret laboratory' of lordship and possession of the world, at the same time as he forms the new lords and possessors.

The fact that one can see that the writing of this great world-book, *Capital*, was never completed is not enough to capsize the scheme: it will be completed. Mankind is a great man who writes unceasingly and constantly re-reads what he has written: we shall enter upon our careers when our elders are no longer there, and kiss the trace their virtues have left in the dust. Around 1900 Marxists and anti-Marxists strove to get the accounts right, since the 'balances' of Marx's drafts didn't work out. About 1930 it was the imbalances that became all the rage, and the left-wing calculators, pen in hand, announced as having been predicted by the Book the final catastrophe which they thought they saw before them. Today, the scattered bits and pieces are being stuck together again with the seccotine of the human sciences. If the economic description of the Machinery of Capital breaks down, it is reinforced with psycho-socio-sexology: all the more irrefutable will be the proof of the inevitable re-absorption effected by that great Thing which is supposed to rule the world.

Marx tried to formulate in his economics the unity of a world domination. Criticizing the narrowness of his point of view amounts to dangling the prospect of a generalized economics expressing an even more dominant standpoint. Spitting oneself still further upon the fixed idea of the master thinkers: there is a language which enables one to master everything, and I have penetrated its most arcane secrets. Mathematical language, dialectical science, universal circulation of money, world power of capital, Testament of Dr Mabuse.

The Capital doesn't exist, and nobody cares. What matters is to talk about it: thereby one can talk smoothly about everything, judge all, decide the significance of any event whatsoever, raise down-to-earth antagonisms to the height of theoretical debates, and know, through having 'before us', in generalized economics, what is and what is not. Thus, the commentaries, refutations, additions, patchings, sewings, cuts, linings, clarifications, illuminations, transcendings, interpretations, counter-interpretations and symposia engaged in around Capital are the continuation pure and simple, even though unconscious, of the traditional 'general metaphysics'.

It matters little who is talking – sometimes it is the representative of the Responsible Organizations – the generalized economics of 'beyond Marx' always claims to judge, in its uniform language, what happens, what is, and all those who are living at the same time as it proclaims itself the science of this language reserved for the initiated: a science of masters *and* a science of beings (of that which can be conceived most generally about what happens, knowledge of *being as such*, according to the Ancients). In that little conjunction, 'and', lies the entire heritage of the German master thinkers: there are interlinked the science of domination and the domination of science, while again and again the prospect is reformulated of an integral and exclusive subjugation of the world accompanied by a language which is supposed to express this subjugation.

It is knowledge of a twofold destruction. On the one hand the system of domination puts forward its proof by the vacuum. Capitalism is constantly 'revolutionizing' the datum – 'the revolution in industry and agriculture has necessitated a revolution in the general conditions of the process of social production, that is, in the means of communication and transport', etc. Peasants driven from their land, workers out of work, all have to be programmed for the *cogito* of modern man, his: 'I think, therefore I think of myself as being shut up in my atomized solitude.' On the other hand, the revolution is going to destroy this destruction, to master Master Capital.

Is this just a play on words? Perhaps so, but our century revolves continually within it. 'The evening session of the congress was to create a cabinet of ministers. M-i-n-i-s-t-e-r-s? What a sadly compromised word! It stinks of the high bureaucratic career, the crowning of some parliamentary ambition. It was decided to call the government the Soviet of People's Commissars: that at least had a fresher sound.' A pamphlet, a comedy? Not at all! It is the cheerful account of the installation of the first Bolshevik government in October 1917 given by Trotsky, who was one of its kingpins. It was 'decided' ... that the Commissar would give off less of the stench of bureaucratic careerism, that the powers of ownership delegated to the Comrade Organizer would sound socialist instead of bourgeois, that the 'revolution in the means of communication' would be regarded as a people's revolution when it established the monopoly of a small minority over all the means of communication (information, circulation of men and ideas, publications, exchanges).

By describing domination of the earth and of mankind as if it had already been accomplished and completed, by proclaiming 'all power to capital' as the absolute law of the 'old world', Marx put into orbit the prize of the century: all power. As a revolutionary, he was to imagine that he saw the Paris Communards storming heaven. More prosaically setting out to storm the seat of government, the Winter Palace, the Bolsheviks were to make of that seat the heaven wherein 'all power' resided, including the power to decide that 'all power to the Soviets' and all power to the Bolshevik ministers meant the same thing.

The revolutionary moment of the Great Leap Forward and the reformist moment of progress with measured steps always alternate where 'revolutionaries' are concerned, and often in the case of reformists too (they rarely decline to engage in bloody showdowns). The formidable drive of the Marxist leader did not fail to 'return to its bed', when he framed his N.E.P. and moved from enthusiastic speeches about revolution to cool consideration of 'economic realities'. A few years after he had hymned the Paris proletarians storming heaven, Marx observed, icily, that with a little more common sense on both sides an agreement between Paris and Versailles would not have been out of the question. History is played out between those who hold power, that power which *the* Capital has, so to speak, wholly monopolized beyond the reach of the dominated. Whether they be reformist or revolutionary, it is always the 'general headquarters' that, according to the theory, carry on the great game.

An absence of ideas which makes its way in the world

Marx devoted a number of writings to the revolutions which took place in his time, and these writings he completed. Apart from the articles written when he was involved in the 1848 revolution in Germany, they were essays written after the event, like obituaries – reports of failure, with 'scientific' explanations thereof. He experienced even 'his own' German revolution as an ineffective repetition of 1789. Regarding projects for the future, Marx, keeping all 'utopianism' at bay, remained extremely dry.

This silence of his can be appreciated, in that he refrained from putting forward demagogic programmes; but his respect for the masses did not go so far as to explain *why* any communist programming of the future must become demagogic in proportion as it becomes more precise. Scattered through Marx's economic writings we find sibylline references to the 'associated producers' who are to plan production (how?) or to Aristotle's self-moving shuttles. Was Saint Technology to lead us out of the realm of the necessities of labour into that of freedom and leisure? It is hard to see in these rare passages anything but stop-gap solutions. The 'free association of the producers', without further explanation, presumes as having disappeared, as though by a wave of the magician's (or the prefect's) wand, those formidable charges of hostility which capitalism, according to Marx, causes to circulate between war and economic conflict. As for technological solutions solving all problems through the creation of plenty, this also implies that the capitalist powers are not powers of destruction and parasitism, working out a technology which is aimed at ensuring opulence for the dominators, and not for the dominated. Through what miracle were the technology and the passions cultivated by the capitalist 'hell', and reproducing this, to turn around so as to produce and reproduce the socialist 'paradise'?

Once and once only did Marx allow himself to toy with projects for the future – in his *Critique of the Gotha Programme*. At last he was to say how the values of things were to be calculated: how exchanges and their equivalence would be regulated: why people would work, once capital's hash had been settled. The result, looked at a century later, is not without some sinister anticipations of the tricks the future had in store. Fundamentally, as though he had nothing to say about communism, Marx again refused, as always, to offer anything precise regarding the organization of life after liberation. Even after taking power, the working class as ruler class would be able to say no more than: 'We'll see, later.' It would postpone to a 'higher' phase of communist society the concern of fundamental importance. 'After labour has become not only a means of life but life's prime want; after the productive forces have also increased with the all-round development of the individual, and all the springs of co-operative wealth flow more abundantly – only then can the narrow horizon of bourgeois right be crossed in its entirety . . .' Words, words: not even a poem. Ah, the 'all-round development', the 'flow of wealth': Marx is inspired! When the problem has been solved there will be a solution to the problem – that is, essentially what he has to say.

While awaiting the arrival of that time, it is assumed that we have already smashed, once for all, the power of Capital. In which case, we shall still be living within 'the narrow horizon of bourgeois right', Marx admits. He supposes, however, that it will be possible to introduce 'certificates' testifying that the worker 'has furnished such-and-such an amount of labour'. The labour of each individual is thus valued directly as useful labour: 'Now, in contrast to capitalist society, individual labour no longer exists in an indirect fashion, but directly as a component part of the total labour.' Who, then, judges the utility of a particular labour?

When other economists had proposed to replace money by labour-certificates, Marx showed a crushing severity, which he failed to apply to himself. Mentioning Gray's idea that labour-time be treated as a currency unit, certified by a national central bank, Marx's caustic comment was that 'bankruptcy would in such a case fulfil the function of practical criticism'. 'Labour-money' was 'a pseudo-economic term' – even, and perhaps, especially, when given a socialist content, something that 'was left to M. Proudhon and his school'. When, twenty years later,

Marx had to formulate the socialist programme, did he become a pupil of Proudhon?

Actually, Marx was trapped. Against Gray he had argued that the labour-certificate could function only if everyone's labour became immediately 'communal labour-time' or 'labour-time of directly associated individuals', but he added, at that time, that this presupposed the complete overthrow of bourgeois relations: 'In that case ... exchange-value would not be turned into price; but neither would use-value be turned into exchange-value and the product into a commodity, and thus the very basis of bourgeois production would be abolished.' What does this mean, if not that, in order to avoid the contradictions of Gray's labour-money, it is necessary to be already in that 'higher' phase of communism wherein we have crossed, 'in its entirety', the 'narrow horizon of bourgeois right' – that phrase of Marx's which, as soon as he is obliged to explain it, puts us off till the Greek Kalends!

This was the first manifestation of an intellectual procedure which was to enjoy great success a century later. If you can't extricate yourself from your contrasting concepts (not any old concepts, but 'socialism' and 'capitalism'), then define a 'transition period', and let history operate this transition which you can't manage to conceive conceptually. We obtain this 'lower phase' – neither fish nor flesh, neither capitalism nor communism – in which bourgeois right (and that which makes it necessary) survives ... but not capitalism! In Scopecolor: how a nullity of thought became historic ... It is not by coupling in a thousand different ways the words 'collective labourer' with the words 'bourgeois right' that you can advance the solution of the problem by one inch. Are you getting out at the first floor or at the second? If you can't get out either at 'capitalism' or at 'socialism', this is perhaps because the lift of reality doesn't stop at the floor where your concepts are.

Capital has all the powers, since it has the supreme power of separating the workers and atomizing them in 'bourgeois' relations. We take all its powers away from it, but, for a time, individuals continue to be enclosed within the 'narrow horizon' of bourgeois right. Who, then, will wield in the meantime the absolute powers of Capital (organizing production, deciding whether a particular labour is useful, etc.), who will have a 'sufficiently wide horizon' to be up to the level of this historic task? The thinker? The Party? The state? (which, in this so-called transition phase 'can be nothing but the revolutionary dictatorship of the proletariat'). Willy-nilly, when the master thinker falls silent, he leaves it to the state of the future to differentiate between capitalism and communism and to counterpose to the dictatorship of private economy its dictatorship of public service. The world will belong to the officials. Marx, who was no statist by inclination, would have been in despair.

Having to take up a position on the programme of the German socialists, he tugged on all the strings that the future was to strengthen and strengthen ... For example, he argues that, by changing from capitalist to socialist, the 'mode of production' changes everything. But whenever he has to explain just what exactly it is that changes in this 'everything', he evades the issue and talks about something else. Marx could have counterposed his own programme to a programme whose ambiguities he condemned, but he preferred to run away, talking round the subject, splitting the hairs of communism into a number of unclearly defined phases. Nothing could be more incoherent than this 'critique'.

And yet he does put forward the enormity which lies at the very depths of his thinking. What, in fact, does he admit? In the first, 'socialist' phase of post-revolutionary society, we are to retain relations that are regulated by right, and are therefore unequal and bourgeois. 'Right, by its very nature, can consist only in the application of an equal standard; but unequal individuals (and they would not be different individuals if they were not unequal) are measurable by an equal standard only in so far as they are brought under an equal point of view, are taken from one *definite* side only, for instance, in the present case, are regarded only as workers and nothing more is seen in them, everything else being ignored. Further, one worker is married, another not; one has more children than another, and so on and so forth.' Consideration of these concrete data, and not merely of the abstract worker, is postponed by Marx to the so-called communist phase, in which everyone will receive 'according to his needs'. Here is the enormity. In a first, 'lower' stage we pay everyone on the basis of the time he spends at work: we are able to do that. But we can't take account of differences in the sphere of private life (marital status, number of children, etc.)! In other words, 'we' can determine without apparent difficulty what is socially useful labour and what is not, what is to be counted as wasted time and what as double time, and can do this for society as a whole just as for each person in particular. It's easy! And yet taking account of each person's everyday needs exceeds society's competence: the facts that you have five children and I have three are harder to compare than are your work as an engineer and mine as a joiner.

Exercising all the powers formerly attributed to Capital, levelling out inequalities, abstracting abstract, socially useful labour from the infinitely various concrete labours, extracting the abstract worker who is hidden in concrete, differentiated men, determining in common the objectives of each branch of production, the usefulness or otherwise of each product, settling the disputes which all this presupposes – these tasks would be easier to accomplish than taking account of differences in the sphere of private life (number of children, for instance)! We see here how Marx opens, more yawningly wide than ever, the split between public and private life, between social labour and individual needs. All the powers wielded by capital over public life pass to . . . whom? We can know only one thing, about that: these problems dominate the private person, a slave to his needs, who is assumed not to be capable of reckoning with the needs of a neighbour who has two children more than he has. Though the bourgeois exploiter has departed long since, there remains the official man who regulates the organization and distribution of social labour, and the private man who submits to this.

Here Marx indulges in an idyll. What has been gained by substituting an official for the capitalist? Axiom: masters hand over power only to masters. Not through ill-will or egoism, but because, whether it be the power 'of capital' or 'of socialism', power remains power to abstract, and, through abstracting, to conceive, that is, to 'dominate' (Hegel). The master thinkers never went in for any but delicate, subtle and interminable commentaries from the standpoint of the dominator: in their eyes, the dominated one, shut up in his particularity, has no standpoint of his own.

'*Concerning the future of the workman.* Workmen should learn to regard their duties as soldiers do. They receive emoluments, incomes, but they do not get wages!' To this proposal of Nietzsche's, Marx would have replied: soldiers, yes, but soldiers of the Revolution!

So what? For being a soldier of the revolution is one any the less a soldier?

6 Whereby I Am above Everything
(Nietzsche for the Lot)

'The poet arouses with his naked sword
His age fright-stricken for not having known
That death was triumphing in that strange voice!'

MALLARMÉ

The beyond-Marx

What was still needed was to burn behind one the last vessels
of the old world, to let the modernity of the master thinkers
reveal itself frankly, to display all at once the true colour of the
coming century. It was Nietzsche, the late arrival, who under-
took the final mopping-up operations and dynamited whatever
made for reticence in his predecessors. 'A monarch but not
subjects?' Hegel had asked. Certainly no subjects! The oppressed are crafty oppressors who enjoy not recognizing themselves
as such: the oppressed have been swept away, they have gone up
in smoke.

But why *a* monarch, *a* capital? Are we not entering into the
republic of the masters? The game of the great powers? Every
struggle is the last, and so on endlessly: each battle is decisive...
for the next battle. If power is measured by power to annihilate,
as they all think, as Nietzsche proclaimed before Mao did –
'always doth he destroy, who hath to be a creator' – then there
will be no power-centre that will not be smashed, no capital not
subjected to capital punishment... Giving place to other
powers and flying into capital pieces. Organizations, States, but
also Science, Art, Politics and Religion are seen by Nietzsche
as 'formations of domination', structures of the will to power.
The world is made up of Copernican suns, it is a grouping of
General Headquarters: 'Every centre of force – and not only the
human being – constructs the rest of the world on the basis of itself: that is, estimates it in relation to its own strength, sounds it
and moulds it...'

The master behind the property owner

Abolition of private property! What a long-drawn-out complicity between the intelligentsia and the state, even in the bloodiest
massacres of this century! The grocer and his petty-bourgeois
mentality were ridiculed and small-peasant ownership was swept
away – without there being observed the advance of the great
public property-owner, the hierarch whose gold braid is equivalent to title deeds of ownership. Marx, already embarrassed,
noted in passing that the 'commanders' of industry, with or
without property-rights, embody the decisive authority, 'This
authority reaching its bearers ... only as the personification of
the conditions of labour in contrast to labour'. But managers,
senior engineers, salaried administrators are, Marxistically, only
variations on the central theme of the private property-owner.
Marx remains in agreement with Hegel that 'possession (is) the
subject's simplest juridical relation'.

This is still a source of confusion to the Chinese Marxists, who,
trying to conceive where lies the possibility of a 'restoration of
capitalism', continue to see it appearing mainly in the form of an
extension of small-scale private economy (the plot of land and
the street-stall) and refuse to think the matter through to realization that the main *locus* of the Red bourgeois is to be found where
power is wielded over society, command over labour, decision-
taking on what each person needs – that this *locus* is the Party
itself.

This fascinated and blind focusing upon private ownership
runs through all German thought until we get to Nietzsche.
Yet some of the revolutionaries of 1789 had a less narrow conception of property and its powers. Barnave, for instance: 'The
prestige attached to knowledge, which is always the greater in
proportion to the ignorance of the masses, gives rise to the first
aristocracy, that of the elders, the priests, soothsayers and
doctors, it is the origin of the Brahmins, Druids and Augurs –
in short, of every aristocracy based upon science, which has
everywhere preceded the aristocracies of arms and of wealth,
and which from the beginning of human society has always
acquired great power by means of some real services rendered,

together with a great deal of deception.' Naturally, the Girondin
Barnave was more naïve than our 'Marxist' trade unions, which
classify all our modern Brahmins and Augurs as 'workers', and
'unite', without difficulty, detail workers and managerial
executives in their single grid!

Seen from within

Perceiving beneath the temporarily abandoned clothing of the
property-owner the very promising outline of the modern
master presupposes that one looks the relations of domination
in the face, no longer as concealed in the guise of relations between things. The employer does not steal *something*, he vampi-
rizes *someone*, he 'sucks out' living labour, said Marx already,
without daring to break completely with the tranquil metaphor
by which relations between men are depicted as relations between things. And yet it is indeed relations directly between men
that he exposes in the 'secret laboratory' of exploitation, relations between the cadres and the rank-and-file. What else is
'surplus-value' or the 'unpaid labour' of the exploited but the
result of this dissymmetry of powers which decides the duration
and intensity of labour to the disadvantage of the underdog?

The idyllic picture of a society in which man relates to things
before he encounters other men was painted by the calm thought
of liberal England. It was from Locke that Hegel took the idea of
the primitive *simplicity* of private ownership. In keeping to the
hypothesis that power-relations are ultimately measured by
relations between things, Marx did not break with this conception, although his appreciation of 'factory despotism'
brought in the automatic and autocratic master.

Past the walls of the factory, the relations of domination
continue: relations between things merely give expression to
them sometimes, without being independent of them. The
luxury of the ruling class consists not so much in the enjoyment
of things as of the difference: what is expensive and prestigious
constitutes surplus value in the sphere of consumption which
reproduces – culturally, pedagogically, aesthetically – the surplus value of production. We need to abandon the idea of

objective measurement of relations of domination by way of economic 'things': the dominator measures without letting himself be measured, it is he who fixes the norms – fat in the 'under-developed' countries, thin in the advanced ones, a lover of tulips in the Holland of Vermeer, of vintage cars, of war, of police, and sometimes of good music.

The relations between things are still relations between men: we never escape from the relations of domination. '"Will" can naturally only operate on "will",' says Nietzsche, completing the formulation of the programme of the master thinkers: 'The world seen from within ... would simply be "Will to Power" and nothing else.'

Beyond fetishism

Production for production, consumption for consumption, accumulation upon accumulation: this is 'the Law and the Prophets' of the modern world, says Marx, not without seeming to take these redoublings for a sign of collapse in the proximate future. He argues within the horizon of a settlement of accounts in which consumption will be paid for in cash by production and liquidities backed by solid assets, whereas the artificial structures of credit for credit and advances upon advances will finally crash down in *the* crisis or *the* revolution.

This great decision which is expected to bring ideas and things, intentions and deeds, the subjective and the objective, definitively into correspondence one with the other, does not apply to the will to power. It is not that the will always runs behind the event, perpetually failing to make idea and thing, plan and execution, square with each other. The apparent 'flight forward' of the will to power shows, on the contrary, that it seeks, through its objectives, above all *itself* – the will of the will, as Heidegger says. Hence the affirmative side of the pseudo-flight, which is really transcendence, surpassing of oneself. The will to power does not look for correspondence, it *is* that: 'Aye, for the game of creating, my brethren, there is needed a holy Yea unto life: *its own* will, willeth now the spirit: *his own* world winneth the world's outcast' (*Thus Spake Zarathustra*).

Molière and Marx were aware of the paradox of the miser who lets himself be possessed by his cash-box, or of the hoarder who wants to shut up all the riches of the world in his hoard: 'Qualitatively, or formally considered, money is independent of all limits, that is, it is the universal representative of material wealth because it is directly convertible into any other commodity. But at the same time every actual sum of money is limited in amount, and therefore has only a limited efficacy as a means of purchase. This contradiction between the quantitative limitation and the qualitative lack of limitation of money keeps driving the hoarder back to his Sisyphean task: accumulation' (Marx).

Is this contradiction between the powers of money really Sisyphean? Sisyphus always recommenced his accumulation from zero, pushing his boulder towards the summit from which the divine curse caused it to roll down again. But the will to power's accumulation is of the 'expanded' sort. Even if its movement proves to be as interminable as that of Sisyphus, it pushes its stone from the summit up to higher, ever higher summits. This pebble – target, terminus, objective, aim, cause, thing – is no longer thought of as measuring the effort made, it is only a provisional limit, to be surmounted in its turn, not an end but a springboard.

Adding that it is with the hoarder 'as with the conqueror whom each new conquest merely brings to a new frontier', Marx shows himself very grumpy in his attitude to the conqueror. Did he not previously hail the conquests of a bourgeoisie which has to its credit greater prodigies 'than the pyramids of Egypt or the aqueducts of Rome'? Unlike the hoarder and Sisyphus, the modern power extends its domination unceasingly: each new frontier leads only to a new conquest. Always a new frontier, laments the passive nihilist: always a new conquest, laughs the 'active nihilist' dear to Nietzsche. 'What does Nihilism mean? *That the highest values are losing their value*. There is no bourne. There is no answer to the question: "To what purpose?"' Nothing sets limits to the dominating will, which thereby, precisely, dominates everything. By showing itself to be the ultimate formulation of lordship and possession of the planet, the active nihilism of production for production, consumption for consumption and accumulation upon accumulation makes felt the will of the will, that of a master, who wants to be alone in the world.

Plain speaking

On his travels, Zarathustra meets a gloomy old man, the last Pope weeping for his last god. Zarathustra breaks into his lamentations: 'When gods die they always die many kinds of death ... He is gone! He was counter to the taste of mine ears and eyes; worse than that I should not like to say against him. I love everything that looketh bright and speaketh honestly (*was ... redlich redet*).' God and all the modern idols are put to death virtuously, if one is capable of seeing in plain speaking – honesty, candour (*Redlichkeit*) – the virtue of virtues: 'Where mine honesty ceaseth, there am I blind, and want also to be blind. Where I want to know, however, there want I also to be honest – namely, severe, rigorous, restricted, cruel and inexorable.'

The master thinkers were all masters of language, to the point that each of them tended to fabricate a language of his own, so as the better to control it scientifically. Languages of a mastery that 'mathematically' masters itself, they always move in the circle of a 'tautology' and proceed from the similar to the same in Fichte's initial principle (Ego=Ego) as in Hegel's speculative proposition. Such, in Marx, is not only the 'dialectical' movement of capital but also that of the revolution which, 'always going to the root of things', always finds there ... itself. (This was, moreover, one of the favourite games of the young Left-Hegelian scholars around Marx: solving all problems by merely putting the prefix 'auto', or 'self', before the name of a problem. Emancipation is resolved in self-emancipation, creation in self-creation, management in self-management, the mobile in the automobile ...)

Nietzsche carried to extremes this movement of a language that wraps itself in its own mastery and subjects itself no longer to any identity, because it imposes all of them – which feels no need to embody itself in a supreme being: god, the spirit, *the* capital or *the* revolution. All these frontiers are no more than the sign of fresh conquests to be achieved, all the closed domains governing certain languages are overwhelmed by the language which masters them.

God, the states, good, evil, the true are all 'idols'. In the Age of the Enlightenment a quite different view was put forward: the limits which reason acknowledges for itself preserve it from the urge to go capering off into the beyond. Thenceforth it is no longer in the name of the limits to reason that the idols are overthrown, but because they set limits to reason. It is no longer a question of remaining critically 'on this side', but of leaping beyond. Nietzsche's 'free thought' may sometimes clothe itself in the sceptical attire of classical reason, it remains none the less modern, the assertion of a conquering mastery which is far from being restrictive and moderate. The same observation applies to a much more naïve approach, twenty years later than *The Twilight of the Idols*, when Lenin, in *Materialism and Empiriocriticism*, sides with the atheism of Diderot, and in so doing introduces his theory of the 'materialist supposition'. The 'decisive' starting-point which is supposed to provide a rational foundation for all scientific discourse is taken from Hegel, not from Diderot: it is the scientistic translation of a will to mastery learnt from the German masters (which was where Lenin found the Fichtean idea of the 'supposition': the most idealist of the philosophers inspiring the most barbarous materialists . . .).

The 'crossing of the limits' effected by Nietzsche in relation to all the 'idols' is profoundly akin to a procedure which mathematicians (Cantor) were engaged in working out in that same period – not without intense dramas.

How does one count infinity? How to distinguish between different infinite numbers? Strictly speaking, one cannot count any of them, since they are by definition infinite. The general procedure which clarifies this problem – 'diagonalization' – consists in making precise what is meant by 'the impossibility of counting an infinite number to the end', and in making from this very impossibility a procedure for constructing the said infinite number.

One can, for example, adopt a way of arranging figures in

rows, vertical and horizontal, such that in the square so constructed the number formed by the figures in the diagonal is not that of any of the rows – and this whatever the length to which the rows are extended. To put it crudely: it is possible with countables (the rows) to construct an uncountable (the diagonal) which is perfectly defined by the construction, and therefore itself a number, even though it cannot be counted on any number of fingers. What matters is not recognition that one judges the construct only by its rule of construction – which is, properly speaking, true of any mathematical entity – but recognition that there exist realities which, though no less definite than the rest, are yet never graspable as completed, constructed. Realities which, by their very construction, do not allow themselves to be constructed. This is the case with the 'highest values', according to Nietzsche. They are not built to last, but last the time it takes to build them: 'Valuing is creating: hear it, ye creating ones! Valuation itself is the treasure and jewel of the valued things.'

The great journey

The 'absence' of God is not Voltairean. It is present to the poet that Nietzsche bears within him – or that bears Nietzsche. It is not a matter of being satisfied with less than God, but of giving more than God: the modern man must be *gifted* in order to identify the absence of God. 'When this is necessary, man can remain fearless and alone before God: his simplicity protects him, he needs neither weapon nor stratagem, whenever the absence of God comes to his aid' (Hölderlin). If 'God' is dead, enthusiasm isn't.

The deconstruction (diagonalization) of the idols is affirmative: knowledge, religion, the state, are all poetic creations – idolizing them means forgetting their origin, no longer tracing their poetic genealogy. In the anarchist workers' libraries of the early part of this century Nietzsche occupied a place of honour. He still occupies this place with those who challenge the existing order: acknowledging the idols means opening them up, bringing to light the poetry that they enclose, as the Pyramids en-

closed the bodies of the Pharaohs. Nietzsche's 'frankness' frees
us; by making the 'higher realities' speak, it speaks out. It
challenges in a quite different way from the denouncing of a lie,
à la Voltaire: 'The poet sees in the liar his foster-brother whose
milk he has drunk up; the latter has thus remained wretched, and
has not even attained to a good conscience.'

The most poetic, clearest and frankest of the master thinkers
is on the point of thinking beyond the sphere of mastery, of letting his tongue and his feet take him where they will – which does
not mean blindly, since it is only in this way that the modern
world lets itself be discovered: ' *In the horizon of the infinite.* We
have left the land and have gone aboard ship! We have broken
down the bridge behind us! Well, little ship, look out! Beside
thee is the ocean; it is true it does not always roar, and sometimes
it spreads out like silk and gold and a gentle reverie. But times
will come when thou wilt feel that it is infinite, and that there is
nothing more frightful than infinity. Oh, the poor bird that felt
itself free and now strikes against the walls of this cage! Alas, if
homesickness for the land should attack thee, as if there had been
more *freedom* there – and there is no "land" any longer!' (*The
Joyful Wisdom*).

This side of any 'Copernican revolution', we set out again on
the great journey of a Pantagruel. However gigantic, the travel-
ler of the *Fourth Book* did not yet possess the scientific authority
attributed to a Copernicus: he did not master 'the horizon of the
infinite' but sailed within it. There is a 'stellar' affinity between
Rabelais's great guffaw and the voyager of the nineteenth century who blamed German scholars for their inability to laugh.
Nietzsche, too, is the only master thinker who does not proclaim
that 'art... is a thing of the past', something transcended
(Hegel), but who, on the contrary, assigns to it all sorts of
missions of exploration in the horizon of the infinite. Thereby
he surpasses, both forward and backward, the complacency of
dominating reason.

Up to what point?

'There is a lot more to language than is imagined, and man
betrays himself much more frequently than he would like. All
speaks! But very few know how to listen, so that man, as it were,

pours out his confessions into the void, wasting his "truths" as
the sun wastes its light. Isn't it a pity that empty space has no
ears?'

A master, even if he be Nietzsche, cannot hold back from the
fight against 'waste': he will be on the alert for it even in empty
space!

After God . . .

Contrary to what applies in the case of their epigones, the com
placency of the master thinkers was always, on one side or
another, outflanked by their actual thought, because they taught
something other than mastery, even if it was only this mastery
seen from without. Book-burners, take note! Even Nietzsche
poeticizes farther than he means to.

In his eyes – if not in his writing – poetry and all art remains
an activity of mastery, an assertion of will to power. He judges
poetry by its 'utility', which he sees as going back to the earliest
times: 'It was intended that a human entreaty should be more
profoundly impressed upon the gods by virtue of rhythm . . .'
The Beautiful, the Good, the True are instruments by means of
which a civilization subjects men and things: 'The essence of
any morality, what gives it its inestimable value, is that it is a
prolonged metrical constraint, a tyranny of rhyme and rhythm.'

This 'tyranny', the hidden spring of art, morality and politics,
has to be discovered at the origin of all human intercourse: we
understand each other easily when we understand each other
quickly: 'the history of language is the history of a process of
abbreviation,' says Nietzsche. Incidentally, he takes this notion
of 'abbreviation' from Hegel, who so described his own philosophical language, but did not extend the concept to language in
general.

Thenceforth, it is necessary to seek in the multiplicity of the
vernaculars the efficacity (which formerly was speculative) of
reason, that is, a tyranny which is not persuasive but *dissuasive*. After defining language as a process of abbreviation,
Nietzsche explains: 'The greater the danger, the greater is the
need of agreeing quickly and readily about what is necessary:

not to misunderstand one another in danger – that is what cannot at all be dispensed with in intercourse.' One might be
reading an argument in favour of the 'hot line' linking the
super-powers, presented by an advocate of thermo-nuclear
dissuasion. It is not a matter merely of understanding one
another negatively. Nietzsche thinks he has here the basis of any
and every agreement, since it is the only basis, the positive one:
'in all loves and friendships', he goes on to say, one has this
same experience.

In this climate, that virtue: with this natural setting, that
kind of man – so calculated the determinists of the Age of
Enlightenment, listing causes and adaptations. The master
thinkers affirm, less naïvely, that one is not determined by
whatever it is, but determines oneself in face of it. 'Verily, my
brother, if thou knewest but a people's need, its land, its sky
and its neighbour, then wouldst thou divine the law of its sur-
mountings, and why it climbeth up that ladder to its hope.'
The thousand-and-one aims of the peoples always reveal the
same dissuasive abbreviation: the situation is a challenge to
mastery, the highest mastery is mastering this challenge: 'It is
laudable, what they think hard.'

While every civilization lets itself be determined by a single
principle, the multiplicity of peoples and principles, having
become a danger to the world, requires that we programme the
single principle which will regulate their conflict: 'A thousand
goals have there been hitherto, for a thousand peoples have there
been. Only the fetter for the thousand necks is still lacking; there
is lacking the one goal. As yet humanity hath not a goal. But
... if the goal of humanity is still lacking, is there not also still
lacking – humanity itself?'

The horizon of the infinite must be understood as that of the
single aim pursued by a single mankind, the sole object of the
sole subject. Here, the metaphysician ousts the poet.

Because, in his ship, the bold sailor is not so bold that he
doesn't feel the need for a master, after God? Because a master
cannot meditate without premeditating a Great Helmsman?
Whose *grand style* Nietzsche invites us to recognize at the centre
of all art: 'This style has in common with the great passion which

it disdains to please, the fact that it forgets to persuade, that it commands, that it wills itself ... to master the inner chaos, to compel its own chaos to take shape, to act in a logical, simple, categorical, mathematical way, to make itself law, that is its great ambition.' The ambition of all the master thinkers.

How printing was invented

Let us reflect upon the conditions under which a dissuasive truth seems to be true. In appearance, it presents itself rather as the opposite of a truth. If it helps life, its reality is help, not truth. If the end and the means, the cause and the effect, the subject and the object, are beliefs necessary for life, these categories are true by virtue of their will to exist, and not by respect for truth. If truth is dissuasion, if we understand each other only in order not to dispute among ourselves, if we agree together only so as to cross the abyss on a rainbow of concepts, then the footbridge of truth is made of necessary fictions held out by a falsifying will. 'We thought we had in the categories of reason a criterion of reality, whereas they ought to serve to enable us to master reality, to deceive ourselves intelligently on the subject of what is real...'

Attention! We need to pick up with all the delicacy of Nietzsche's tweezers this attempt to carry through to its ultimate consequences the idea, launched by Hegel, that 'to conceive is to dominate' ... 'And now, behold, the world has become false through the very qualities that constitute its reality: change, becoming, multiplicity, contrast, contradiction, war.' No: dissuasive truth is a fiction because it says something is white which in fact is black, because it talks of peaceful coexistence when in reality war is raging. Nietzsche is more subtle: dissuasive truth is not less than being but more, it does not give a pale image of reality but imposes and imprints itself thereon. It is itself that which changes change into stability, becoming into being, multiplicity into unity, contrast into organization, contradiction into structure of domination, war into imperial peace, and all that through change, becoming, multiplicity, contrast, contradiction and war.

Dominating dissuasion neither finds nor seeks its truth outside itself, in a reality to which it ought to correspond. It has no need to look for a mirror in which it may laugh to see itself so beautiful, and good, and one, not even when identifying itself with 'absolute knowledge', or counter-identifying itself with 'the' capital. Dissuasion *signifies*, commands, makes a unity of the things it embraces, without awaiting its own unity from these things: 'All unity is unity only in so far as it is organization and co-operation ... It is thus a structure of domination which signifies unity but is not itself unity.' Dissuasive truth equalizes, simplifies, makes cruder: it causes the logical and pacified world to appear by starting to make it logical through terror and war – unceasingly. It cultivates the fiction of the stable being by imposing itself as the will to being – not an unstable equilibrium but a stabilizing disequilibrium.

The will of the master masters itself. It does not close itself upon an object – God, capital – or upon a single event – the speculative Good Friday or The Revolution. It closes itself upon ... nothing? Is the abyss, is terror its ultimate truth? Let the Generals declare with all the needful solemnity: 'It's me or chaos.' Nietzsche's Dionysos knows more about it than they do, and whispers: me, the Ego, *means* chaos. The master does not 'find' the abyss, he digs it deep so as to give more height to his heaven. The Generals do the same, but without being able to say so. The will of the master closes upon itself: 'To imprint upon becoming the character of being – that is the highest will to power.' This is what it discovers everywhere: was not the earliest poetry already an attempt by means of rhyme and rhythm, 'to impress a human entreaty more profoundly upon the gods'?

The ring

Here is the circle of circles: the master fabricates all the truths – his fictions – but none the less claims that *that*, at least, is true, and that he is a true master. How does he move from the truths which he masters in an arbitrary way to the truth of his mastery and his arbitrament? And what if this should also turn out to be fiction?

The master seems trapped. God was no problem: one could 'diagonalize' or deconstruct him by affirming the existence of gods more divine than the gods themselves. Here, however, paradoxes arise which are unavoidable because they bear upon what is affirmed about the affirmation itself. If I say that truth is fiction, is this statement itself fictitious? It is the paradox of the liar who says 'I lie', the paradox of the true world which becomes a fable, and of this fable which is true: 'We have suppressed the true world: what world survives? The apparent world, perhaps? ... Certainly not! In abolishing the true world we have also abolished the world of appearance!'

At grips with this circle, the master assumes a two-fold attitude:

(1) *In* the circle he plays about, becomes 'superficial by virtue of profundity', shrugs his shoulders and dances: 'What, for me, is now appearance? Certainly not the opposite of a being ... Appearance means for me life and action itself, the life which mocks itself sufficiently to make me feel that it is only appearance, a will o' the wisp, a dance of elves and nothing more: that, in the midst of so many dreamers, I too, who *know*, am dancing the same step as the others ...' Fine, but whence do I know that dancing is the step most appropriate for following this 'duration of a dream' that the world's course seems to be? What unshakably dancing foundation will there be for my *tango ergo sum*? Nietzsche asks himself this question, and so we get:

(2) *Before* the circle, 'I' find myself 'at six thousand feet above any inhabited locality', in a place and time truer than the rest. 'Noon: the moment of the shortest shadows; the end of the longest error; mankind's zenith; *Incipit Zarathustra*.' Is this still fiction?

Am I inside or outside? Inside, if any view over the world effects a certain preliminary division of this world in relation to my project, to the perspective in which I dance. Outside, since I say: everything is a matter of perspective, I must look down from on high in order to take account of it. Very well, dance now! Necessarily inside, and Nietzsche deduces from this the argument: 'The total value of the world cannot be evaluated, and therefore philosophical pessimism is comical.' The pessimist leaps above the world in order to judge it, and 'therefore' he is comical. But isn't this 'therefore' just as comical? The optimist, too, leaps above the world. And this leaping is just as comical. Already, by saying 'the' value, and, what is more, 'the total' value 'of the' world, has one not been the first to leap above the world, in order to treat it as *one*? And even if one chooses plurality (rather than unity), difference, worlds (in the plural), where is one situated when one makes this choice? Somersaulting off again above the worlds? Necessarily outside? Comical! 'In short, we do not have the right to represent our intellect to ourselves in this contradictory fashion, as a belief and at the same time as knowledge that this belief is only a belief.'

At this point in the argument, if one wants to remain sound in body and mind, one denounces a sophism. And thereby honours the Sophists by sitting them on the same bench of infamy between great thinkers and modern mathematicians. The thinker has questioned the truth of fiction-truths, the world of worlds, in the same way as the mathematicians of the beginning of this century 'fell upon' paradoxes (including that of the Liar) by developing the 'naïve' theory of wholes. The 'total value' of the world is impossible to evaluate for the same reason as one cannot state whether the whole of all the wholes which do not contain themselves contains itself. If yes, no: if no, yes. Is the world, which contains everything, contained in its own evaluation, or does it contain this? And if it contains it, how can it be an evaluation of the world? And if it does not contain this, how can it be called the world?

Though new for mathematics, these paradoxes possess ancient nobility in philosophy: '*That is true which can be proved.* It is an arbitrary definition of the world "true", it cannot be proved ... That means that the axiom: *what can be proved is true* presupposes truths given in advance.' While Nietzsche is not frightened of falling into the circle, still less does he avoid it. He makes us see there the classical *locus* of the principles, axioms, truths given in advance (*a priori*), all notions translated or borrowed from the Greek thinkers who made them turn by removing the undergrowth from the clearing of their 'first meditations'.

Nietzsche was not frightened by seeing the master go round

and round in the circle of his mastery. He cheerfully pointed to this as the sign that a dominator will always need to have a philosophy. It remains to ascertain which philosophy meets this need.

Zero hour

Order is dissuasively ensured in the world by the reciprocal terror of the opposing powers, with much better effect than if one camp were to try to determine it persuasively, by referring to common interest or respective strengths. This was known before the coming of thermo-nuclear weapons. Power is based upon opposing chaos, while stirring up chaos when necessary. All grand policies are put into action 'on the brink of the abyss' and all grand decisions imposed because it is 'that or nothing'. Peace seems to be positive, whatever its nature, because it seems to suspend total catastrophe, and it is perpetuated by actually suspending that catastrophe ... over its head. A peace is strengthened the more as war comes to entail greater risks, a war is turned into peace when it becomes increasingly dangerous, an escalation is halted as it nears the climax, the ever-nearer possibility of the ultimate catastrophe brings ever-nearer the possibility of perpetual peace. Thus, the power to destroy dominates the power to construct. These beautiful truths of dissuasive strategy did not have to wait for the experts of the Pentagon or the Politbureau to discover them. The master thinkers pondered over these truths of mastery in the conditions of the modern age, the age when one dominates by dissuasion rather than persuasion. Nietzsche was the one who expounded these truths most freely: '... One needs to have tyrants opposing one in order to become a tyrant oneself, that is, a *free* man. It is no small advantage to have a hundred swords of Damocles hanging over one's head: it teaches one to dance, it gives "freedom of movement".

'The thinker who has appreciated that within us, alongside all growth, the law of destruction also prevails, and that it is indispensable that everything be destroyed and dissolved pitilessly in order that other things may be created and come to birth –

he will have to learn to find in contemplating this fact a kind of joy, if he wants to be able to *bear the idea of it*: otherwise, he will no longer be able to know. He needs, therefore, to be capable of refined cruelty and to prepare himself for that with a resolute heart.

'Apollo's misapprehension: the eternity of beautiful forms, the aristocratic prescription, "Thus shall it ever be!"'

'*Dionysos*: sensuality and cruelty. The perishable nature of existence might be interpreted as the joy of procreative and destructive force, as *unremitting creation*. Transvaluation of all values. Taking pleasure no longer in certainty but in uncertainty: neither "cause" nor "effect", but a continuous creation: the will no longer a will to preserve but to dominate: no longer that humble saying: "It's all only subjective!" but this declaration: "It's all our work too – let's be proud of it!"'

Mastery and mathematics

Nature becomes an object of mastery in the modern sense as soon as it lends itself to mathematicization (Galileo, Descartes). Mastery of society, in its turn, requires mathematics, even when it aims to transcend mathematics in a speculative language more rigorous still. The high style of mastery always aims at being 'mathematical'.

Does this mean, reciprocally, that the project of mastery is internal to mathematics? Mathematicians thought so, and were still at the beginning of this century programming (Hilbert) the perfect mastery of their own language – this perfection to be guaranteed not only by excluding all contradiction (that always applies) but also by excluding the very possibility of encountering contradictions and antinomies. Mathematics would thus be established as the highest science of law (Husserl's 'nomology').

We know that this did not happen, that mathematicians eventually formulated their method in a different way, abandoning the ideal without abandoning rigour altogether. And they gave themselves the additional pleasure, in a celebrated theorem (Gödel), of demonstrating that unless its domain was confined to the poorest and least interesting fields, mathematics could not aspire to obtain absolute mastery of itself and exclude in advance all possibility of antinomic statements.

Interpretations of the various solutions proposed for the 'crisis' in mathematics are even more numerous than the solutions themselves. However, it is not impossible to divine what it is that will enable mathematics to evolve freely, with the ideal of absolute mastery set aside. In itself, mathematics has never claimed to say everything about everything, although it has been accused of this. The mathematical logician can avoid the reefs of antinomy by not engaging in piracy on two oceans of language, which he excludes at the outset of his plans for voyaging. Thus, for Tarski, there is, 'underneath' mathematics, colloquial language which says everything about everything in an ambiguity which no logic can make univocal: and, 'above' it, nonexistent except as something rejected, a theory of theories which would also speak about everything, pronouncing upon truth in general: 'The language of the general theory of truth would then contain a contradiction for exactly the same reason as does colloquial language.'

The logicians construct subtle and diverse hierarchies, crisscrossings of languages, with the superior language (metalanguage) controlling the inferior one (language-object). But the logicians expressly exclude the possibility that this hierarchy has a firm hold on its basis (the common language) or that it has a summit which dominates everything (a general theory of truth, a nomology). Broadly speaking, mathematics 'emerges' from this by agreeing to let itself be overwhelmed by the vulgar, common, ordinary language, which it no longer aspires to absorb or dominate. Mathematics has, in its own way, internalized this common vulgarity: by agreeing never to master everything, itself included, mathematics has acquired the possibility of talking in its own way about everything, including its own limitations. The language will not possess the universality of mathematics, as this was dreamt of by the philosophers who followed Descartes (an end to *mathesis universalis*): but, on the other hand, mathematics, immersed therein, will profit by the ambiguous, un-masterable universality of a colloquial language which, as Plato already put it, 'makes all things move about'. Henceforth, if he really tries to imitate mathematics, the master will drown.

Mastery and theology

It is said that all the unhappiness of modern man is due to his imagining that he is God, or that his master is God ('the cult of personality'). A convenient explanation, this: we are dying of religion, we aren't scientific enough yet. Funny! The greatest crimes of our century have been committed to that tune. Not funny at all!

If we are to believe the augurs of theory, to deduce respect for the master from respect (unadmitted, unconscious) for God is scientific and materialistic. Bravo: the respect we show on earth derives from our respect for heaven. The shattering materialist interpretation of the Gospels is discreetly accompanied here by an evangelical interpretation of materialism. By spending one's time wondering which is the true god, God or matter, one forgets to ask why this true god and this true matter always present themselves with the real authority of a true master. How many final solutions are yet to come and dance on the point of that sword?

And what if, instead of seeking God in the master, one ought to pursue the master even so far as God? To ask when and how the master recognized himself in God. Perhaps one ought to inquire whether that did not happen at the expense of the gods, just as with every 'object' that the master claimed to subject to his mastery?

Mathematics provides a model of mastery because it seems to dominate a language completely, by 'constructing' it. Even before mathematics thereby became the emblem of power, and later on in rivalry with it, theology tried its hand in the same role. 'Proving' the existence of God means binding the highest realities in the chains of a language. Declaring that 'God is dead' asserts the same power, which is why Nietzsche called to mind there an act too great for those who had committed it. Whether one proves God or refutes him, one ensures, by hypothesis, that 'everything' is to allow itself to be dominated by a language which dominates itself by providing its own 'proof'.

It has been observed that the efforts of rational theology stumbled against antinomies akin to those encountered by the 'naïve' theory of wholes. 'The antinomy which imagines the concept of *that which is such that nothing greater can be conceived* is mathematical,' notes J. Vuillemin, examining St Anselm's 'proofs'. One finds, each time, the ambition of a language that claims to cause to exist that of which it speaks, moments in which reason has been 'led to reflect upon its creativeness and to realize its extent and power', arriving thus at 'the rational idea of God' (ibid.). This ambition will be recognized in rational theology just as in the naïve theory of wholes. The principles are similar: the principle of comprehension (Quine) or of abstraction (Russell). They consist, when we conceive a condition (a property), of supposing the class, the whole, the elements of which are the things that fulfil these conditions (or which are defined by these properties). The 'ontological proof', which deduces God's existence from his essence, thus crystallizes a claim of a more general order: it haunts the language of a modern reason which wants to possess what it talks about, and to dominate its possessions.

God or Not-God matters little as soon as, on this point of existence or non-existence, a language masters everything that exists: 'God remains dead! And we have killed him! ... Is not the magnitude of this deed too great for us? Shall we not ourselves have to become gods, merely to seem worthy of it?' (Nietzsche). Conceiving 'that which is such that nothing greater can be conceived', and thinking that he conceives this, it is his own greatness that a master measures, whether in God or in the absence of God.

When God died, he had been replaced long before by a double.

A metaphysical passage

'Above "you must" there is "I want" (the heroes), and above "I want" there is "I am" (the Greek Gods).' No reader of *Thus Spake Zarathustra* is unaware that Nietzsche's thinking revolves around a doctrine which, though unformulated, is central ('its place in history is at the centre'), namely, the enigmatic Eternal Recurrence. This crazy-mystical aspect of Nietzsche is to be stressed because he finds nothing to say about this supreme key – unless we note that Marx doesn't say much more about his final revolution and that Hegel is careful to state that he has absolutely nothing to say about the buckskin breeches monarchically installed at the summit of his Philosophy of Right. The Eternal Recurrence, the Revolution, the Monarch, all are just what they are, and so much alike that they become the same thing when the eternal recurrence of the revolution is monarchically affirmed by Mao 'for 10,000 years and more'.

The master thinkers enclose everything within the ring of their mastery and their way of embracing everything is elliptical, because it always includes two *foci*: Will to Power and Eternal Recurrence, Capital and Labour, Bourgeoisie and Revolution, In-Itself and For-Itself, Spirit and Nature, Ego and Non-Ego. The great principles go two by two, polarizing battles and paradoxes, but, even more, conditioning the thought of all. Mastery of the whole: Will to Power. The whole of mastery: Eternal Recurrence. The whole of domination: Capital. Domination of the whole: Revolution, the class struggle as the 'driving force' of history, and so on.

A circle like this is logical by the antinomies that it causes to circulate, and is theological in that it defines 'supreme' realities which it at once subjects to itself by reasons and the proofs of its reasonings. Even more, it shows itself onto-theo-logical, to follow the very useful commentary made by Heidegger on Nietzsche's fundamental categories. It invites us to see in the Will to Power the classically limited domain, like that of the essence (*essentia*), whereas the Eternal Recurrence raises the questions of existence (*existentia*) traditionally projected in the Existent of existents, God. The relation between these two *foci* of examination, more complex than that imagined in the scholastic pseudo-evidence of 'existence' and 'essence', constitutes those circles which are avoided by no modern philosopher, beginning with Descartes when he guarantees by God the truth and eternity of the certainties found by 'I'.

We begin to divine the ways by which the master thinkers adapted themselves to apparently insurmountable difficulties. For example, that one can say hardly anything about the Revolution or the Eternal Recurrence: these realities correspond to the question 'what', not to the question 'how', to the 'practical' question of what exists, not to the theoretical question of what it is. The division between these two ways of questioning seems, as such, to be perfectly arbitrary, but this arbitrariness is rooted in the tradition of Western metaphysics. The division between general and special ontology still clearly subjects to its arbitration both Marx and Nietzsche: 'The twofold question: "What is Being?" is asked, on the one hand, as: "What (in general) is Being?" and, on the other, as: "What is (that which is absolutely) Being"?' (Heidegger).

'To be radical means to grasp the matter by the root' (Marx). And where is this root to be found? In God, who talks Science and Logic to himself before creating the world (Hegel). In man, for whom 'the root is man himself' (Marx). In the world which reproduces itself Dionysiacally (Nietzsche). When the three chapters of special metaphysics have been exhausted, one turns to general metaphysics to obtain a similar programme of radical mastery of everything that is, that moves, that passes. Being is a masterpiece.

Every modern domination is metaphysical at bottom. The master revolves within the circle of his mastery, leaping gaily from the logical to the theological circle and from the supreme beings to the science of beings in general: he plays on the three keyboards of onto-theo-logy. Does this mean, reciprocally, that every metaphysics is, at bottom domination? The master thinkers all said so: not, however, without suggesting that the strictly modern recasting of thought has catastrophical aspects. There was Nietzsche declaring that we live in the authoritarian tradition and in the imperial translation of the *Imperium Romanum* rather than in the looser framework of Greek thought. There was Marx joking about the worship offered by his contemporaries (and himself) to productive labour, which both Aristotle and Caesar would have ridiculed. Master of himself and of the Universe, Racine's Augustus is strictly modern, dubiously

Roman, and certainly not Greek. Metaphysics managed for a long time without the master thinkers: inquiring *how* would necessitate another investigation. But the master thinkers cannot do without metaphysics, even if it becomes with them increasingly unadmitted. The masters are modern in their will to dominate everything, their own discourse included. Thereby they strive to will themselves unique and solitary. Consequently they are blind to the links that bind them one to the other, and all to the past of the West of the masters, except when they scent, as though in spite of themselves, that the will to dominate dominates them too. At once lost in their ambitions, and saying more than they would ever know, in a century which has not ceased to echo them.

The final opera

Whom does one fear one may meet upon the Wagnerian scene? Hitler, perhaps, but, no less likely, Lenin, Marx, a certain Freud, and some anti-Freudians. Though the nineteenth century experienced few social and political upheavals, it programmed a good many of them. Order, Labour, Revolution, Ultimate Chaos – the ideas that are dominant today were produced in that period. All that we have done that's new is to apply them. Wagner alone puts them on the stage, unreal as yet, but already palpable: questions of power, money, sexuality and death. The meeting of music, poetry and gesture is the work, suggests Wagner, of the 'Knowing of the Unconscious'. *What Wagner puts on the stage is thought*, the thought that goes on in the back of the head. These thoughts of the century are not innocent, for they brood upon *domination of the world*, explains Nietzsche, the iconoclastic disciple of the great Sachem of Bayreuth.

Politically, Wagner is not original. He was on the Dresden barricades in 1849, with Bakunin: prosecuted and exiled, he abominated property, the state and religion, and declared himself a communist – one in a thousand, neither more nor less than Marx and Co. But what is of more than anecdotal significance is that his great work *Der Ring des Nibelungen* was, in the main, conceived during this period in which Wagner was on familiar terms with the 'goddess Revolution'. He aimed to erect his barricades upon the lyric stage, challenged opera as an invention of palace-bound aristocrats, announced that 'no longer shall "Prince and Princess" be sung', that the people, disalienated and communist, were to rediscover themselves in the *musical drama*, 'the work of art of the future'. A cultural revolution, in short.

Except that the Peking opera is, by comparison, *chi-chi* and conventional. Wagner did not get his inspiration from the Maos of his time, but from Oedipus: 'When he stabbed the light from eyes which had flamed wrath upon a taunting despot, had streamed with love towards a noble wife – without power to see that one was his father, the other his mother – then he plunged down to the mangled carcass of the Sphinx, whose riddle he now must know was yet unsolved. It is *we* who have to solve that riddle, to solve it by vindicating the instinct of the Individual from our society itself; whose highest, still renewing and re-quickening wealth that Instinct is' (*Opera and Drama*). Siegfried, the Individual, was to be born of the love of Siegmund and Sieglinde, consciously brother and sister.

All the Marxist interpretations of Wagner are insipid. The subtlest, Adorno's, does not refrain from labelling the pettybourgeois primitivism of this 'representative of a class condemned by history'. But suppose one were to try it the other way round, interpreting Marx by Wagner?

How do *the capitals* gather together into a territorial unity of 'vampire' quality, called Capital? How does this 'universal power' enclose within its circle all that is diabolical in our society? This 'truth' promised by the title of the book, which we search for in vain as we study each page, pre-exists over and above any proof, beyond the reach of any refutation: what matters is not to read *Capital* but to listen to its music, the *leitmotiv* of 'the curse of the ring', that is, of money. Shakespeare, who had some kind feelings for the women of the streets, called it a universal whore; Goethe said it was black magic; the nineteenth-century thinkers taught the following century that it was the source and the sum of all evil.

'The' Revolution against 'the' Capital – so begins the myth of the Ring and of Siegfried. Who is Siegfried? A child, a barbarian? Yes, and yet also 'the very opposite of a simpleton, a being who lives and acts in the highest consciousness' (from a letter of Wagner's). We recognize here the child of all German metaphysics, the union of theory and practice, the disalienated one who is 'freer than the gods', the individual reconciled with nature, which he hears and understands, integral mankind without fear or envy, total man. Who invented Siegfried – Wotan, or Hegel, rather? The death of the gods brings about the birth of man!

Wagner swells out this dream, swells it out until it bursts: he displays it and he smashes it. At the beginning, everything seemed to derive from the one conflict between inhuman gold and human love (*Das Rheingold*). Then there enter in the difficulties of a god, Wotan, who has to enforce respect for the laws, and therefore to seem to respect them himself: he has need of a reliable man who will not compromise him, and who must therefore be 'free' (*Die Walküre*). This man, self-managed and self-made, makes his appearance (*Siegfried*). Then, a *coup de théâtre* at the beginning of the final episode (*Götterdämmerung*): we learn that the story of the theft of the gold is a trivial affair compared with the initial crime of a god who, through his will to power, has begun an endless series of rapes and acts of violence. The central problem is not the gold at all, but Wotan. Suddenly, Wagner rises in the end above all the little Marxist laurel-wreaths that anyone might wish to crown him with.

Behind the theft of the Ring is Wotan's enterprise. Behind the fantasm of capital is the question of power. The gods with long teeth have need of final battles. If Valhalla, power, the Forbidden City, the palace of the Central Committee burn, then everything burns. Me or chaos. The *tabula rasa* as a method of government. Hiroshima my desire. Power does not persuade but dissuades. Why does it assert itself in the planning of catastrophes? Why does it know only one history, that of an endless count-down? Why do the states keep Apocalypse-time? Why are the gods born fit for twilight?

The Wotan-state had concealed its own monstrosity by focusing all hatred upon 'the gold'.

Who is Wotan? Wagner defines him as 'the totality of the intelligence of the present time'. The nineteenth century programmed for us poor creatures – technocratized, Marxized, managed – a discourse which takes account of everything and says everything: about the one who speaks and the one who listens, about every object that can be evoked. The power whose discourse this is presents itself as absolute, in that it allows of nothing outside itself, no contrast. It has the hard gaze of the Valkyrie, this power which reveals itself only to tell us that our end has come.

> But fated men
> My form may look on:
> To whom 'tis shown
> Full shortly must leave this life.
> On the war-plain alone
> The warrior sees me ...

The strong state reflects itself in its twilights: that of Hiroshima or that of Cambodia. The death of others, the death of itself, power blooms in its congealing blood.

> With silent sign
> Walhall's warriors
> Sent he to hew
> The world-ash-tree in pieces.
> With the mighty fragments
> He bade his heroes build him
> A towering wall
> Circling the shining hall.
> The gods to council
> He commanded.
> In state on his throne
> Wotan sat;
> By his side
> In torturing fear they assembled,
> In ring on ring
> And row on row stood the heroes.

Wagner might have remained a prisoner of this programme. His plans for an 'integral' work of art emphatically bear its imprint. But he frees us with his disintegrated masterpieces.

Wotan will never cease to get bogged down in the dead-ends of power. Brünnhilde vacillates between her father and her half-brother. Siegfried confuses his women. We shall never know whether Tristan and Isolde die or make love. This is the revenge of music, which does not let itself be integrated, and of drama in which whoever tries to pull the strings gets his feet caught in them. Isolde the witch, Tristan the traitor, Parsifal the fool, Wotan punished at last, all sail far away from Total Man. The twilight can descend, men and gods are not any more cunning than each other. When love shines forth death laughs in its beams; the reverse is no less true, sings Brünnhilde.

Burning what he had worshipped, and detesting the Wagnerites above all, Nietzsche nevertheless suspected the truth. 'Is Wagner's "Parsifal" his secret laugh of superiority at himself, ... is it Wagner able to laugh at himself?' (*Nietzsche contra Wagner*). Laughing at himself and at us, at his time and therefore at ours.

A man sets out upon a stage the grand machinery of modern power: he launches the speeches, prepares the imbroglios, puts the fantasms into action. It works. In his miracle of Bayreuth he realizes the philosophy of Hegel and of Marx, that of the Kremlin, the Pentagon and the Forbidden City. He guffaws in our faces.

The Finishing of History

'... not like a fish in the water, but loaded like a
U-boat. Both within and to one side. The water supports,
holds, contains. Being at one's own density and yet all
made of steel, T.N.T., a nuclear slug. Hypocrite!
Definitely, all the vices! Bara, cut-throat, saint,
assassin ... policemen.

'Policemen ... yes. An extra curse, the people can
be cut down by the people.

'You go up to a mobile security company and say:
"Let the sons of barristers, doctors, industrialists,
professors step out of the ranks!"

'Nobody, you may be sure, nobody at all will step
forward. There you have a troop which, if it did not come
out of the land and the factories, would never advance.
Quite the contrary, marvel of marvels, it charges. The
father bashes the son and the son the father, in splendid
set-tos of the under-developed; after drinking,
truncheons and bloody double hits: if you want it, here it
comes.'

IPOUSTEGUY

I

Subtle, refined, crafty and complex as it is, the doctrine of the master thinkers does not seem an unfathomable mystery. It expounds the implicit philosophy of the civil and military general staffs. This doctrine becomes universal when these general staffs are renewing themselves all over the world.

This would be perceptible were it not for the blinkers provided by the 'critique of totalitarianism'. Some American intellectuals attempted to set out under this heading the responsibilities common to Stalin and Hitler. What was wrong with this way of presenting the matter was that it let the 'non-totalitarian' regimes off the hook, to the point of blindness to all filiation (intellectual or historical) as well as to all kinship (practical and contemporary) linking harsh methods of domination employed both in the West and in the East.

The critique of totalitarianism shows a tiresome tendency to boil down always to a critique of totalitarianism *elsewhere*. In contrast to the United States and Britain, celebrating the peaceful liberalism of the Glorious Revolution of 1688, Continental Europe is said to dream only of Terror and Counter-Terror (cf. Hannah Arendt or J. L. Talmon). In contrast to Europe, there is the U.S.S.R. and its glacis. In contrast to the U.S.S.R., there is China. Around China, there is, sometimes, the entire world. Totalitarianism means the others.

Out with totalitarianism? Totalitarianism at one's own door! The technique of the concentration camps was systematized at the very dawn of our century by liberal Britain, when her generals had to put down the (white) rebellion of the South African colonies. Since then, Britain's methods have entered into widespread use, while the former Boer rebels are developing them for application to 'their' blacks. The mentality which causes them to be accepted goes back even further in time. When he put a Texan hat on that officer of his who, astride the Bomb, launches the Apocalypse, Stanley Kubrick in *Dr Strangelove* seems to have had a much clearer perception of the true genealogies. Instead of seeking in the Jacobin tradition of Continental Europe the sole example of historical and cultural violence in modern times, the theoreticians of totalitarianism would have done better to take a look at the Westerns of their dozen T.V. channels. They would have discovered there how a genocide became a founding myth. They had observed correctly that on one side of the Atlantic people started, or re-started, their history by killing a certain percentage of wicked aristocrats, or of *petroleuses*, depending on changes in opinion. They might have admitted that, on the other side, they had begun by killing all the Indians, followed by a good proportion of vagabonds, bandits and girls of dubious virtue. Not to mention the Negroes. Two different versions of 'the origins of totalitarian democracy', capable of preparing the way for similar operations carried out against what remains of the Indians, against the Vietnamese, the South Americans ... or the inhabitants of Dresden, Hiroshima or Nagasaki.

Neither the producers of Westerns nor the master thinkers invented out of nothing the stories that are told when a genocide is carried out. The massacre of the New World began with its discovery, as is testified by Montaigne, an already horrified witness. The master thinkers systematized and made strategically manageable ideas and tactics that were widely diffused before their time, in societies that were in process of becoming rationally disciplinary. The kernel of their doctrines (the idea that in the modern age one does not persuade but dissuades) was universally accepted. The main principle of their strategy (not so much to constrain as to terrorize) became that of every respectable general staff. Their grand design (the drilling and selection of the world's *plebs*) is on the agenda all over.

Here is the occasion for smelling out what is distinctive about the modern powers. It is not the absence or presence of state ('totalitarian') terrorism, which we find everywhere, but rather the conditions under which it is possible to *struggle against this* – the very concrete possibilities of communicating one's opinion, of going on strike, of demonstrating, of examining the records of the powerful, of stopping a colonial or imperial war, or of preventing its secret commencement. No general staff granted these liberties: here and there they were seized, to a greater or less degree, never complete, always provisional – these differences, neglected in the History which the master thinkers organize, are what make up the rough and the smooth of *our* century. For those, at least, who do not philosophize as members of a general staff.

2

The present day variants – Russian, American, Chinese – of the doctrine of the master thinkers are numerous, but the end-effects are always the same. Between the bomb falling from a B52 and the bullet spurting from an automatic rifle of Russian or Chinese make, between the proclaimed Marxist motivation of the latter and the unproclaimed Hegelianism of the former, the Cambodian peasant, transplanted, starved and massacred, has little leisure to note the differences which from afar seem to be so important. Such great concern to preserve these differences proves much in favour of an effective education (civic, political, metaphysical and theological) and leaves few illusions regarding the gentleness of Western ways.

Cannon-fodder everywhere, never his own ruler, insubordinate and therefore an animal to be tamed, the peasant of Europe was the first embodiment of the *plebs* that the authorities aim to drill. From their birth, the workers' organizations cultivated bourgeois contempt for the clodhopper, displaying thereby their urbanity and the modern, scientific character of their different shades of socialism. The fact that Europe's peasants are no longer the majority of its population does not prevent the majority in present-day society from being still the target of a very fantastic and learned contempt. This contempt beats down from the élite upon everyone who does not form part of that élite, and also beats laterally, from one stratum to another: contempt for the workman, for the office-worker ('unproductive', 'bureaucratic', 'pansy'), contempt for the muck-shifters. Contempt felt by each category for the others, and even for itself. Since they present as obvious the image of the *plebs* who have no destiny unless they let themselves be guided theoretically, the master thinkers can be very properly cultivated by this epoch of scientific contempt.

The proof that the *plebs* are incapable – whether only for the moment, or permanently, the result is the same – of deciding for themselves always proceeds by way of proof by The Revolution: whether this revolution is to be made or re-made, or has been definitively accomplished, whether it is good or bad, is of little importance once it has been recognized as a deed too great to fall within the capacity of a *plebs* without a shepherd. There is a discourse on revolution the various *nuances* of which glimmer in a rainbow display which always closes in upon the same conclusion: the people, in this difficult transition, needs to be held by the hand – whether the leader be a professional revolutionary, an expert in psychology, a licensed official, or a star-spangled Pentagon General.

The matrix of this proof by revolution was very carefully constructed in the three canonical phases of the master thinkers: the revolution of minds prepared by the science of the intellectuals, the terrorism of the masses against the masses, and the final establishment of a new order by the new officials. Just as the German masters gave systematic form to ideas that they found scattered around them, so are variants of this matrix of order invented without its being necessary to have read Hegel and Marx (who, whether studied or not, thus remain universal).

The circulation of ideas in France provides a good example of linkage between revolutionary experiences, ideas about these experiences and theories about these ideas. The Marxists announce every ten years that Marxism has been poorly implanted in this country, that it 'cannot be found' or that, at any rate, it lacks the scientific character, philosophical rigour or culture which it is alleged to possess under more favourable skies. Actually, Marxomania is no less widespread in Paris than elsewhere: for a century there have been a thousand and one 'chapels' which are more or less Marxizing, Marxian, Marxological, crypto-, pseudo-, or hetero-Marxist. All that the French might have grounds for lamenting would be their not having known the hegemony of a single school of Marxism – more or less united – dominating an organized and responsible labour movement. This was (not without *nuances*, and looked at from a distance) the situation in Germany and Austria down to 1930, and also the situation that 'Gramscian' Italy is supposed to be in today. As for the Russian and Chinese Marxisms, which imposed their hegemony through the criticism of weapons before bringing about the triumph of the weapons of their criticism, *their* example cannot, without retrospective (or prospective) illusions, serve to illuminate the situation in France.

If Marxism was for a long time less 'hegemonic' there than in the neighbouring countries, that was for a simple reason – the place had been taken. The 'great lessons of the Revolution' did not wait for Marxists to draw them – they were drawn by historians, argued over by intellectuals and diffused on a mass scale by the educational system. Jaurès grasped admirably this national peculiarity: he endowed 'his' labour movement with a 'socialist' history of the Revolution, thus translating into French the operation which Kautsky began, in the German way, on the other side of the Rhine, by splitting theoretical hairs. Having become the leader of a 'great party of the working class' Thorez could not but repeat, on a lower intellectual level, the same attempt, by mingling the strains of the *Marseillaise* and the *Internationale*. In France Marxism is not 'impossible to find' – it had already been found before Marx: the traditional 'history lesson' gave voice, from the primary school onward, to the song of the master thinkers. If they wanted to achieve recognition in their own names, they would have to choose this exclusive means for conquering the French ear. A misunderstanding, perhaps, but not a misdeal: in getting themselves accepted as commentators on the Great Revolution, what were the masters finding but the imprints of the first intellectual steps they had taken? Had they not begun with a fascinated contemplation of 1789?

3

The theory and the history of the Revolution are twin sisters. Were they born of the same event? Or of its interment? By wishing itself one and indivisible, national and world-wide, definitive, and therefore concluded, did not *the* Revolution, in inaugurating its own commentary, place in orbit these theories and histories which set it out of reach? This is a problem which presupposes quite different studies, direct and historical in character, of the events concerned. Here I propose merely to surround it with some questions.

Far from having invented the canonical scenario of the revolution, the master thinkers systematized and absolutized standpoints which appeared in the course of the events: they embraced theses that were put forward by the actors in the drama – not without giving them greater solidity and conferring upon them a somewhat ossified legitimacy. The idea that the revolution was, in its first stage, prepared by the entire century of the Enlightenment was shared by many members of the Constituent Assembly and by all those of the Convention. Some swore by Montesquieu, others by Voltaire, yet others by Rousseau, but all were agreed in exploiting their inheritance of an intellectual Authority. As for the thesis of a second phase, one of necessary terror, of struggle by all against all, and mistrust and egoism on everyone's part, Saint Just expounded this himself, from the tribune: 'It is a question of the ills of a revolution, a question of making a republic out of a dispersed people with the débris and the crimes of the monarchy, a question of establishing confidence, a question of instructing in virtue hard men who live only for themselves' (29 February 1792, speech on 'the impossibility of free trade'). The governments of revolutionary France did not wait for Lenin or Mao before proceeding to carry out revolutionary requisitions, to swing the levelling scythe, or to 'fight against selfishness' among the masses. As for the final phase, that of the establishment of a new order, few revolutionaries and fewer historians doubt the need for this. All that they argue about is the date when the revolution came to its end. One or other of those turning-points of the Terror in which the decisive intervention of the Paris masses seemed to reach its climax? The liberal republic of the Directory? The restoration of state authority by Napoleon? Since the summer of 1791, when Barnave declared: 'The revolution is over,' the debate about the place and the time when this happened has continued lively, first among contemporaries and then among historians. Few doubt that the revolution was a single event, with a beginning and an end.

As such, the unity of *the* Revolution, conceived as a 'single' whole, seems to be mythical. The idea of a 'telescoping of several revolutions' (Furet and Richet) seems to sum up fifty years of investigations which have enabled historians to stress the original aspects of the *sansculotte* revolts and the great peasant insurrections: 'It seems to us impossible to show that the aims of the élites grouped in the academies and intellectual societies were the same as those of the peasants of the Sarthe or those of the Paris artisans' (ibid.). The events of 1789 here lose the so-to-speak substantial unity accorded to them by past historians who spoke of the undifferentiated unity of 'the people'. Today's historians endeavour to transfer this unity from the substance to the event: the Revolution has a beginning and an end, and so remains one and indivisible.

(i) In the beginning the 'telescoping' occurs. It is therefore not at *that* moment that we should look for the unity of the revolution. Even if we were to suppose, through retrospective illusion, that the culture of the élite (the Enlightenment) prepared the Revolution of the élite, the peasants' Revolution had other sources, as had, often, the urban Revolution too. When the historian G. Lefebvre records the plundering and arson carried out by the peasants at the start of the Revolution, he is careful to emphasize that 'these are not acts of collective madness, as has so often been suggested. The people always has its own way of dealing with things. In 1792, for instance, a miner from Littry was killed by a *garde seigneurial* and his comrades went in most orderly manner to the seigneur's farms and place of residence, which they then proceeded to destroy and burn in a very methodical way, one after the other, carefully evacuating anything belonging to the farmers and the servants so as not to damage the property of those not involved. All the peasant revolts followed this pattern.'

Jacqueries in the countryside and *émotions* in the towns not only belonged to a lengthy tradition of popular upheavals, con-

tinued over several centuries. In them were manifested deeply
rooted popular cultures: 'There was no shortage of laughter
among the threats and the violence. At Collonges, the Macon-
nais rebels on their way to Pollet's country house put themselves into a great good humour by saying that they were going
to *fricasser ce poulet* (cook this chicken), a play on words which
gave them enormous pleasure; they sometimes dressed up – a
belt tied round a sheet, a curtain cord or a bell-pull; a cockade
made out of a lotto card. There was no sort of viciousness, no
attacks against women . . . Taine's "lewd and bloodstained
monkey" made no appearance here.' We see that 1789 does not
merely telescope several series of violent events but also, through
these events, several sets of customs and cultures, and starts off
the divergent cultural revolutions which can perhaps be perceived in the great de-Christianizing movements (not entirely
inspired from above) and in the Chouannerie (almost entirely
inspired from below).

(ii) Does the opacity of these telescopings become transparent
when they merge in a second phase? With the evidence of intervention by the popular masses, who, during their *journées* in
their *sections* are supposed to have raised directly 'the question
of power', the Jacobin Terror often figures as the moment when
the Revolution becomes one and universal. This was the 'plebeian way' of accomplishing the Revolution, said Marx – who also
said the opposite, namely, that the Terror was a panic reaction
on the part of leaders who had lost their way. Marx hesitated,
but not his epigones, who reconcile the two contradictory
appreciations with a cheerful: 'The time wasn't ripe; we'll do
better next time.' Could this be the eternal moment of the
Revolution? '. . . Who does not realize that some of the problems which confront a revolutionary movement today were
there already, in some other form, at the heart of the complicated and terrible situation, social and political, of the Year Two?
. . . The revolutionary path or the path of compromise? Total
destruction of the old economic and social system, or preser-
vation of the old mode of production within the new society?
We know how, between 1789 and 1794, the French Revolution

decided that debate' (A. Soboul). Do we really know that? Is it supposed that the hopes of today can be made transparent through the dreams of yesterday? Or the dreams through the hopes?

Let us quote one example, only one, but a significant one, that of the famous 'September massacres'. They caused both blood and ink to flow. Scrupulous historians have rejected the thesis of administrative preparation of the massacre and manipulation of the massacrers: here, a relatively spontaneous mass movement caused 'people's tribunals' to operate in complete sovereignty. What do we see? The bloodstained ape of Monsieur Taine? Or the 'acculturated' masses who are capable at best, when deprived of the leadership of a liberal and enlightened bourgeoisie, of believing in the magic solutions of violence? This is what Richet and Furet suggest: 'Revolutionary patriotism had become a religion and already had its martyrs. Before long, as France lost ground in the war with Prussia, it was also to have its Inquisition and its public executions.' Or should we recognize, in Marxist–Leninist style, that, at grips with a catastrophic situation, the people reacted with vigour, beginning to 'exercise authority in all matters', an initiative the secret of which the Jacobin dictatorship was to pass on to the future dictatorship of the proletariat?

The thesis of the historian Pierre Caron on *Les Massacres de Septembre* does not give a direct answer to any of these three questions, but makes them seem irrelevant because its very detailed account of the event compels us to formulate quite different ones. The men of September set to work on nine prisons containing about 2,800 prisoners, of whom they killed between forty and fifty per cent. Of those massacred, two-thirds were common-law criminals (four of the prisons involved had no political prisoners in them): mostly very young persons and petty thieves. 'The people put to death individuals charged with stealing a tablecloth, or a piece of flannel, or a few chattels, a watch, a horse, a handkerchief, etc. Massacred also was a cook accused of theft within the household ...' At Bicêtre thirty-three inmates of the children's reformatory were killed, the youngest aged twelve and the oldest seventeen.

The massacrers were not at all 'the dregs of the population', and not exclusively people of the lower class. We find amongst them also the usual militants of the *journées parisiennes*, members of the 'middle class'. They had been prepared by the opinion-formers: the newspapers summoned them to their task, and respectable persons like Bishop Thomas Lindet gave their approval, while the passivity of Roland, the Minister of the Interior, no less than that of Robespierre, indicates that mental complicity was quite general.

Everything points to the fact that what happened was not so much a change of justice as a temporary substitution of judicial personnel, with these 'judges for a day' playing their parts in a way that respected the mental and social categories, no less than the severity, of the old justice. 'Specifically judicial consider-ations possessed, in the September events, an importance which has been overlooked: it was to the mass of the prisoners without distinction – and not to a particular category among them, the rest being only accidental additions – that the justice of the *Prévôté de Paris* was to be broadly applied. And the massacrers were to show even more severity towards the wretched "straw-ies" of the Châtelet or the convicts of the Bernardins, and more severity also towards the hated nonjurors of the Carmes or of Saint-Firmin, than towards the lay counter-revolutionaries of the Abbaye or La Force.'

The people's justice of the Year Two was not aimed especially at the aristocrats, it was not political: nor in the main at the 'class enemy', it was not social. Its target was the enemy of society in general and it functioned as state justice temporarily under-taken by the people. The enemy is at our gates, we must go to the frontiers; the prisons are full, the prisoners are plotting to take advantage of our absence to violate our property and our women: we will give a hand to the government, help it expedite its business; this is not a matter of lynch-law. Speeded-up pro-cedure, citizen judges, interrogations, sometimes acquittals: it functioned more quickly than usual, but always in accordance with classical justice. In former times, the King could take the place of the courts: this theory of the 'retained power of justice' was transferred from the King to the sovereign people. When this happened, the state did not become the people; the people acted in the role of an occasional, temporary functionary of state.

We can see why historians concerned to explain the event fail to encounter any of the 'major questions' for which it served as pretext. The popular hydra spoken of by Taine does not show itself here. The mental participation of the great majority is ensured, that of good society, of its newspapers, and of its ministers. Whether the Terror is Red or White, the massacres in the prisons are all alike and bring into play the same moral categories. As for the Marxist-Leninists, they present as 'people's power' this moment when the panic-stricken Parisians imitated the ancient justice of their *Prévôté*, at the expense of the humblest handkerchief-thieves! Finally, it seems superficial to ascribe (as Furet and Richet do) to religious simplicity, millenarianism or the people's 'acculturation', a form of conduct so perfectly historical, dated and *cultivated*. Frequentation of the prisons did not begin with the Revolution. The reason, usages and morality of the classical epoch, the age of 'the great locking-away', were honoured in these days of September 1792, by the men of order, from the greatest to the least, on the backs of the massacred, and, in particular, of the most pitiable of them. Bourgeois and police reason triumphs here. 'We understand the mistake made by the historians who write of a "show", a "parody" of justice. They have misunderstood certain intentions. Tribunals of blood, hasty judgements, hatred, cruelty, yes, as much as you like: but caricature, mockery of the courts, no. On the contrary, a grave task carried out with all the seriousness of fanaticism' (P. Caron).

The fanaticism of reason against unreason, of good society against the 'bad' sort, of those who are not in prison against the lepers who are locked away there, all without distinction, creatures who in prison are still dangerous, contagious, given to plotting. The massacres were, as Michelet put it, a 'great and radical moral purging': this had been administered steadily for two centuries to the good people of Paris, until now, when they were administering it to themselves, at a time when the royal authority had disappeared and the new authority was not yet firmly established. With the revolutionary tribunal and Dr Guillotin the purging became once more a job for professionals.

During the Revolution the state continues and grows stronger. The centralized state, created by the absolute monarchy, goes on functioning, rationalizes its administration, multiplies its grips upon the population. No historian has shown this better than De Tocqueville. Power was never in abeyance – in the second phase, the *sansculotte* and Jacobin one, any more than in the first. With the Terror there did not in the least emerge 'from the darkness of the unconscious the ancient, centuries-old fear of the wretched of this world' (as Furet and Richet claim). Fear, yes! But the whole of society felt the same fears: that of the 'plot in the prisons', for instance, which kept on reviving, now to the Left, now to the Right, bringing with it, besides September, the *noyades* at Nantes and the great massacres in Lyons and the towns of southern France in the Year Three. This major obsession was to be the justification of the liquidations, one after the other, of the Hébertists, the refractory priests, the Chouans, and then the 'Terrorists' and 'Mathevons'. These are the fears of Reason – reason of state at the same time as classical, moral, philosophical reason, as Michel Foucault has shown. State, put forth one effort more if you want to be republican!

Quite naturally, Terror extends the power of the police, with the methods of the police: 'What an invitation, indeed, to delation, calumny and the gratifying of old grudges is a regime of Terror, whether this Terror be revolutionary or royalist, blue or white!' (R. Cobb). The year 1793 does not show us, all fresh and pink, 'people's power' with everything that it may have about it that is exalting, hideous or naïve, according to taste. The Terror? Not the masses who seize power, but power which seizes the masses: the contradictions among the people systematically and rationally placed at the service of the government. When Lyons was subdued, all 'the inhabitants of this vile city' were treated as victims without distinction: 'We shall still send them our dragoons, to make them dance the *Carmagnole* in the style of the commandant of the place, who politely smashes their faces in with a rifle-shot' – '*Père Duchêne*' thinks like Louis XIV and talks like the Leninists yet to come. *Le dragon, c'est moi*, says the Sun-state, whether revolutionary or monarchical.

The state popularizes its great problems of public order, not all of which, moreover, are artificial (the 'fatherland' is at certain times really 'in danger'). At the same moment, by a different movement, the population, differentiated and divided as it is, puts forward its 'petty' problems and does this publicly (which is what is new in the revolution): the price of bread, the price of soap, the need to eat in order to live. Sometimes it criticizes 'the inequality of possessions'. In the countryside there is refusal to submit to requisitions or conscription. The micro-authorities of everyday life (squires, parish priests, bourgeois men sent from Paris) are challenged, without too much of a claim being made to control the macro-politics of the central authority: it is more a matter of day-to-day living than of the 'major problems', of social life, not of the state, of here and now rather than of eternity. Ever since the *cahiers de doléances* there has been no stopping this tremendous movement of subversion, in which the great majority, still dispersed and full of contradictions but no longer silent, brings its own problems into the open, publishing and sharing them, analysing and transforming them.

Far from being transparent, as the master thinkers and numerous historians suppose, the *sansculotte* phase of the Revolution accumulates 'telescopings'. To the previously existing ones, in which the various strata of French society clashed, it adds that of society and the state. While the state revolutionizes society by means of terror, society undertakes to revolutionize itself – two different things.

(iii) The revolution goes 'to the root of things' (Marx): as 'revolution' in its phase of dictatorship by the Mountain (school of Mathiez and Soboul), and as 'bourgeois' in its third phase, that of the new economic order (the Directory, according to Furet and Richet). The two theses are equally Marxist, and the founding father upheld one after the other. Actually, the Marxists-Leninists, who are fascinated by the second, the dictatorial phase, cannot avoid the necessity of a third one (any more than Lenin could avoid the N.E.P.).

The final phase is taken to show a 'relative transparency of bourgeois civil society and of the revolutionary process' (Furet): it is the Thermidorian Directory, for example, which returns, after the 'skid' represented by the Terror, to 'the main road traced out by intelligence and wealth in the eighteenth century' (ibid.): the world of business which is also the republic of the professors, the bourgeoisie is now installed. This theory aroused the fury of the Marxist historians of the Sorbonne: a gigantic 'ideological battle' followed, and the clashing of replies, challenges and rejoinders can still be heard. If he learns of this fracas, the uninitiated person will perhaps be amazed to see so much hostility poured out in defence of one and the same conclusion: namely that the Revolution came to an end, and this end was the France of bourgeois liberty and the fraternity of business deals. The same ultimate reality, with only a difference of date: the Directory for Furet Richet, Louis Philippe for Soboul. The difference is slight and perhaps not insurmountable: 'Louis Philippe was being wished for' when Bonaparte thrust himself in, Furet and Richet have already said.

This history with measured steps makes us regret two great absent ones: the state and the majority of society – in this case, Napoleon and the peasants. 'The liberal bourgeoisie was opposed once more by revolutionary terror in the person of Napoleon,' says the young Marx. In this way he brings together into one the two great trends – social-democratic and Leninist or pro-American and pro-Russian – which argue today about *the* French Revolution. The bourgeoisie is sufficient unto itself with the free mechanisms of the market! It has no more need for the state, it makes the least possible use thereof! A very British, very nineteenth-century myth: in order to cultivate it with regard to 1789 one needs to forget De Tocqueville and the continuity of the strong state which he emphasizes, and to short-circuit Napoleon as a throwback which disfigures the liberal society that is supposed to come forward with the Directory or with Louis Philippe. Napoleon was liberal in matters of industrialization and, within the limits of his situation, in matters of trade as well? The French bourgeoisie remained statist in its wars, civil and foreign? Let's not dwell on these things, mortals...

There are some splinters in our heads: the peasant questions.

If it is One and Indivisible, the French Revolution can only be essentially bourgeois. How so? Why, by anticipation! In fact, capitalism did not dominate French society either in 1788 or in 1800 or in 1830: 'It would still be a long time before capitalism would assert its authority definitively in France: its progress during the revolutionary period was slow, the size of enterprises often remaining at a modest level ...' (Soboul). Well? Soboul gets out of his difficulty by means of a metaphor: the Revolution 'had none the less uncompromisingly cleared the path for bourgeois relations of production and circulation'. It 'swept the board' by destroying the system of feudal property and the guild regulations. Except that, on this clean-swept board, it installed a huge opaque mass: the peasants and the petty-bourgeois of the towns, who supported the Napoleonic regimes and likewise the Third Republic, but who were obstacles according to Marx and all the liberal economists, in the path of development of modern capitalism. That path which had just been represented to us as having been 'uncompromisingly cleared' was blocked by the horde of independent producers whom Soboul goes on to describe as the result of a compromise, of an alliance between the big bourgeoisie and a section of the people.

From the Marxist standpoint the Revolution was bourgeois because it cleared the path leading to the capitalist market, because it set face to face 'free' sellers of labour-power and capitalist buyers thereof who were no less free. But when did it do that? Was it necessary to wait until 1950 to establish that 1789 was a bourgeois revolution? In the meantime, far from 'freeing' the peasant from his land, in the English manner, the Revolution fixed him upon it by guaranteeing his (often pretty miserable) property-rights.

Less embarrassed by the demands of orthodoxy, the exegetes of the other camp are all the more acrobatic in their efforts to stay faithful to the common basis of the Marxist and liberal tradition, namely, the English model of the free market. The bourgeoisie was 'pre-capitalist'? Never mind, retort Furet and Richet: 'Everything happened as though it felt itself to be already in control of the economy, and aimed to use this position to advance still further. For its intellectual maturity was more undeniable than its economic maturity.' Splendid! This intellectual maturity which was capable 'already' of anticipating control of an economy which did not yet exist shows that 'the' bourgeoisie of 1789 was not only ready to lead 'its' revolution but also to look forward to the situation in 1960, a 'France without peasants'. Meanwhile the consolidation of peasant ownership resulting from the alliances of the Year Two was to enable 'nineteenth-century France to experience both stability in the countryside and backwardness in agriculture ... These were lasting restraints upon the spread of capitalism ...' This capacity ascribed to the bourgeoisie for leaping over two centuries is well worthy of the science-fiction presciences which Soboul distributes even more generously: 'The popular masses were well aware of the fate awaiting them, which was why they showed themselves hostile to the economic freedom that opened the way to concentration and capitalism.' What giants confronted each other in that Revolution! Between a bourgeoisie able to control an economy which did not begin to exist until a hundred years later and popular masses who were already resisting this control of a non-existent market, the peasants cut but a poor figure. Or is it, perhaps, these historians who lack imagination – where the countryfolk are concerned, though not elsewhere?

Why these trips to the moon? Because it is convenient to end the Revolution, as Barnave said in 1791, and Bonaparte too, in so many words, on 18 Brumaire, and others who offer the flower to the Directory, or to Louis Philippe, or to the period when they are writing, or to the moment when they expect to be read. An unending revolution is not a revolution: with telescoping after telescoping one would never emerge from it. And have we emerged?

The only point of view which makes it possible to bring into unity the telescopings of the Revolution of 1789 is the point of view of the one who puts an end to it. There is no single voice of the People expressing itself indivisibly and intelligibly at each great moment. For a long time now, historians have ceased to claim that they hear this voice. Divergent and opposite ruptures

have destroyed the unity of French society. That majority of
'fringe people' who do not form a majority, that third of the
French people who do not speak French but who are beginning
to concern themselves with their own affairs, those ninety per
cent of 'barbarian' peasants, with 'limited horizons', who are
grouping themselves, hamlet by hamlet ('war to the *châteaux*,
peace to the cottages'), all those little peoples who are putting
forward their illiterate questions – how can one make of them
one great event? Patient research has enabled us to glimpse the
immensity of this explosion, and yet, when called upon to produce a synthesis, historians allow themselves to adopt the point
of view of whoever they see as the one who puts the full stop –
either the Directory, or Napoleon, or Louis Philippe, or
General de Gaulle. For lack of being able to define a *substance*,
one concludes the event, so as to provide a completed *period*: the
bourgeois revolution.

Free (oh, how free) from any philosophical presuppositions,
our historians set their feet, at the moment of conclusion, in the
prints left by the master thinkers. They end their works with that
same New Year's landscape in which the snow covers up the
disturbances caused by the *plebs*, now reduced to silence, while
the bell-tower of the state gazes down upon the vast plain of the
economic free market. On the back of this card are various
seasonal wishes. The state must dominate the market by becoming a 'closed commercial state' (Fichte), or socialism in a
single country; the market must cause the state to disappear; a
higher force (the Spirit, the Revolution, the Eternal Recurrence)
must subject to itself both market and state: 'Only the fetter for
the thousand necks is still lacking; there is lacking the one goal.'

What is lacking? Why, that which has been hidden under the
hoarfrost of learning, those thousand faces, revolting against
fetters, who do not all speak with the same voice. They seem
monstrous to those who can make them out through the crack
in the learned monologue of the supreme thinkers and the
masters of the world. Yet they are there, and history is never
anything else but what happens to them.

A thousand scattered insurrections, fantastically condensed

into a 'seizure of power', a variety of revolts by oppressed people obliterated by *the* bourgeois revolution – this entire optical device proves incapable of suppressing the great opaque mass at the centre of the X-ray picture of the events of 1789. It is a cancer in the well-pasteurized and scholasticized universe in which the state focuses the question of power while the economic market locks everyone away in his own solitude. Precisely! The events of 1789 in France, and other more scattered revolts, across the centuries, from the first riots in Florence to the 'doubtful battle' of the workers before the New Deal, to the struggles of the Blacks and the students in the U.S.A. during the Vietnam war – all these disorders are more decisive than the waltz of rulers and regimes or the determinisms of an economic market about which, in the end, it is admitted that they always function too soon (1789) or too late (today) to be really determining.

Between the newly privileged and the majority of the population, 'the' French Revolution settled down in a compromise. A compromising one, which brought 'rural democracy' (Jaurès) and an uncertain number of freedoms, but also the military brutalization to which the peasant soldier was subjected, from the sun of Austerlitz to the mincer of Verdun and the twilights of the Riff. In 1930 came the great crisis, economic upheaval, a fresh compromise, the New Deal. The great opaque mass lost its peasants, and became filled with white-collar employees, underpaid typists and needy students – the great army of the poverty-stricken. There was the no less equivocal compromise of an incomplete democracy, which bore within it the danger of various forms of fascism consolidating from below upward the hierarchies of petty bosses, but also opportunities for antifascist movements, and then for liberation movements bringing changes in men and ideas, more or less breaking up authority and hierarchy in the instability of a constantly renewed contestation. In Europe, cultural revolutions did not wait for 1789, nor did they end then: telescoping the privileged against the unprivileged, and the latter among themselves, they remain like successful psychoanalyses according to Freud: *unending*.

In order to hold back a contestation that might prove too

sweeping, the élites of Western society had to decide between two methods. The soft method was to share out, as inequitably as possible, the privileges that were being challenged, so that everyone, apart from the immigrant detail-worker, might enjoy a few crumbs: credit, consumption, a place in some hierarchy or other, and for one-third of the population the advantages – slight, and yet culturally and socially undeniable – associated with 'brain-work' in its many forms. The peasants and artisans, the former middle classes, had melted away, but others, more numerous, had come to fill these middle positions, the buffer zones which prevent society from being polarized. 'In the capitalist mode of production . . . the independent peasant or handicraftsman is cut up into two persons. As owner of the means of production he is capitalist; as labourer he is his own wagelabourer. As capitalist he therefore pays himself his wages and draws his profit on his capital; that is to say, he exploits himself as wage-labourer, and pays himself, in the surplus-value, the tribute that labour owes to capital.' Here Marx is amusing himself in the role of master thinker: he treats as an *exception* what was the rule for the great (peasant) majority in nineteenth-century Europe, and as a *rule* the theoretical polarization between those who have nothing to lose and those who acquire everything . . . It is a rule without an example, a rule which the master imposes on a reality that escapes from his mastery, and Marx was to explain why, by way of exception, industrial Britain in its turn cocked a snook at the rule, since the numbers of its 'unproductive' workers (employees in the tertiary sector) grew faster than the numbers of the 'productive' ones.

For all that it is more rarely peasant than it used to be, the West of today is no less than before 'cut up into two persons', and engaged in 'exploiting itself'. This does not mean – *pace* Marx! – that there are only those who exploit and others who are almost exclusively exploited. In that 'almost' lies the whole secret, not only of the classical peasant but also of modern society: *everyone* participates in the reproduction of exploitation – for example, by going on strike to *prevent* an armaments factory from going out of business, or waging a trade-union campaign to ensure that a costly giant aeroplane, of no use to ninety-nine per cent of the people, is 'saved'. If one takes account of this internal division it becomes impossible to imagine a single, ultimate revolution, wherein good and bad face each other in a decisive battle. If no one escapes completely from the reproduction of relations of exploitation, if everyone is 'dual', then the majority have their own guns trained on themselves.

The central zone appears opaque to the master thinkers and to the systematizing historians. It escapes from their conceptual slicings. Confrontation is always happening there *already*, but never, perhaps, for the last time. This history without beginning or end overflows that zero line in time (revolution, terror) from which the master thinkers start their reasoning, and fails to direct our gaze towards the Apocalyptic occasion which is to decide the government of the world, or the Great Good. The State does not dominate the market, nor does the world market absolutely dominate the states, and furthermore, there is no higher power – Hegelian, Marxian or Nietzschean – dominating *these* powers. This history takes place 'in between': the language makes everything move about among this diverse population where people find themselves – like Marx's peasant or handicraftsman – 'cut up into two persons', neither everything nor nothing, and yet not a throw-back. There one resists or one yields, but without ever evading the struggle against oneself.

This middle zone of men who are not exclusively exploited and yet not themselves exploiters was in former times acknowledged by Socrates and by Panurge. Others stride about in it, recruiting-sergeants through whom an élite mobilizes its masses for the 'war to end wars', either national or social. Some set up their scenery with great sweeps of Apocalyptic contrast: gold and virtue, private life and public good, the monologue of science and the stammering lips of lost children.

Under colour of learning, the master thinkers erected the mental apparatus which is indispensable for launching the grand final solutions of the twentieth century – and they did this on a large scale and quite openly. There are no grounds for blaming the honest frankness of a Nietzsche: he says everything, and the twentieth century has only to read him literally, to listen to his every word, and light the lantern of the Gulags from his plain speech. The master thinkers raised to the level of the speakable that will to power which inspires, more pettily, more covertly, the bosses and under-bosses of disciplinary societies. Because I have not only been subjected to their *mise en scène* but have also played a minor role in setting it up, I cannot hope to be able to draw the curtain with the ironical magic of a Prospero:

> ... These our actors,
> As I foretold you, were all spirits and
> Are melted into air, into thin air:
> And, like the baseless fabric of this vision,
> The cloud-capp'd towers, the gorgeous palaces,
> The solemn temples, the great globe itself,
> Yea, all which it inherit, shall dissolve
> And, like this insubstantial pageant faded,
> Leave not a rack behind.

Paris, 2 January 1977

Notes and References

IN THE BEGINNING WAS THE INTERRUPTION

1. **Panurge Outside the Walls**

Quotations from Rabelais are taken from the Penguin translation. The interpretation of the Thélème episode accepted and honoured in the universities, as 'an act of faith in the excellence of human nature' (Plattard), is not the one advocated here. However, studying *Les Langages de Rabelais*, François Rigolot has noted the 'enigmatic' aspect of this abbey of Cockayne: 'These *liberated* people possess every liberty except that of differing from others ... Theirs is *life in unanimity*, with all its false promises' (*Études rabelaisiennes*, Geneva, Droz, 1972).

3. Jean Pasqualini (Bao Ruo-wang), *Prisoner of Mao*, London, André Deutsch, 1975. A. Solzhenitsyn, *The Gulag Archipelago*, London, Collins-Fontana, 1974, p. 419.

4. M. Foucault, *Discipline and Punish*, London, Allen Lane, 1977, pp. 172, 208, 209.

5. Every book on modern logic devotes a chapter to antinomies and paradoxes (including that of the famous Cretan also known as the Liar), so that no bibliography is needed here. Works that may be consulted are: Jules Vuillemin, *Leçons sur la première philosophie de Russell*, Paris, Armand Colin, 1968, and, by the same author, *Le Dieu d'Anselme et les apparences de la raison*, Paris, Aubier, 1971. A. Tarski, *Logic, Semantics, Metamathematics*, Oxford, Clarendon, 1956: W. Quine, *The Ways of Paradox*, New York, Random House, 1966.

On Rabelais's laughter, see M. Bakhtin, *Rabelais and his World*, Cambridge (Mass.), M.I.T. Press, 1968, p. 72.

Hegel, *The Phenomenology of Spirit*, Oxford, Clarendon, 1977, p. 27.

6. M. Bakhtin, op. cit., pp. 81–2. Marx, *Collected Works of Marx and Engels*, Vol. 6, pp. 486–9, and *Capital*, I, Penguin edn, 1976, p.103.

7. Marx, *Contribution to the Critique of Political Economy*, London, Lawrence and Wishart, 1971, p. 146. Marx, *Capital*, Vol. I, Penguin edn, pp. 235–6; Vol. III, F.L.P.H. edn, 1959, p. 449. Lenin, *Collected Works*, 4th edn, Eng. version, Vol. 22, p. 276. Clausewitz, *On War*, Vol. I, London, Kegan Paul, 1911, pp. 44–5. G. Sorel,

Reflections on Violence, London, Allen and Unwin, 1916, pp. 22, 127.

Plato describes, in *The Laws*, V, 739 c, an ideal city of communal life very similar to Thélème (*The Laws of Plato*, Eng. trans., London, Dent, 1934, pp. 121–2). Compare, from a different standpoint, C. Jambet, *Apologie de Platon*, Paris, Grasset, 1976, pp. 128–9.

2. Siegfried Without Knowing It

Fritz Lang's film *The Testament of Dr Mabuse* (1933) was banned by the Nazis. The sole activity of Dr Mabuse, locked away as a madman, was writing: he laid the foundations of 'the empire of crime', conceived in accordance with the general principle of 'order through chaos'.

Thomas Mann, *Betrachtungen eines Unpolitischen* (French translation, *Considérations d'un apolitique*).

The Kant quotation comes from his *Anthropology from a Pragmatic Point of View*, The Hague, Nijhoff, 1974, p. 179. The Engels quotation is from Marx and Engels, *Selected Works in Three Volumes*, Vol. 3, London, Lawrence and Wishart, 1970, p. 376.

The cradle of bureaucracy

The etymology of 'territory' is mentioned in P. Legendre, *Jouir du pouvoir*, Paris, Minuit, 1976, p. 246 n. [Cf. O.E.D.: 'The original form (of the word) has suggested derivation from *terrere*, to frighten, whence *territor*, frightener, territorium, "a place from which people are warned off"' – Trans.]

E. Vermeil, *L'Allemagne*, Paris, Gallimard, 1945, p. 100. W. Scheel, 'Friedrich Ebert was our first opportunity of democracy': speech on the centenary of the Bayreuth Festival, 23 July 1976 Vermeil, op. cit., p. 24. R. Musil, *The Man Without Qualities*, Eng. trans., London, Secker and Warburg, 1954, Vol. 2, pp. 258, 259.

Revolution by means of texts

Trotsky quoted from I. Deutscher, *The Prophet Unarmed*, London, O.U.P., 1970, pp. 342, 343–4.

The game of the law

Rousseau quoted from *The Social Contract*, London, Dent, 1973, pp. 193, 195, 196.

Being in the good books of the powers that be

On the MacNamara strategy, see A. Glucksmann, *Le Discours de la guerre*, Paris, l'Herne, 1967, p. 371. Kafka quoted from *The Castle*, London, Secker and Warburg, 1942, p. 82. Legendre, op. cit., pp. 157–9.

The game of truth

Kafka quoted from *The Castle*, op. cit., p. 21, and from *The Castle* (definitive edition), London, Secker and Warburg, 1953, p. 322 [one of the quotations is from the 'additional material', included in the definitive edition, which was not in the original translation – Trans.]; also from *The Trial*, London, Gollancz, 1937, pp. 13–14. Legendre, op. cit., p. 69; J. P. Sartre, *Situations VIII*, Paris, Gallimard, 1972, pp. 468–9.

Trading in influence

Legendre, op. cit., pp. 169–70.

The class of the law

A. Thierry, *The Formation and Progress of the Tiers État*, London, Thomas Bosworth, 1855, Vol. I, p. 17. Stalin, *Works*, Eng. edn, Vol. 6, p. 47. Marx, *Collected Works of Marx and Engels*, Vol. 3, p. 186.

The Germany within

Mehring quoted from *Absolutism and Revolution in Germany 1525–1648*, London, New Park Publications, 1975, pp. 31–2. A. and M. Mitscherlich, *Le Deuil impossible*, Paris, Payot, 1972, p. 56 [the original of this is *Die Unfähigkeit zu trauern*, 1968 – Trans.]. Nietzsche, *Umwertung aller Werte*, Vol. 2, Munich, DTV, 1969, p. 674.

3. The Impossible Mr Socrates

A first attempt at a survey of 'contestation' inside the American Army will be found in David Cortright, *Soldiers in Revolt*, New York, Doubleday, 1975. W. Sombart quoted from *The Quintessence of Capitalism*, London, T. Fisher Unwin, 1915, p. 358. P. Clastres, *La Société contre l'état*, Paris, Minuit, 1974. Mao quoted from *Quotations from Chairman Mao Tse-tung* (vest-pocket edition), 1968. Hegel quoted from *Philosophy of Right*, Oxford, Clarendon, 1965, p. 7: *Lectures on the History of Philosophy*, Vol. I, London, Routledge, 1955, pp. 384, 441, 442–3; and *Verhältnis des Skeptizismus zur Philosophie*, in *Werke*, Vol. 2, Frankfurt, 1970, pp. 248, 252. Kierkegaard quoted from *The Concept of Irony*, London, Collins, pp. 203, 285–6, 286. Éluard, *Tout dire*, in *Œuvres complètes*, Vol. 2, Paris, Gallimard, 1968, p. 363. Céline, *Journey to the End of the Night*, London, Chatto and Windus, 1934, pp. 6, 7, 146. Socrates quoted from Plato, *Four Socratic Dialogues*, trans. Jowett, Oxford, Clarendon, 1903, p. 63. Solzhenitsyn and others, *From Under the Rubble*, London, Collins and Harvill, 1975, p. 275. [The French edition of this book is called *Des Voix sous les décombres*, i.e., 'Voices under the rubble' – Trans.]

THE FOUR ACES

Fichte (1762–1814) came from a poor family of country folk and looked after cows until he was seven. A rich benefactor made it possible for him to study. A miserably paid tutor but a gifted thinker, he was sometimes helped financially by Kant. Like Kant, at the peak of his fame, he fell foul of the censorship. He published at Zurich his *Considerations Aimed at Correcting the Views of the Public Concerning the French Revolution* (*Beiträge zur Berichtigung der Urtheile des Publicums über die französische Revolution*: French trans., Paris, Payot, 1974, *Considérations sur la Révolution française*), which gave him the reputation of being a Jacobin. This caused Fichte to be summoned by Goethe to the University of Jena, where he made his mark as *the* philosopher of a new epoch. A few years later he was dismissed on grounds of 'atheism'. After considering the possibility of teaching at Mainz, in the part of Germany occupied by the French, he went to Berlin, where he gave lectures at his own home, before professors, ministers and high officials of a Prussia which was then undergoing reform. He maintained ambiguous relations with the young romantics, and made himself the herald of German anti-Napoleonic patriotism (*Addresses to the German Nation*, 1808), offering his services to the reforming ministers. His theory of 'the closed commercial state' aimed at ensuring control of the economy by the central government through a state bank and a monopoly of foreign trade – an ideal of autarky which the various versions of 'socialism in a single country' were unconsciously to revive. When he died he was Rector of the University of Berlin: a moderate patriot, opposed to Napoleon, whom he accused of betraying the Revolution, but not a royalist.

The life of Hegel (1770–1831) is better known (cf. F. Châtelet, *Hegel par lui-même*, Paris, Seuil, 1968). A student revolutionary who, along with his friends the future poet Hölderlin and the future philosopher Schelling, greatly admired the French events of 1789, he became editor of a newspaper and then head of a school in the part of Germany occupied by Napoleon, whom he respected and served. He ended in Berlin as the dominating figure in German philosophical life.

Marx was born in 1818 in Trier, in a Jewish family, German and liberal, which converted to Christianity as a matter of convenience. He died in 1883. His life story is nowadays well-known. Those who find wearisome the hagiographical tone of his usual biographers should consult, in order to discover a Marx like everyone else: Françoise Lévy, *Karl Marx, Histoire d'un bourgeois allemand*, Paris, Grasset, 1976.

Friedrich Nietzsche's life story is also well-known – often, indeed, better known than his work. Born in 1844, he was from 1870 to 1874 friendly with Wagner, who was then at the height of his glory, and became the composer's quasi-official (and unconditional) philosopher, as may be seen from his *The Birth of Tragedy*, and, to a lesser degree, *Thoughts out of Season*. It was after estrangement from Wagner that he produced his major works. Put away as insane in 1889, he died in 1900.

Kafka quoted from *The Trial*, etc., London, Secker and Warburg and Octopus, 1976, p. 566.

1. The New Greece and Its Jew

Kafka quoted from *Letters to Milena*, London, Secker and Warburg, 1953, pp. 219–20.

The eternal youth of thinkers

Heine quoted from *Religion and Philosophy in Germany*, Boston, Beacon Press, 1959, pp. 158–9, 161. Nietzsche quoted from *The Birth of Tragedy* (in *Complete Works*), p. 12. Fichte's life, see X. Leon, *Fichte et son temps*, 3 vols., Paris, Armand Colin, 1922–7. Hegel, *Lectures in the History of Philosophy*, London, Routledge, 1955, Vol. 3, p. 425.

The height of perversity

For Hegel on the Jews, see his *The German Constitution*, in *Political Writings*, Oxford, Clarendon, 1964, p. 242. Hegel also quoted from *Philosophy of Right*, op. cit., p. 134. Himmler: see Leon Poliakov, *Harvest of Hate*, London, Elek, 1956.

I think, therefore the madman doesn't think

Descartes quoted from *Meditations*, in *Discourse on Method, etc.*, Penguin Books, 1960, p. 102. M. Foucault, *Histoire de la folie*, Paris, Gallimard, 1976, pp. 57–8. [The English translation, *Madness and Civilisation*, London, Tavistock, 1967, is an abridgement of an earlier edition of this book – Trans.]. This disrespectful cleaning up of a famous passage has greatly distressed the modern Cartesians and professors of philosophy. So far as the passages are concerned, I think Foucault's is to be preferred. So much the worse for prejudice.

What does a Jew lack ?

Hegel on Judaism in *The Spirit of Christianity and its Fate*, in *Early Theological Writings*, University of Chicago Press, 1948, pp. 185, 201–2, and in *The Philosophy of History*, New York, Dover Publications, 1956, p. 197.

No life outside the state

Fichte, *Considérations sur la Révolution . . .*, op. cit., pp. 160–61. For the play on words, see the German original in *Schriften zur Revolution*, Berlin, Ullstein, 1971, p. 176.

The German sickness

Hegel, *The German Constitution*, in *Political Writings*, op. cit., pp. 146–7. Nietzsche, *Nachgelassene Fragmente*, *Werke*, III:3, p. 80.

The Revolution and the State

Hegel, *The German Constitution*, in *Political Writings*, op. cit., p. 182. Also *The Philosophy of History*, op. cit., p. 447. These are notes taken at old Hegel's lectures and published after his death Nietzsche, *Die Geburt der Tragödie: Der griechische Staat*, Stuttgart, 1964, p. 214.

The State and the Revolution

Lenin, *Collected Works*, Vol. 20, p. 46. R. Marienstras, 'Les Juifs ou la vocation minoritaire', in *Les Temps modernes*, Aug.-Sept. 1973. M. Molner, *Marx, Engels et la politique internationale*, Paris, Gallimard, 1975. Lévy, op. cit., p. 153, Marx to Engels, 14 June 1853, in *Selected Correspondence*, F.L.P.H. edn, 1956, p. 104. Engels, in *Neue Rheinische Zeitung*, 13 January and 29 April 1849, in *Collected Works of Marx and Engels*, Vol. 8, pp. 234-5, and Vol. 9, p. 360.

The philosophical baptism of Karl Marx

Hegel, *Political Writings*, op. cit., pp. 180-81, Marx, *Collected Works of Marx and Engels*, Vol. 3, pp. 170-72.

The new order

Fichte, *Considérations . . .*, op. cit., p. 228. Hegel, *Political Writings*, op. cit., pp. 161 and 220-21, and *The Philosophy of History*, op. cit., pp. 173-4.

A disciplinary machine

Hegel, *Political Writings*, op. cit., pp. 159-60, and *Philosophy of History*, op. cit., p. 279. For Hegel on Antigone, see *Phenomenology of Spirit*, op. cit., pp. 286-7. Fichte, *Considérations . . .* op. cit., p. 246.

The panoptic apparatus

Hegel, *Philosophy of History*, op. cit., pp. 450, 456, and *Philosophy of Right*, op. cit., p. 289. On 'panopticism', see M. Foucault, *Discipline and Punish*, London, Allen Lane, 1977, Chapter III, section 3.

The high places

Hegel, *Philosophy of History*, op. cit., p. 221.

I think, therefore the state is

On 'conceiving is dominating', see J. Wahl, *Le Malheur de la conscience dans la philosophie de Hegel*, 2nd edn, Paris, P.U.F., 1954, p. 154, and D. Janicaud, *Hegel et le destin de la Grèce*, Paris, Vrin, 1975,

p. 65. On Chronos, see Hegel, *Philosophy of Nature*, Oxford, Clarendon, 1970, p. 35.

The beggars of Europe

D. Goldstein, *Dostoïevski et les Juifs*, Paris, Gallimard, 1976, pp. 226, 264. L. Poliakov, *History of Anti-Semitism*, Vol. 3, London, Routledge, 1975, pp. 150, 377, 505. See also Nietzsche, *Nachgelassene Fragmente*, *Werke*, VIII: 2, p. 177: 'The profound contempt with which the Christian was treated in the ancient world, which had remained noble, is found again today wherever an instinctive repulsion is felt regarding the Jews: this is the hatred of classes which are free and conscious of themselves towards those *who sneak in* and who combine timid gestures with a ridiculous self-conceit.'

The statesman and his 'other'

Hitler, *Mein Kampf*, Eng. trans., London, Hurst and Blackett, 1939, pp. 58–9.

The ideological multiplier

Hegel, *Philosophy of History*, op. cit., p. 98. For a detailed description of antisemitic crises, see L. Poliakov's *History of Anti-Semitism*, op. cit. However, this author fails to emphasize the decisive role played by mass statism ('nationalism').

2. Why I am So Revolutionary

Nietzsche, *Thus Spake Zarathustra* (in *Complete Works*), p. 329. Hölderlin, *Hyperion*, in *Werke und Briefe*, Vol. I, Frankfurt, 1969, p. 300.

Apologia for the masters who lead nowhere

Briefe von und zu Hegel, Vol. I, Hamburg, 1952: letters of 13 October 1806 and 23 January 1807. Nietzsche, *Ecce Homo* (in *Complete Works*), p. 131, and *Thus Spake Zarathustra* (in *Complete Works*), p. 353.

Extraordinary

L. Althusser, *Essays in Self-Criticism*, London, New Left Books, 1976, pp. 115, 116. Hegel, *Phenomenology of Spirit*, op. cit., pp. 3–4. Nietzsche, *Thus Spake Zarathustra*, op. cit., pp. 358–9. Fichte in A. Philonenko, *Théorie et praxis dans la pensée morale et politique de Kant et de Fichte en 1793*, Paris, Vrin, 1968, p. 78, and Fichte, *Considérations . . .*, op. cit., p. 8.

The adventures of Copernicus

Marx, *Contribution to the Critique of Hegel's Philosophy of Right*, in *Collected Works of Marx and Engels*, Vol. 3, p. 187, and *The Class Struggles in France, 1848–1850*, in *Selected Works*, op. cit., Vol. I (1969), p. 213. Nietzsche, *Der Wille zur Macht*, Stuttgart, 1964, p.565.

The new universal and university gravity

Kant, *Schriften zur Anthropologie, Geschichtsphilosophie, Politik und Pädegogik*, in *Werke in 6 Bänden*, Vol. 6, Frankfurt, Inselverlag, 1964, pp. 355, 356. On necessity in Fichte, see B. Willms, *Die totale Freiheit*, Cologne, 1967, p. 96.

Between brackets, for the academics

Marx, *Collected Works of Marx and Engels*, Vol. 3, p. 176.

The eternal three phases of revolution

Hegel, *Philosophy of History*, op. cit., pp. 12, 446–7, and *Vie de Jésus*, trans. Bosca, Paris, Gambier, 1929 (reprinted 1976); *Phenomenology of Spirit*, op. cit., pp. 237 ff. Plato, *Four Socratic Dialogues*, op. cit., p. 242. Engels, 'On the History of Early Christianity', in *Marx and Engels on Religion*, F.L.P.H., 1957, p. 313. It was in connection with the Napoleonic phase that Nietzsche took up the teaching of the masterthinkers: 'The Revolution made Napoleon possible: that was its justification. For such a prize one would be willing to see the anarchical collapse of our whole civilization. Napoleon made nationalism possible: that was his limitation' (*Werke*, VIII: 2, p. 137). The masters feel cramped within nationalism – they think in terms of an Empire, of an International, or of world domination. On the place of Napoleon in Hegel's *Phenomenology of Spirit*, see my book *Le Discours de la guerre*, op. cit. Valéry, *Le Cimetière marin*, trans. C. Day Lewis, in *Selected Writings*, London, New Directions, 1950, pp. 44–5.

One can no longer get out of the sun

Trotsky, *History of the Russian Revolution*, London, Gollancz, 1932–1933, Vol. I, pp. 16–17, and Vol. III, p. 167. Also quoted in Deutscher, *The Prophet Unarmed*, op. cit., pp. 461–2.

More rigorous than mathematics

Hegel, *Phenomenology of Spirit*, op. cit., p. 406. Nietzsche, *Der Wille zur Macht*, op. cit., p. 401.

Revolution around a crown

Shakespeare, *Richard II*, Act III, scene 2, lines 160–65.

Master through dread

Hegel, *Phenomenology of Spirit*, op. cit., pp. 116, 117, 119, and *Philosophy of History*, op. cit., pp. 99, 407. Marx, *Contribution to the Critique of Political Economy*, op. cit., p. 36.

Necro-logical

Hegel, *Science of Logic*, London, Allen and Unwin, 1969, pp. 129–31. Nietzsche, *Human, All Too Human* (in *Complete Works*), p. 131, and *The Joyful Wisdom* (in *Complete Works*), pp. 9–10. M. Foucault, *La Naissance de la clinique*, 2nd edn, Paris, P.U.F., 1972.

Death in labour

Hegel, *Gesammelte Werke*, Vol. 6, Hamburg, F. Meiner, pp. 297–300, and *Science of Logic*, op. cit., pp. 178–84.

From persuasion to dissuasion

Hegel, *Gesammelte Werke*, Vol. 6, op. cit., pp. 303–6, 312. Nietzsche, *The Genealogy of Morals* (in *Complete Works*), p. 201, and *Umwertung aller Werte*, op. cit., Vol. 2, p. 810.

The final duel

Hegel, *Philosophy of Right*, op. cit., pp. 209–10, and *System der Sittlichkeit*, Hamburg, 1967, p. 88. Engels, in *Collected Works of*

Marx and Engels, Vol. 7, p. 159. See also Lévy, op. cit., p. 287.
Nietzsche, *The Joyful Wisdom* (in *Complete Works*), p. 320.

3. Why I Am So Clever

Lewis Carroll quoted from *The Lewis Carroll Picture Book*, ed.
S. D. Collingwood, London, T. Fisher Unwin, 1899, pp. 198–9.

Paris time

Hegel, *Philosophy of History*, op. cit., p. 447.

The world's clock

Nietzsche, *Thoughts out of Season* (in *Complete Works*), Vol. 2, p. 98.

The plebs

Fichte, *Considérations* ..., op. cit., p. 110. Hegel, *Phenomenology of
Spirit*, op. cit., pp. 335–6, and *Philosophy of Right*, op. cit., pp. 196–277.
Nietzsche, *Umwertung aller Werte*, op. cit., Vol. 2, pp. 510–11, and
Werke in 3 Bänden, Vol. 3, p. 425.

The strategy of enforcing literacy

Lenin, *Collected Works*, op. cit., Vol. 26, p. 414, and Vol. 33, p. 497.
Solzhenitsyn, *The Gulag Archipelago*, Vol. 1, London, Collins, 1974,
p. 27. Fichte, see A. Philonenko, *La Liberté humaine dans la philosophie
de Fichte*, Paris, Vrin, 1966, p. 230.

One lord and no serfs

Hegel, *Philosophy of History*, op. cit., pp. 104, 399.

The vocation of the scholar

Fichte, *The Vocation of the Scholar*, in *The Popular Works of J. G.
Fichte*, London, Chapman, 1848, Vol. I, pp. 215, 217, 222.

To everyone his own plebs

Marx, in *Collected Works of Marx and Engels*, Vol. 3, p. 186.

Fidelity to the State and to the Revolution

H. Marcuse, *Reason and Revolution*, 2nd edn, London, Routledge, 1955, pp. 136, 218, 219. Heine, *Religion and Philosophy in Germany*, op. cit., p. 13. Hegel, *Political Writings*, op. cit., p. 173.

Education for life and for death

Willms, op. cit., pp. 158–9. Hegel, *Gesammelte Werke*, Vol. 6, op. cit., pp. 301–6.

Shrouding the night in darkness

Hegel, *Jenaer Realphilosophie*, Hamburg, 1967, pp. 180–81, and *Gesammelte Werke*, Vol. 6, op. cit., pp. 301–6. Also *The Logic of Hegel*, Oxford, Clarendon, 1892, p. 379.

Making the heart the heart's grave

Marx, *Collected Works of Marx and Engels*, Vol. 6, p. 497. Hegel, *Lectures on the Philosophy of Religion*, Vol. 3, London, 1895 (reprinted 1968), p. 278.

The mortuary

M. Heidegger, *Hegel's Concept of Experience*, New York, Harper and Row, 1970, p. 62. Shakespeare, *Richard III*, Act I, scene 2, lines 71–2.

The terrorist theory

Hegel, *Phenomenology of Spirit*, op. cit., p. 208.

4. Why We Are So Metaphysical

A Hiroshima love

Hegel, *Phenomenology of Spirit*, op. cit., p. 19, and *System der Sittlichkeit*, op. cit., p. 43. Nietzsche, *Thus Spake Zarathustra*, op. cit., p. 374.

What is German idealism ?

Nietzsche, *The Twilight of the Idols*, in *Complete Works*, p. 66.

Very homely

Pascal, *Pensées*, Penguin Books, 1970, p. 247. Descartes, *Discourse on Method*, op. cit., pp. 57, 58. Hegel, *Lectures in the History of Philosophy*, op. cit., Vol. 3, p. 217.

On the bill-board

See the commentary by Philonenko in *Théorie . . .*, op. cit., pp. 101 ff, and the same author's *Liberté . . .*, op. cit., p. 284. Marx, *Collected Works of Marx and Engels*, Vol. 3, p. 482, and *Grundrisse*, Penguin, 1973, p. 105. Nietzsche, *Thus Spake Zarathustra*, op. cit., pp. 10, 11. Hegel, *Philosophy of History*, op. cit., p. 79.

There and back

Heidegger, *Nietzsche*, Vol. 2, Stuttgart, Neske, 1961, pp. 165, 165–6. M. Bloch, *Strange Defeat*, London, O.U.P., 1949, p. 51.

The great Western

Hegel, *The Logic of Hegel*, op. cit., p. 103. Nietzsche, *Umwertung aller Werte*, op. cit., Vol. 2, p. 674.

I can, therefore I am

Fichte, *The Science of Knowledge*, New York, Appleton-Century-Crofts, 1970, p. 133. Nietzsche, *The Will to Power* (in *Complete Works*), part 2, p. 106, and *Werke in 3 Bänden*, op. cit., Vol. 3, p. 680.

The promised wealth

Nietzsche, *Ecce Homo* (in *Complete Works*), chapter headings. Fichte, *The Science of Knowledge*, op. cit., p. 7. Marx, *Collected Works of Marx and Engels*, Vol. 3, p. 304 (*Manuscripts of 1844*), and Vol. 5, p. 394 (*The German Ideology*).

Exclusion–inclusion

Fichte, *The Science of Knowledge*, op. cit., p. 105.

God as vicious circle

Hegel, *The Logic of Hegel*, op. cit., pp. 57–9. Marx, *Collected Works of Marx and Engels*, Vol. 3, pp. 296–7.

The speculative proposition

Hegel, *Phenomenology of Spirit*, op. cit., pp. 38, 40. Nietzsche on science, *The Joyful Wisdom* (in *Complete Works*), p. 44.

How a master thinker assembles his ideas

Hegel, *Phenomenology of Spirit*, op. cit., pp. 27, 40, and *Lectures on the Philosophy of Religion*, op. cit., Vol. 3, p. 271. Heidegger, *Vier Seminare* Frankfurt, Klostermann, 1977, p. 53.

Unseemly questions

Hegel, *Phenomenology of Spirit*, op. cit., p. 43, and *Lectures on the Philosophy of Religion*, op. cit., Vol. 3, p. 250. Marx, *Collected Works of Marx and Engels*, Vol. 3, p. 305. Heidegger, *What is a Thing?* Chicago, Henry Regnery, 1967, pp. 117–18. Nietzsche, *Werke in 3 Bänden*, op. cit., Vol. 3, p. 685.

The major affirmation

Hegel, *Phenomenology of Spirit*, op. cit., pp. 22, 159. Marx, *Collected Works of Marx and Engels*, Vol. 6, p. 174 (*The Poverty of Philosophy*), and *Capital*, Vol. 1, French trans., Éditions Sociales edn, Vol. 2, p. 168. (This passage is not included in the English version of *Capital*.) Nietzsche, *Beyond Good and Evil* (in *Complete Works*), p. 74, and *Thus Spake Zarasthustra*, p. 193.

The minor affirmations

Hegel, *Encyclopedia of Philosophy*, New York, Philosophical Library, 1959, pp. 261, 263. Nietzsche, *The Will To Power*, op. cit., part 2, p. 239.

Why this long way round ?

See R. Davezies, P. Cantier and J. M. Trillard, *Échanges et dialogues ou la mort d'un clerc*, IDOC-France, 1975. Hegel, *Encyclopaedia of Philosophy*, op. cit., p. 266.

5. How I Became a Fatality

Ecce Maestro!

Hegel, *Faith and Knowledge*, Albany, State University of New York Press, 1977, conclusion, and *The Difference between Fichte's and Schelling's Systems of Philosophy*, Albany, State University of New York Press, 1977, pp. 147–8. Bakunin on Marx in *Socialisme autoritaire ou libertaire*, Paris U.G.E., Collection 10/18, Vol. I, 1975, p. 216. On the Chinese-type bureaucracy, see C. and J. Broyelle and E. Tschirhart, *China: A Second Look*, Harvester Press, 1979. Dostoyevsky, *The Devils*, Penguin Books, p. 404. Nietzsche, *Thus Spake Zarathustra*, op. cit., p. 361.

The order for mobilization

Trotsky, *Kak vooruzhalas revolyutsiya*, Vol. I, 1923, p. 251 (French trans., *Écrits militaires*, Paris, l'Herne, 1967, p. 288). Nietzsche, *Nachgelassene Fragmente*, Werke VIII: 2, p. 431.

A science of great resources

Marx, *Collected Works of Marx and Engels*, Vol. 6, p. 212 (*The Poverty of Philosophy*), and Vol. 9, p. 205 (*Wage – Labour and Capital*); also *Selected Works*, op. cit., Vol. I, p. 405 (*The 18 Brumaire*) and Vol. 3 p. 271 (*Fictitious Splits in the International*). Lévy, op. cit., p. 400. Nietzsche, *The Will to Power*, op. cit., part 2, p. 359.

Learning to play the Great Game

Marx, *Capital*, Vol. III, p. 259, and *Grundrisse*, p. 107.

The power of the separating power

Marx, *Capital*, Vol. I, op. cit., p. 80; *On the Jewish Question*, in *Collected Works of Marx and Engels*, Vol. 3, p. 170: and *Contribution to the Critique of Political Economy*, p. 34.

Property is rape

Marx, *Capital*, Vol. I, pp. 274, 280, 450, 451 and 492 ff. ('Machinery and Large-Scale Industry').

The Hegelian factory

Marx, *Capital*, Vol. I, p. 549. Foucault, *Discipline and Punish*, p. 228. François Ewald, who is preparing a major work on the place of the miners in the history of the French labour movement, has drawn attention to this one-sidedness in Marx's approach.

Capital does not exist

Marx and Engels, 31 July 1865, in *Selected Correspondence*, 1934, Lawrence and Wishart edition, p. 204; *Capital*, Vol. III, pp. 47, 248, 361.

Nor does labour

Marx, *Capital*, Vol. I, p. 308: the phrase 'a property by virtue of which it differs from all other commodities' is in the French version of *Capital*, Vol. I, but not the English one – see Éditions Sociales edition, Vol. 2, p. 211; *Capital*, Vol. III, p. 795; *Grundrisse*, pp. 104, 105, 296, 361; *The Poverty of Philosophy*, in *Collected Works of Marx and Engels*, Vol. 6, pp. 127, 130.

Yoke against yoke

Trotsky, *History of the Russian Revolution*, Vol. 3, London, Gollancz, 1933, p. 317.

An absence of ideas which makes its way in the world

Marx, *Critique of the Gotha Programme*, in *Selected Works in Three Volumes*, Vol. 3, pp. 17–19, and *Contribution to the Critique of Political Economy*, pp. 85, 86. Nietzsche, *The Will To Power*, op. cit., Vol. 2, p. 208.

6. Whereby I Am Above Everything

Mallarmé, *Le Tombeau d'Edgar Poe*, trans. Roger Fry, in *Poems*, London, Chatto and Windus, 1936, pp. 206–7.

The beyond-Marx

Nietzsche, *Thus Spake Zarathustra*, p. 67.

The master behind the property owner

Marx, *Critique of the Gotha Programme*, in *Selected Works in Three Volumes*, Vol. 3, pp. 18–19; *Capital*, Vol. III, p. 859; and *Grundrisse*, p. 102.

Seen from within

Nietzsche, *Beyond Good and Evil* (in *Complete Works*), p. 52.

Beyond fetishism

Nietzsche, *Thus Spake Zarathustra*, p. 27, and *The Will To Power*, part 1, p. 8. Marx, *Capital*, Vol. I, pp. 230–31.

Plain speaking

Nietzsche, *Thus Spake Zarathustra*, pp. 305, 318. Lenin, *Collected Works*, Vol. 14, p. 37.

The great journey

Nietzsche, *The Joyful Wisdom*, pp. 167, 200.

After God…

Nietzsche, *The Joyful Wisdom*, p. 117; *Beyond Good and Evil*, pp. 242, 243; *Thus Spake Zarathustra*, pp. 66, 68; *Nachgelassene Fragmente*, *Werke* VIII: 3, pp. 38–9.

How printing was invented

Nietzsche, *Der Wille zur Macht*, op. cit., pp. 383, 400, and *The Joyful Wisdom* (in *Complete Works*), pp. 116–20.

The ring

Nietzsche, *The Twilight of the Idols* (in *Complete Works*), p. 25; *Umwertung aller Werte*, I, pp. 84–5; *Werke in 3 Bänden*, Vol. 3, p. 895.

Zero hour

Nietzsche, *The Will To Power* (in *Complete Works*), part 2, p. 415; *Umwertung aller Werte*, Vol. 2, p. 717; *Werke in 3 Bänden*, Vol. 3, p. 497.

Mastery and mathematics

Tarski, op. cit., p. 264.

Mastery and theology

Vuillemin, *Le Dieu d'Anselme* ..., op. cit., p. 134. Nietzsche, *The Joyful Wisdom* (in *Complete Works*), p. 168.

A metaphysical passage

Nietzsche, *Werke in 3 Bänden*, op. cit., Vol. 3, p. 425. Heidegger, *Wegmarken*, Frankfurt, Klostermann, 1967, p. 277. Marx ('ruling and using are a *single* conception'), to Ruge, May 1843, in *Collected Works of Marx and Engels*, Vol. 3, p. 138.

The final opera

This message was published in *Le Nouvel Observateur*. Inspired by Patrice Chéreau and Richard Peduzzi, it was written in homage to the lengthy and learned preparation of their *mise en scène* at Bayreuth. Wagner, *Prose Works*, Vol. 2, London, Kegan Paul, 1900, p. 183. Brünnhilde's words, in *Die Walküre*, from the translation by H. and F. Corder. Wotan's words, in *Götterdämmerung*, from Newman's translation. Nietzsche, *Nietzsche contra Wagner* (in *Complete Works*), p. 12.

THE FINISHING OF HISTORY

Works quoted:

F. Furet and D. Richet, *La Révolution Française*, Paris, Fayard, 1973, pp. 21, 86, 204, 209, 277 ff. (English trans.: *The French Revolution*, London, Weidenfeld and Nicholson, 1970). G. Lefebvre, *The Great Fear of 1789*, London, New Left Books, 1973, pp. 119, 120. A. Soboul, foreword to C. Mazauric, *Sur la révolution française*, Paris, Éditions Sociales, 1970, p. 7. P. Caron, *Les Massacres de Septembre*, Paris, Maison du Livre Français, 1935, pp. 58, 59, 102, 110, 442 ff. R. Cobb,

Terreur et subsistances, 1793–1795, Paris, Clavreuil, 1965, pp. 21, 27 ff. A. Soboul, afterword to G. Lefebvre, *Quatre-vingt-neuf*, new edn, Paris, Éditions Sociales, 1970, pp. 273 ff. Marx, *The Holy Family*, in *Collected Works of Marx and Engels*, Vol. 4, p. 124, and *Theories of Surplus Value*, Part I, Lawrence and Wishart, 1969, p. 408. Shakespeare, *The Tempest*, Act IV, scene I, lines 148–56.

See also:

H. Arendt, *On Revolution*, London, Faber and Faber, 1963. F. Furet, 'Le Catéchisme révolutionnaire', in *Annales E.S.C.*, March-April 1971. D. Richet, 'Élites et despotisme', in *Annales E.S.C.*, January 1969. *La Pensée*, no. 186, June 1976. J. L. Talmon, *The Origins of Totalitarian Democracy*, London, Secker and Warburg, 1952.

On the question of the *plebs*, here is a recent *mise au point* by Michel Foucault, in *Recherches logiques*, no. 4, 1977: 'No doubt we ought not to conceive "the *plebs*" as the permanent basis of history, the ultimate objective of all subjections, and the hotbed, never completely extinguished, of all revolts. There is, doubtless no sociological reality corresponding to "the *plebs*". But there certainly always *is* something in the body of society, in classes, groups, and individuals, which in a certain way eludes the relations of authority – something which is *not* the primal matter, more or less docile or restive, but is centrifugal movement, inverse energy, the runaway. "The *plebs*" is non-existent, no doubt: but there is "something plebeian". There is something plebeian in our bodies and in our souls, in individuals, in the proletariat and in the bourgeoisie, but to a varying extent, and with differing forms, energies and irreducibilities. This plebeian part is not so much what is external to relations of authority as their limit, their reverse side, their "rebound". It is what replies to every advance on the part of authority by a movement to separate itself therefrom; and is therefore that which motivates every fresh development of the networks of authority. The reduction of the *plebs* can be carried out in three ways: either by its effective subjection, or by its utilization as a *plebs* (cf. the example of delinquency in the nineteenth century), or by its taking up a fixed position itself, in accordance with a strategy of resistance. Adopting this view of the *plebs*, i.e. seeing it as the reverse side and the limit in relation to authority, is therefore essential if we are to analyse its construction: it is on this basis that we can understand the way it functions and develops.'

Index

About the Author

André Glucksmann was born at Boulogne (Seine) in 1937 and graduated from the École Normale Superieure of St. Cloud in philosophy. Currently he is in charge of sociological research at the French National Center for Scientific Research. He specializes in nuclear strategy and in the economic definitions of monetary crises.

He has published *Le Discours de la Guerre* (a study of strategy from Clausewitz to Mao Zedong), *La Cuisinière et le Mangeur d'Hommes* (a study of the state, Marxism and concentration camps), and numerous magazine articles.